Risk Analysis for Large Projects
Models, Methods and Cases

Risk Analysis for Large Projects
Models, Methods and Cases

Dale F. Cooper

Spicer and Pegler Associates, London

and

C. B. Chapman

Department of Accounting and Management Science
University of Southampton

JOHN WILEY & SONS

Chichester · New York · Brisbane · Toronto · Singapore

Library of Congress Cataloging-in-Publication Data:

Cooper, Dale F.
  Risk analysis for large projects.

  Bibliography: p.
  Includes index.
  1. Reliability (Engineering)   2. Risk.   I. Chapman,
C. B.   II. Title.
TA169.C66   1986   658.4'03   86-15968
ISBN 0 471 91247 6

British Library Cataloguing in Publication Data:

Cooper, Dale F.
  Risk analysis for large projects: models, methods and cases.
  1. Risk management
  I. Title   II. Chapman, C. B.
  658.4'03   HD61
  ISBN 0 471 91247 6

Typeset by Paston Press, Norwich
Printed and bound in Great Britain by
Biddles Ltd, Guildford and King's Lynn.

Contents

Acknowledgements

The structure of this book was conceived while the first author was Visiting Fellow at the Australian Graduate School of Management (AGSM). Much of the material was presented at an Executive Seminar on 'Risk Analysis for Large Projects' at the AGSM. Significant contributions were made by John Stringer, Professor of Management at the AGSM, and Sandro Bignozzi, Managing Director of A. Bignozzi and Associates in Sydney.

A version of Chapter 1 has been published as

> Cooper, D. F., and C. B. Chapman, (1985) Risk analysis for underground projects. *Underground Space* 9(1), 35–40.

Chapters 2 and 12 are based on seminars in the series Modern Management Approaches, conducted for local businessmen and professional advisors by the Department of Accounting and Management Science at the University of Southampton.

Chapters 3, 7, 10 and 11 are concerned with models that have been described in different forms in a variety of publications.

> Chapman, C. B. and D. F. Cooper, (1983) Risk engineering: basic controlled interval and memory models. *J. Operational Research Society* 34(1), 51–60.
>
> Chapman, C. B. and D. F. Cooper, (1985) Risk Analysis. In G. K. Rand and R. W. Eglese (eds). *Further Developments in Operational Research*, Pergamon, Oxford.

Chapter 4 describes work undertaken for a client of Acres International in Canada. Significant contributions were made by Gus Cammaert, the Acres project manager. The 'method' part of Chapter 4 has been published as

> Chapman, C. B., D. F. Cooper and A. B. Cammaert, (1984) Model and situation specific OR methods: risk engineering reliability analysis of an LNG facility. *J. Operational Research Society* 35(1), 27–35.

The President's Medal of the Operational Research Society was awarded to the authors for this paper.

The 'model' part of Chapter 4 has appeared in

> Cooper, D. F., C. B. Chapman, and A. B. Cammaert, (1983) Reliability analysis of an LNG facility. *Proceedings of the 6th National Conference, Australian Society for Operations Research, Brisbane*, 45–53.

Chapters 5 and 8 describe work undertaken for clients of Acres International in the USA. Significant contributions were made by Chuck Debelius and Tee Pecora, who both had project management responsibilities in Acres. A version of Chapter 5 has been published as

> Chapman, C. B., D. F. Cooper, C. A. Debelius, and A. G. Pecora, (1985) Problem-solving methodology design on the run. *J. Operational Research Society* **36**(9), 769–78.

Chapter 6 is based on work undertaken jointly with Will Cumberlidge as an undergraduate project when he was a student at the University of Southampton. An extended version of Chapter 6 was presented as

> Cumberlidge, W., (1983) Encoding Probability Assessments. Dissertation submitted in partial fulfilment of the degree of BSc (Social Sciences), University of Southampton.

Chapter 9 describes work undertaken for a client of Acres International in Canada. A significant contribution was made by Dave MacDonald, Head of Planning and Estimating in Acres. A version of Chapter 9 has been published as

> Cooper, D. F., D. H. Macdonald and C. B. Chapman, (1985) Risk analysis of a construction cost estimate. *International J. Project Management* **3**(3), 141–9.

A version of Chapter 13 has been published as

> Chapman, C. B. and D. F. Cooper, (1983) Risk analysis: testing some prejudices. *European J. Operational Research* **14**(3), 238–47.

Chapter 14 describes how risk analysis studies are conducted in BP International. A version of Chapter 14 has been published as:

> Chapman, C. B., E. D. Phillips, D. F. Cooper, and L. Lightfoot, (1985) Selecting an approach to project time and cost planning. *International J. Project Management* **3** (1), 19–26.

The authors are grateful for help, encouragement and inspiration provided by a number of colleagues not mentioned above. J. Gavin Warnock and Robin Charlewood of Acres were key instigators in many of the studies which are the basis of this book, and we have been supported by many other Acres staff who have been involved in individual studies. Members of the BP International Risk Analysis Group within the BP Engineering Planning and Costs division have played a central role in the development of many of the basic ideas over nearly a decade. More recently staff of Gulf Canada Resources Incorporated have contributed in a substantial manner. All the studies undertaken by the authors have provided important lessons, and in many cases our clients have been our mentors. It would be inappropriate to list all of them and their contributions, but the authors would like to express their gratitude. Only the errors and omissions are entirely our own.

Chapter 1

Introduction to risk analysis

Summary

This chapter introduces some of the main concepts to be used throughout the book. It considers what risk analysis is, the nature of the risk engineering approach to risk analysis, when risk analysis might be necessary, and some of the benefits which arise from its use. It also provides some general guidance for the reader.

THE NEED FOR RISK ANALYSIS

Recent decades have been chacterized by a vast proliferation of risk. The real scale of projects and investment programmes has expanded dramatically, increasingly intractable geographical areas have been developed, and economic instability in growth rates and prices has become endemic.

With this uncertain and volatile environment, the need for risk analysis of potential projects and investments has increased. The need for analysis is particularly apparent when projects involve

Large capital outlays.
Unbalanced cash flows, requiring a large proportion of the total investment before any returns are obtained.
Significant new technology.
Unusual legal, insurance or contractual arrangements.
Important political, economic or financial parameters.
Sensitive environmental or safety issues.
Stringent regulatory or licensing requirements.

For many projects, the additional information needed to reduce risk and uncertainty to an acceptable level prior to commencing the development will not be available, and there may be large costs or delays in acquiring it. These factors increase the need for early assessment of the uncertainties

1

and risks which affect the project before large sums of money are irrevocably committed.

Each major project may be viewed as unique. Some projects involve construction or operation in new or hazardous geographical and geological areas, some involve significant new or untried technology, and some involve risks with very large or potentially catastrophic consequences. Even where the individual risks may be known, their combined effects may not be obvious, as the synergy inherent in large projects frequently leads to quite unexpected consequences.

A DEFINITION OF RISK ANALYSIS

Risk is exposure to the possibility of economic or financial loss or gain, physical damage or injury, or delay, as a consequence of the uncertainty associated with pursuing a particular course of action.

Risk analysis can involve a number of approaches to dealing with the problems created by uncertainty, including the identification, evaluation, control and management of risk.

Risk engineering is an integrated approach to all aspects of risk analysis, used as the basis of discussion here. Its aim is to identify and measure uncertainty as appropriate, and to develop the insight necessary to change associated risks through effective and efficient decisions. Risk engineering uses risk analysis, defined in a very broad and flexible manner, for the purpose of better *risk management*.

RISK ENGINEERING APPLICATIONS

Risk analysis of this risk engineering form has many applications. They range from the evaluation of the risk from seismic hazards for a nuclear power station, through the optimization of a major offshore oil development programme, to the assessment of the risk of default on a bond offering. 'Engineering' is used in the sense of a 'synthesis of ends and means', with no intention of suggesting only technological aspects of large projects are relevant.

The risk engineering approach to risk analysis was first developed for and tested by BP International, for programme development for their North Sea projects, in the late 1970's. It is now applied to all major sensitive BP projects for project time and cost planning. Studies which formed the basis of this approach and its generalization to other application areas have involved a number of organizations in the UK, Canada and the USA, including Acres International Limited, Spicer and Pegler Associates, Gulf Canada Resources Incorporated, Petro-Canada, Alaska Power Authority, Alberta Utilities Consortium, Petroleum Directorate of the Government of

Newfoundland and Labrador, Northwest Alaska Pipelines, Fluor Engineers and Contractors Incorporated, Potomac Electric Power Company, US Department of Energy, Newfoundland and Labrador Hydro, Canadian International Project Managers Limited, Canadian Arctic Gas Study Group, and the Channel Tunnel Group.

Risk engineering is a synthesis of a number of other approaches to risk analysis, many of which can be treated as special cases. In particular, it draws upon key ideas from decision analysis, safety analysis of fault tree and event tree forms, generalizations of Program Evaluation and Review Technique (PERT) like Graphical Evaluation and Review Technique (GERT), Markov process modelling, reliability analysis, and 'futures' or 'scenario' modelling.

Risk engineering provides a structured means of looking ahead in the life of a project. It differs from many conventional approaches, such as sensitivity analysis, in three key areas:

It subdivides a project into a relatively small number of major elements, and then analyses the uncertainty associated with each in detail.

It identifies the causes of time delays, cost changes and other impacts, and it evaluates responses to associated potential problems, prior to assessing net effects.

It considers degrees of dependency between risks and between the project elements.

REQUIREMENTS FOR RISK ANALYSIS

There are five somewhat different circumstances in which uncertainty may be a major factor and in which suitable forms of risk analysis may be appropriate.

In the *pre-feasibility appraisal* of a proposed project or investment, a decision may have to be made, often on the basis of minimal information, to discard the project, to postpone it, or to proceed with more detailed feasibility studies.

A decision may be required concerning whether or not to undertake or become involved with a *marginal project*. This is the case when the rate of return calculated on the basis of the best estimates of capital requirements and cash flows is close to the opportunity cost of capital, or the net present value is close to zero.

When a project or investment involves *unusual risks or uncertainties*, which may lead to a wide range of possible rates of return, risk analysis may be appropriate.

Strategic decisions may be necessary when *choosing between alternative projects or investments*, for a project or investment concept which has already been justified at an earlier pre-feasibility or feasibility stage.

Risk analysis may be appropriate for *tactical decisions*, when developing a detailed plan or optimizing project specifications, for a project concept already given approval.

Within this broad framework, there may be formal requirements for risk analysis for many reasons:

Economic viability assessment, for high level strategic decision making within an organization or in relation to a government decision process.

Financial feasibility assessment, for the bond or debt market when a finance package is being assembled.

Insurance purposes, to assess premiums for unusual risks for which there may be little statistical or actuarial information.

Accountability, for major project managers to demonstrate that they have fully assessed all the material risks, that the measures taken to control risk are appropriate, and that the economic reward for taking on the risk that remains is adequate.

Contractual purposes, to assess alternative contractual and legal frameworks for the project, in the context of deciding who should bear what risks and determining an equitable allocation of risks and rewards between project owners, contractors and insurers.

Tendering, when deciding whether or not to bid for a proposed project, and at what level.

Regulatory purposes, for legislative, judicial or licensing agencies of government, or for public enquiries, to demonstrate accountability in a public or social context.

Communication purposes, to provide information for project owners, contractors or joint venture partners, or to demonstrate capability and competence in an area.

BENEFITS OF RISK ANALYSIS

Risk analysis may be required initially for a limited range of purposes. However, the experience of many organizations suggests a risk engineering approach provides other benefits which may prove far more important in the long term. These benefits include:

Better and more definite perceptions of risks, their effects on the project, and their interactions.

Better contingency planning and selection of responses to those risks which do occur, and more flexible assessment of the appropriate mix of ways of dealing with risk impacts.

Feedback into the design and planning process in terms of ways of preventing or avoiding risks.

Feedforward into the construction and operation of the project in terms of ways of mitigating the impacts of those risks which do arise, in the form of response selection and contingency planning.

Following from these aspects, an overall reduction in project risk exposure.

Sensitivity testing of the assumptions in the project development scenario.

Documentation and integration of corporate knowledge which usually remains the preserve of individual minds.

Insight, knowledge and confidence for better decision making and improved risk management.

Of these benefits, *it is the reduction in project risk exposure which provides corporate management with the bottom-line justification for undertaking risk analysis studies.* At the project management level, better insight is one critical aspect, leading to better decision making and better risk management. Another is a control and reporting framework which avoids sudden surprises and losses of confidence. A third is a framework for the justification of prudent risk avoidance and mitigation measures which may involve early expenditure of substantial sums of money.

PERFORMING RISK ANALYSIS

Although risk analysis is usually thought of as quantitative, a risk engineering approach need not be about measuring risk, and it need not use probabilities. Risk analysis should be concerned with understanding what might happen and what should happen. As an aid in developing and communicating this understanding, structured verbal models can be extremely useful, especially when the nature of the risks and the associated responses may cause confusion or misunderstanding if an agreed definition is not provided.

Effective and efficient performance of risk analysis involves a number of contributing elements. These include models, methods and computer software, as well as less tangible skill-related elements such as methodology design, specialist expertise and study team management.

RISK ANALYSIS MODELS

Risk analysis is concerned with uncertainty and its consequences. Mathematically, risk analysis models manipulate probabilities and probability distributions, in order to assess the combined impact of risks on the project. The exact manner in which this is done depends on the purpose of the analysis.

A flexible set of verbal, graphical and mathematical risk engineering models has been developed for risk analysis tasks. They form a general family of models applicable in a wide range of specific risk analysis contexts. They are based on Controlled Interval and Memory (CIM) representations of probability distributions. The nature and use of CIM models is described in detail throughout this book, beginning in the next two chapters.

Risk analysis models other than CIM models are discussed briefly in the next chapter, to provide a simple basis for comparison. However, a detailed treatment of alternatives is beyond the scope of this book.

There is no single all-purpose risk analysis model. Some models are very simple, while others may be very complex, embodying not only uncertainty about events or activities, for example, but responses to that uncertainty and the consequences of the responses. In general it is advisable to start with simple models, and make them more complex only if doing so seems cost effective. CIM models allow a very wide range of levels of complexity, and a flexible structured approach to introducing complexity, as discussed in the final chapter, and demonstrated throughout the book.

RISK ANALYSIS METHODS

Risk analysis involves a method or a systematic series of steps. A detailed risk engineering method for project duration risk assessment is illustrated in Figure 1.1. Using this method involves an iterative approach, and the step sequence may not be strict. Such a method is necessary if the process of risk analysis is to be efficient and effective.

Phase	Step
Scope	Activity identification
	Primary risk identification
	Primary response identification
	Secondary risk identification
	Secondary response identification
Structure	Minor and major risk identification
	Specific and general response identification
	Simple and complex decision rule identification
	Risk/response diagramming
Parameter	Desired parameter identification
	Scenario identification and probability estimation
Manipulation and	Risk computation
interpretation	Risk efficiency decision rule assessment
	Risk balance decision rule assessment
	Budget contingency sum assessment

Figure 1.1   The phase and step structure of a risk analysis method for project duration assessment

Risk analysis methods must be designed to suit the model and the circumstances in which it is used. There is no single all-purpose method for risk analysis. Families of related risk engineering methods have been developed, involving similar concepts and characteristics. Like the method of Figure 1.1, they follow a systematic series of steps, but the steps are related to the specific risk analysis context. Different risk analysis methods are described in the case studies through this book, beginning in Chapter 4.

RISK ANALYSIS COMPUTER SOFTWARE

Some standardized risk analysis software packages are available. However, appropriate computer software must reflect the choice of model and method, and there is no one best approach for all forms of risk analysis.

Families of related programs have been developed for associated families of risk engineering models and methods. They are sophisticated, interactive program suites which provide a means of entering information in a wide range of different formats and synthesising it in any required manner. They are designed to take advantage of the general characteristics and terminology of the application area being addressed. More basic general risk engineering software is also available.

RISK ANALYSIS METHODOLOGY DESIGN

Methodology design involves choosing or developing an appropriate model/method/software combination for a particular kind of risk analysis in a particular context. The time and money available to perform the analysis, and the expected future use, are obviously important considerations, as well as the immediate task. Methodology design is a process which is necessarily dependent upon experience and intuition, but a comparison of the case studies in this book provides an introduction to some of the key issues, as does the final chapter.

RISK ANALYSIS AND SPECIALIST EXPERTISE

Risk analysis models, methods and software provide valuable tools for project planning and design, but obtaining the right answer still depends upon specialist expertise. Judgements must be made, in some cases based upon hard data, in some cases based on sound conventional guidelines, in some cases based on creative innovation and well schooled intuition rooted in a wide range of relevant experience. Expertise involving an effective and efficient blend of all these aspects is not made less important by adopting risk engineering methodology: it is simply made use of more effectively.

Risk analysis requires many forms of expertise. Economics, finance, environmental issues, contractual issues, and so on are clearly involved in most major projects. What is not always appreciated is that they may directly impact the way the design and planning is done, and they should be properly considered in a timely manner. Risk analysis helps to provide this integration.

RISK ANALYSIS STUDY TEAM MANAGEMENT

Risk analysis study team management requires special consideration. Like the model/method/software aspects of risk analysis methodology, it must be adapted to the circumstances. For example, one organization the authors have worked with uses an in-house Risk Analysis Group in an internal audit role most of the time. Analysts examine a project plan and project cost estimates in detail over a period of six to eight weeks. Their work then provides useful immediate feedback to the project staff, but they report to the project manager and the head of the planning and costing function group. Other organizations the authors have worked with used large teams over several months to perform a complete analysis, externally to the project team, and they used the analysis to make recommendations based upon fundamental judgements which went beyond the risk analysis itself. Very different kinds and styles of management are clearly necessary for such diverse operations. Proper treatment of these issues is beyond the scope of this book, although some insights are provided, in Chapter 5 especially.

SOME GUIDANCE FOR THE READER

This book is based upon a risk analysis special short course developed for an executive seminar in a business school. It draws upon a number of technical papers published and in progress, and a more technical text in progress, but it does not attempt a detailed technical treatment. Its concern is providing an understanding of key issues and concepts, for managers and clients who may want risk analysis performed for them, as well as for managers and their staff who may want to undertake risk analysis. It does not require a highly mathematical or technical background, but it does assume a degree of comfort with numbers, and familiarity with organizational decision processes and concerns. Further, it assumes readers who are familiar with other forms of risk analysis will suspend judgement of the risk engineering approach until they have finished this book and examined some of the more technical issues in the references provided. Finally, it assumes any reader who wishes to implement risk analysis studies based upon the suggested approaches will study the technical references provided or seek advice.

Chapter 2 provides an introductory overview of basic approaches to risk analysis, the only chapter which does not limit itself to a risk engineering perspective.

Chapter 3 introduces the controlled interval and memory (CIM) models which are central to a risk engineering approach. They are introduced in their simplest form, assuming the individual sources of risk that are of interest can be added assuming independence.

Chapter 4 provides a case study which sets these simple models in a realistic context, and introduces aspects of the risk engineering methodology. It concerns the reliability of an LNG facility.

Chapter 5 provides another case study which builds on the discussion of the risk engineering methodology, and introduces an important modelling complexity, concern for multiple criteria. It considers the best way to cross a river with a large diameter gas pipeline.

Chapter 6 deals with an issue which most readers will be concerned with by now: the elicitation of probabilities for risk analysis.

Chapter 7 introduces the treatment of dependence in a CIM modelling framework.

Chapters 8 and 9 provide case studies concerned with project costs and estimates of contingencies, extending the earlier discussion of the methodology and illustrating how some aspects of dependence can be handled in practice.

Chapters 10 and 11 consider more complex dependence modelling issues, concerned with structural dependence in a cost or duration estimation framework and dependence induced by a project planning network.

Chapter 12 considers project appraisal in terms of economic risk evaluation for large projects, building on all the previous material. Chapter 13 discusses related applications.

Chapter 14 provides an overview, considering the selection of an appropriate approach to project time and cost planning.

A glossary of terms, references and an index follow.

This material, and its sequence, has been selected to allow simple modelling concepts to be considered first and then gradually built upon, in parallel with the development of the key concepts of the risk engineering methodology, providing practical sources of motivation based on case studies throughout. The reader may find it useful to skim through the book before more careful reading, but sequential treatment of the material is important, and much of the later material will not be intelligible if earlier material has not been assimilated.

A final word of advice: understanding uncertainty and risk in depth is not a simple matter, and there is no simple way to acquire such understanding. This book attempts to provide a much deeper understanding than most introductory books and many very technical books, and it attempts to make its acquisition as painless as possible, but it is not light reading.

SUMMARY

Successful risk analysis requires:

A flexible and general set of verbal, graphical and mathematical models, supported by sophisticated interactive computer software.
A family of related methods, designed to suit the models, which link the models and the circumstances in which they are to be used.
A wide range of relevant expertise and specialist skills.
The experience and leadership to design and integrate models, methods, and software for specific risk analysis tasks, to organize and manage risk analysis study teams, and to successfully execute large risk analyses for major projects.

The risks in large projects may have consequences which involve physical loss or damage, commercial loss, environmental damage, and third-party liability. The risk analysis methodology described in this book helps to identify the sources of risks, possible responses to them, and their consequences, including any secondary risks which arise as a result of the response mode chosen. This explicit identification of risk sources permits a reasoned assessment of who should appropriately bear each risk if it arises—the insurer, the owner or the contractors—and how much it might be worth to do so. The detailed examination of the project risk structure usually also leads to better contingency planning, and hence to an overall reduction in risk, to the benefit of all parties.

Basic approaches to risk analysis

Summary

This chapter provides a brief survey of the main basic approaches to project risk analysis, outlining a variety of modelling frameworks for handling uncertainty. The emphasis is on ways of combining independent distributions. Approaches covered include: simple adjustments and sensitivity analysis; 'analytic' methods like moment-based approaches; simulation or sampling based methods; numerical methods, discrete probability interval distribution methods and interval or histogram representation methods. This forms an introduction to the controlled interval and memory (CIM) models considered in the next chapter.

INTRODUCTION

This chapter looks briefly at some of the main basic approaches that have been used for project risk analysis. Most of them have been used for the financial appraisal of capital investments, in various forms of financial models. The intention is an examination of some of the effects of uncertainty which indicates how it has been handled within a variety of established basic modelling frameworks, to provide an appropriate background for consideration of the controlled interval and memory (CIM) approach introduced in Chapter 3.

Project investment appraisal uses a set of measures or predictions about the project and its environment, such as initial capital expenditure, projected demand, projected market share, and projected cash flows. These are combined in a financial model of the project in order to derive some measure of the worth or return from the project. This can then be used as a criterion for decision, or at least as a major input to the decision process. Such criteria include the payback period of the project, its accounting rate of return, the net present value and the internal rate of return.

If the initial measures of predictions are uncertain, then the criterion will be uncertain as well. This raises two kinds of issue: how to incorporate the uncertainty about the initial predictions in the model, and how to use an uncertain criterion to make a decision. This chapter concentrates on the first of these issues. In particular, if the uncertainty in the initial predictions can be expressed in the form of probability distributions, what is the distribution of the criterion? The second issue, concerning decision making, is discussed in outline here and in more detail in Chapter 12.

The first problem can be stated formally as

Determine the distributional characteristics of a derived variable which is a function of a set of uncertain base variables.

The underlying important general assumption is that it is easier and more accurate to specify the individual base variables and the relationships between them than it is to specify the derived variables directly. This is likely to be particularly important if the tail areas of the distributions of the derived variables are of interest. In practice it appears that low probability high consequence events represented by the tails are critical for decision making, even though they may contribute little to the expected value of the derived variable.

The general method for approaching this problem involves three steps:

(1) Specify the base variables.
(2) Specify the relationships between them.
(3) Calculate the derived variable.

This simple three step method indicates some of the issues to be addressed in what follows. Different methods will be examined for specifying uncertainty in terms of base variable distributions, and for specifying the relationships and interdependencies between base variables, thinking about the flexibility of different specification forms and the specification errors associated with them. Calculation processes, and their implications in terms of computation error and computation effort, will also be considered.

Simple adjustment methods and sensitivity analysis are considered first, in the context of discounted cash flow models. Cost-volume-profit and breakeven analysis are used to introduce 'analytic' methods like moment-based approaches. Simulation or sampling methods are discussed in the context of project appraisal, where there are complex relationships between the base variables. Various numerical methods are examined, leading to discrete representations of base variable distributions, and interval or histogram representation methods.

SIMPLE ADJUSTMENTS AND SENSITIVITY ANALYSIS

Discounted cash flow models

Assume an investment requires an initial cash outlay C, after which it produces returns $F_1, F_2, \ldots F_n$ at the end of years $t = 1, 2, \ldots n$. Assume that at the horizon at the end of year n, the investment has a residual or scrap value S. If the discount rate is d, the investment has a net present value (NPV) given by

$$\text{NPV}(d) = -C + \sum_{t=1}^{n} F_t (1 + d)^{-t} + S(1 + d)^{-n}.$$

The internal rate of return (IRR) of the investment is that discount rate d^* for which $\text{NPV}(d^*) = 0$.

The most common decision criterion in this discounted cash flow (DCF) framework is that the investment is worthwhile if the net present value is positive using a discount rate defined by the return on the next-best use of capital, or if the internal rate of return exceeds the return from the next-best use of capital.

Adjustment for risk

When there are uncertainties with the values of key parameters, a simple adjustment of the DCF criteria may seem to provide an easy solution. For example, a larger discount rate might be used in the NPV calculations, or the IRR might be required to exceed the return from a relatively risk-free form of investment by some 'risk margin'.

However, *ad hoc* approaches of this kind do not help the decision maker to assess the degree of risk involved, and they give no indication of whether the safety margin is appropriate. Further, there are sound reasons why they may bias decisions against long term comparatively safe projects in favour of short term high risk projects, the opposite effect of that intended.

Parameter bounds

Where a parameter lies within a known range, the calculations can be repeated with the parameter set to its pessimistic and optimistic values, as well as its most likely value or its expected value. This gives a range for the NPV or IRR criterion measure, but little distributional information. Where two or more parameters can vary, interpretation of the distribution shape becomes even more speculative.

Sensitivity analysis

A more general form of sensitivity analysis determines the bounds on a specific parameter for which the criterion is still acceptable, with all other parameters set to their expected values. This enables the most important parameters to be identified for further analysis, more detailed monitoring or more sophisticated forecasting (Hull, 1980). Analysis of this kind can be extended to determine limits for one parameter as one or two others vary within their respective ranges (for example Figure 2.1, from Chapman and Cooper, 1983b), but again little distributional information is obtained.

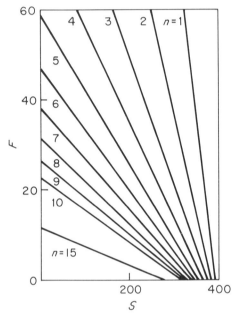

Figure 2.1 Minimum horizon (*n*) for given levels of annual fuel saving (*F*) and scrap value at the horizon (*S*), from a DCF example in Chapman and Cooper (1983b)

Distributional results

Where just one parameter can vary, and its distribution is known, then it is possible to determine a distribution for the criterion. For example, Warszawski (1982) used DCF methods to evaluate the effect of inflation on the profit from construction contracts. If V_s is the profit associated with an inflation rate s, and $p(s)$ is the probability that the inflation rate will be in the anticipated range, then we have distributional information about V_s, from which an expected value can be calculated: $V^* = \Sigma_s\ p(s)\ V_s$.

Warszawski went on to determine expected utilities under various assumptions about the contractor's risk aversion: $U^* = \Sigma_s\, p(s)\, U(V_s)$. In effect, this is a simplified form of the numerical integration methods to be examined in a later section.

ANALYTIC METHODS

Cost-volume-profit analysis

Assume a firm sells Q items at a selling price P. If the variable cost per item is V, and the fixed costs are F, the profit is

$$Z = Q(P - V) - F.$$

The related breakeven problem is to determine the minimum sales Q for which the profit is positive.

Under uncertainty, cost-volume-profit (CVP) analysis requires subtraction of random variables and multiplication of random variables. It is the multiplication which causes the main problems.

Two-moment approaches

The simplest analytic approaches to the stochastic CVP problem use the first two moments (mean and variance) of the base variables Q, P, V and F to calculate the mean and variance of the profit Z. The distributional form of Z is assumed known, and so the probability of any particular profit value can be determined.

Jaedicke and Robichek (1964) made the first major attempt to tackle CVP analysis under uncertainty. They began by assuming that one base variable, sales volume Q, was a Normal random variable. The other base variables were assumed to be deterministic. They then derived a profit distribution which was also Normal, using a method akin to the example of Warszawski (1982) cited above. When all four base variables were assumed to be independent and Normally distributed, they calculated the mean and variance of the profit, which they again assumed was distributed Normally. However, while the subtraction of Normal variables yields a Normal result, the product of two Normal distributions does not. Ferrara, Hayya, and Nacheman (1972) showed empirically that the product of two Normal variables is approximately Normal only if the sum of the coefficients of variations (the standard deviation divided by the mean) of the two base variables is less than or equal to 12 per cent. Hence, the Jaedicke–Robichek result has restricted applicability.

A variety of similar methods has since appeared. For example, Hilliard and Leitch (1975) assumed that quantity Q and contribution margin $(P - V)$

were lognormal, with F deterministic; profit Z is then lognormal (a simple analytic result), and its first two moments are sufficient to enable probability statements to be made about particular profit levels. Hilliard and Leitch allowed simple dependencies in the form of correlations.

Johnson and Simik (1971) extended the analysis to the multi-product case, where they allowed correlated demands for different products. They avoided the multiplication problem by assuming that the contribution margin for each product was constant over the relevant volume range.

King, Sampson and Sims (1975) specified an analytic form for the sum, product, and quotient of independent random variables whose 10-, 50-, and 90-percentiles are given, and justified it numerically. They used a 'binormal' cumulative density form for the result. This has a Normal cumulative density function (c.d.f.) on one side of the mean (m), and a different Normal c.d.f. on the other side: that is,

$$f(X;\ m,\ \sigma_1,\ \sigma_2) = \Phi((X - m)/\sigma_1) \quad \text{for } X \leqslant m$$
$$= \Phi((X - m)/\sigma_2) \quad \text{for } X > m,$$

where $\Phi(.)$ is the c.d.f. of the standard Normal distribution.

Starr and Tapiero (1975) derived analytic solutions for special cases of the breakeven problem, particularly when the base variables are uncorrelated or correlated Normal variables. Hillier (1963) used two-moment methods in the context of the DCF problems discussed in the previous section.

Four-moment approaches

A large increase in generality can be achieved by considering the first four moments of the base variable distributions, and using these to calculate the first four moments of the derived variable. Kottas and Lau (1978a) and Kottas, Lau, and Lau (1978) gave four-moments formulae for use in the CVP problem under different restrictive assumptions (Normal distributions in one case, independence in the other). Kottas and Lau (1982) provided more general formulae for the first moments of the sum, difference, and product of random variables, with a variety of dependence forms: linear or quadratic regression relationships between the variables, and constant, linear, or quadratic scedastic functions.

This approach allows a far more versatile specification of the base variables, and it should be possible to describe most marginal distributions and dependence forms that are likely to be encountered in stochastic CVP analysis. The form of the final distribution is not specified, however, so distributional assumptions must be made before probability results can be derived.

Probability statements and derived variable distributions

One purpose of stochastic analysis is to enable statements to be made about the likelihood of specific values of the derived variable occurring. For example, in the CVP context, questions which a decision maker might ask are: 'What is the probability that a sales volume Q will enable the firm to break even?' or 'What is the probability of achieving a profit of at least Z?'

If the form of the result distribution is not known, then weak probability statements can be made using Tchebychev inequalities. Wagle (1967) used this approach to assess risk in capital investment projects, and it has been applied to CVP analysis by Buzby (1974; and further comments by Hayya, Ferrara, and Saniga, 1975, and Buzby, 1975), Johnson and Simik (1974), and Starr and Tapiero (1975). Tchebychev inequalities, though, are exceedingly conservative. For example consider the probability p that a realized profit Z will be more than two standard deviations from the expected value $E(Z)$: if nothing is known about the distribution of Z, then

$$\text{Prob} \left(|Z - E(Z)| < k\sigma \right) \leqslant 1/k^2,$$

so $p \leqslant 0.25$; if Z is known to be unimodal and symmetric, then

$$\text{Prob} \left(|Z - E(Z)| < k\sigma \right) \leqslant 4/9k^2,$$

so $p \leqslant 0.111$; if Z is known to be Normally distributed, then $p \leqslant 0.045$. For accurate probability statements to be made, the distributional form of the derived variable must be known. There are only a few 'convenient' base variable distributions, and their use in practice frequently requires major simplifying assumptions. Further restrictions are imposed by dependence relationships.

The four-moment approaches generally assume that the derived variable distribution belongs to a general system such as the Pearson family. This is the form adopted by, for example, Kottas and Lau (1978a, 1982) and Liao (1975). It includes a wide range of shapes and combinations of skewness and kurtosis. Percentage points are tabulated by Johnson *et al.* (1963).

Summary

Simple analytic approaches to the problems of combining random variables can be attractive under some conditions: if the base variables have 'convenient' distributional forms, if only simple dependence relationships are involved, or if weak probability statements are sufficiently precise for the purpose.

The four-moment methods are more versatile: they allow base variable distributions to be quite general, so there is no need to force an analytic function onto empirical data; the moments are related to the distributions' shape characteristics, so they can be interpreted readily; and the computational requirements are modest. However, there may be problems with computational accuracy if the base variables are not well-behaved or if the dependence specifications are non-standard. In particular, calculation of the first four moments of a derived variable requires base variable moments higher than the fourth: these higher moments are very sensitive to the distribution assumptions, and they are numerically significant in the calculations in comparison with the lower moments. The form of the result distribution is not well specified, and while the Pearson family appears adequate it is rarely possible to obtain sufficient empirical data to verify the fit.

A major practical disadvantage of the analytic methods in some circumstances is the restriction imposed on the possible forms of interdependence relationships between the base variables. While the dependence forms allowed within Kottas and Lau's (1982) four-moments approach may be adequate for most CVP or breakeven analyses, more general specifications may be required for other forms of financial analysis and project costing applications.

It is not clear that any of the analytic methods can cope with distributions that are multi-modal, such as those which occur commonly in projects with seasonal or weather-window dependencies.

SIMULATION

Where a large number of base variables must be combined, or where there are complex dependence relationships between the base variables, analytic or Monte Carlo sampling (simulation) has been suggested as a preferred alternative (but see Lewellen and Long, 1972, for a dissenting view).

An early application of simulation to the analysis of a capital investment decision was described by Hertz (1964). In his example, Hertz considered nine factors about which there was uncertainty: market size, selling price, market growth rate, market share, investment required, useful life of facilities, residual value of facilities, operating costs and fixed costs. The inclusion of uncertainty provided quite different results from an analysis based solely on expected values. In his example an expected return of 25.5 per cent was calculated using the expected values of the nine factors, but a simulation using 3600 DCF calculations, each based on sampled values for each of the nine factors, indicated that the expected return was only 14.6 per cent. Further, the simulation provided detailed information about the probability of achieving any specific desired rate of return.

Simulation has been used in a variety of financial areas. Economos (1968) examined a range of financial indicators of a subsidiary company: investment, post-tax income, post-tax return on investment, and other DCF measures. Wyman (1973) evaluated financial leases in terms of their post-tax interest cost equivalents, for comparison with the interest cost of long-term debt financing. Spooner (1974) estimated the mean and variance of a construction project cost estimate, and then used simulation to verify that the distribution of the estimate was close to Normal under different assumptions about the form of the base variable distributions. Kottas and Lau (1978b) studied the stochastic CVP problem.

Liao (1975) also studied the stochastic CVP problem using simulation. After an initial set of samples had been used to estimate the variance of the derived variables, the total number of samples necessary to achieve a desired level of accuracy was calculated and the sampling completed. Liao then fitted a Pearson curve to the derived variable distribution, based on its first four moments, as discussed in the previous section.

A similar approach, of simulation followed by four-moment curve fitting, was followed by Crandall and Woolery (1982) to determine the distribution characteristics of milestone dates in a project schedule network. While these applications may seem to utilize a novel combination of simulation and analytic techniques, it should be remembered that there are large standard errors associated with the higher moments of a distribution, and simulation may not be the most efficient approach if they must be estimated very accurately.

Simulation has been criticized because of the often large number of trials that may be needed to reduce sampling errors to an acceptable level, and this criticism becomes even more salient if extensive sensitivity analyses are required. On the other hand, straightforward DCF or CVP analyses can certainly be simulated easily and at low cost, and where the derived variable distribution is expected to be 'well-behaved' some sampling error in the higher moments may be tolerated. Unfortunately, the sampling error will be highest in just those cases where simulation approaches show some of their main advantages: where the base variables have non-standard or empirical distributional forms, linked by complex inter-relationships.

In many risk analysis contexts, the mean values of derived variable distributions may be less important than the extreme or tail values: rare but potentially costly events may contribute little to the mean value, but they may nevertheless be of major concern to decision makers. There are two sources of error associated with the tails of simulated distributions: sampling error, noted above, and modelling error. When rare events arise contingency plans are implemented and 'non-standard' management processes occur; unless the simulation reflects these often complex decision rules and responses, the extreme values of a simulated distribution may be based on an unrealistic management strategy (see, for example, Myers, 1976; Robichek and Van Horne, 1967).

NUMERICAL METHODS

Functional integration

Numerical integration approaches are based largely on functional integration results, functional integration being an analytic approach which is used in problem areas like queueing theory, but normally not for risk analysis. Consider two base variables x and y, with distribution functions $p_x(x)$ and $p_y(y)$, and suppose the distribution function $p_z(z)$ is required, where $z = f(x, y)$. If f has a unique differentiable inverse f^{-1} such that $z = f(x, f^{-1}(z, x))$, then the distribution function is given by the convolution

$$p_z(z) = \int p_x(x)p_y(f^{-1}(z, x) \mid x)|f^{-1}(z, x)| \, dx.$$

For example,

$$p_z(x + y) = \int p_x(x)p_y(z - x \mid x) \, dx,$$

$$p_z(x - y) = \int p_x(x)p_y(x - z \mid x) \, dx,$$

$$p_z(xy) = \int p_x(x)p_y\left(\frac{z}{x} \mid x\right) \frac{1}{|x|} \, dx, \quad \text{for } x \neq 0,$$

$$p_z\left(\frac{x}{y}\right) = \int p_x(x)p_y\left(\frac{x}{z} \mid x\right) \left|\frac{x}{z^2}\right| \, dx, \quad \text{for } z \neq 0.$$

To use these convolution formulae to determine the distribution of a derived variable, it is necessary to integrate a product of the base variable distribution functions. Even if analytic forms for the base variable distributions are available, only in rare cases can an analytic solution be obtained for the integral, and dependencies between the base variables pose a major problem. Numerical methods are then required. These may be directed at the integration itself, or at the underlying base variable distributions.

Numerical integration

If analytic base variable distributions are available, there is a variety of quadrature and finite difference methods for evaluating the convolution integral. However, these do not seem to have been applied to risk analysis problems. A likely explanation for this lies in the nature of the distributions they produce: they are numerical, not analytic, and so if the results from one convolution must be convoluted in turn with a further base variable, a different approach is needed.

Discrete probability distributions

A more flexible numerical approach is to abandon the analytic base variable distribution and to adopt a different representation for it. One such representation is what Kaplan (1981) calls a discrete probability distribution (DPD), or what Winkler and Hays (1970) refer to as a probability mass function.

A DPD is a set of doublets $\{\langle p_i, x_i \rangle\}$, in which p_i is the probability associated with a particular discrete value x_i of the base variable x, with $\Sigma_i \, p_i = 1$. The DPD can be regarded as an approximation to an underlying continuous base variable distribution, or it can be considered more directly, and often more usefully, as a specification of our state of knowledge about the base variable.

Combining two base variables in DPD form yields a result which is also a DPD (Kaplan 1981). If x and y are independent base variables with DPD representations $x = \{\langle p_i, x_i \rangle\}$ and $y = \{\langle q_j, y_j \rangle\}$, then the derived variable $z = f(x, y)$ is the DPD $z = \{\langle p_i q_j, f(x_i, y_j) \rangle\}$. This result generalizes readily to functions with more than two arguments.

A function g with a probabilistic form may also be represented as a DPD: $\{\langle r_k, g_k \rangle\}$. If $z = g(x)$, then z is the DPD $z = \{\langle p_i r_k, g_k(x_i) \rangle\}$.

While the DPD representation is notationally compact and computationally simple to implement, there are three problem areas associated with it.

First, if x and y are DPDs with m and n doublets respectively, then $z = f(x, y)$ has mn doublets, so a series of operations on DPDs will quickly lead to storage problems unless some form of aggregation is taken. Aggregation requires that the range of z be divided into intervals in some way. Doublets with z-values within a specified interval can now be combined into a single new doublet $\langle p, z \rangle$ with $p = \Sigma \, p_i$ and $z = h(z_j)$, where the summation is over the doublets in the interval and h is an aggregation function such as an arithmetic or geometric mean. This is not likely to be a major problem in practice.

The second problem area is serious. Discrete distribution procedures involve inherent bias relative to comparable continuous distribution treatment. Using very large numbers of doublets will limit this bias, but because a DPD approach ignores it, it cannot be controlled. It will accumulate over successive operations, and substantial computational effort is necessary to maintain reasonable confidence in the results.

The third problem area is also serious. The operations on DPDs which have been described above assume independence between the base variables, an important practical limitation.

Interval and histogram representations

An alternative representation of a base variable distribution is a histogram. With this representation the analytic convolution formulae become sums rather than integrals, and the calculations are both simple in concept and straightforward computationally. Several different histogram representations are possible, based on intervals of equal width (Driscoll, 1980; Chapman and Cooper, 1983a) or equal probability (Colombo and Jaarsma, 1980). The controlled interval and memory (CIM) approach is based on histograms with intervals of equal width, as described in the following chapters. Like discrete probability distribution approaches, approaches based on interval and histogram representations involve inherent bias. However, in the CIM framework the bias can be considered and controlled, drawing upon functional and numerical integration techniques, greatly reducing the computation required to maintain confidence in the results. Further, the CIM framework allows flexible treatment of dependence.

REFERENCES

Buzby, S. L. (1974) Extending the applicability of probabilistic management planning and control models. *Accounting Review*, **49**(1), 42–9.
Buzby, S. L. (1975) Extending the applicability of probabilistic management planning and control models: a reply. *Accounting Review*, **50**(4), 832–4.
Chapman, C. B. and D. F. Cooper (1983a) Risk Engineering: basic controlled interval and memory models. *Journal of the Operational Research Society*, **34**(1), 51–60.
Chapman, C. B. and D. F. Cooper (1983b) Parametric discounting. *OMEGA*, **11**(3), 303–10.
Colombo, A. G. and R. J. Jaarsma (1980) A powerful numerical method to combine random variables. *IEEE Transactions on Reliability*, **R-29**(2), 126–9.
Constantinides, G. M., Y. Ijiri and R. A. Leitch (1981) Stochastic cost-volume-profit analysis with a linear demand function. *Decision Sciences*, **12**(3), 417–27.
Craig, C. C. (1936) On the frequency function of xy. *Ann. Math. Statistic*, **7**, 1–15.
Crandall, K. C. and J. C. Woolery (1982) Schedule development under stochastic scheduling. *J. Construction Div. ASCE*, **108**(C02), 321–9.
Driscoll, M. F. (1980) Instructional uses of approximate convolutions and their graphs. *American Statistician*, **34**(3), 150–4.
Economos, A. M. (1968) A financial simulation for risk analysis of a proposed subsidiary. *Management Science*, **15**(12), B675–82.
Eilon, S. and T. R. Fowkes (1973) Sampling procedures for risk simulation. *Operational Research Quarterly*, **24**(2), 241–52.

Ferrara, W. L., J. C. Hayya and D. A. Nachman (1972) Normalcy of profit in the Jaedicke-Robichek model. *Accounting Review*, **47**(2), 299–307.

Hayya, J., W. Ferrara and E. Saniga (1975) Extending the applicability of probabilistic planning and control models: a comment. *Accounting Review*, **50**(4), 826–31.

Hertz, D. B. (1964) Risk analysis in capital investment. *Harvard Business Review*, **42**(1), 95–106.

Hilliard, J. E. and R. A. Leitch (1975) Cost-volume-profit analysis under uncertainty. *Accounting Review*, **50**(1), 69–80.

Hillier, F. E. (1963) The derivation of probabilistic information for the evaluation of risky investments. *Management Science*, **9**, 443–57.

Hull, J. C. (1980) *The Evaluation of Risk in Business Investment*. Pergamon, Oxford.

Jaedicke, R. K. and A. A. Robichek (1964) Cost-volume-profit analysis under uncertainty. *Accounting Review*, **39**(4), 917–26.

Johnson, G. L. and S. S. Simik (1971) Multi-product C-V-P analysis under uncertainty. *Journal of Accounting Research*, **9**, 278–286.

Johnson, G. L. and S. S. Simik (1974) The use of probability inequalities in multi-product C-V-P analysis. *Journal of Accounting Research*, **12**, 67–79.

Johnson, N. L., E. Nixon, D. E. Amos and E. S. Pearson (1963) Table of percentage points of Pearson curves. *Biometrika*, **50**, 459–98.

Kalymon, B. A. (1981) Methods of large project assessment given uncertainty in future energy pricing. *Managing Science*, **27**(4), 377–95.

Kaplan, S. (1981) On the method of discrete probability distributions in risk and reliability calculations—application to seismic risk assessment. *Risk Analysis*, **3**(3).

King, E. P., C. B. Sampson and L. L. Sims (1975) An alternative to Monte Carlo sampling in stochastic models. *Management Science*, **21**(6), 649–57.

Kottas, J. F., A. H.-L. Lau and H.-S. Lau (1978) A general approach to stochastic management planning models: an overview. *Accounting Review*, **52**(2), 389–401.

Kottas, J. F. and H.-S. Lau (1978a) Stochastic breakeven analysis. *Journal of the Operational Research Society*, **29**(3), 251–57.

Kottas, J. F. and H.-S. Lau (1978b) Direct simulation in stochastic CVP analysis. *Accounting Review*, **53**(3), 698–706.

Kottas, J. F. and H.-S. Lau (1978c) On handling dependent random variables in risk analysis. *Journal of the Operational Research Society*, **29**(12), 1209–17.

Kottas, J. F. and H.-S. Lau (1982) A four-moments alternative to simulation for a class of stochastic management models. *Management Science*, **28**(7), 749–58.

Lewellen, W. G. and M. S. Long (1972) Simulation versus single-value estimates in capital expenditure analysis. *Decision Sciences*, **3**(4), 19–33.

Liao, M. (1975) Model sampling: a stochastic cost-volume-profit analysis. *Accounting Review*, **50**(4), 780–90.

Myers, S. C. (1976) Postscript: using simulation for risk analysis. In S. C. Myers (ed.) *Modern Developments in Financial Management*, Praeger, New York.

Robichek, A. A. and J. C. Van Horne (1967) Abandonment value and capital budgeting. *J. Finance*, **22**(4), 577–89.

Spooner, J. E. (1974) Probabilistic estimating. *J. Construction Div. ASCE*, **100** (C01), 65–77.

Starr, M. K. and C. S. Tapiero (1975) Linear breakeven analysis under risk. *Operational Research Quarterly*, **26**(4,ii), 847–56.

Wagle, B. (1967), A statistical analysis of risk in capital investment projects, *Operational Research Quarterly*, **18**(1), 13–33.

Warszawski, A. (1982) Risk element in profit planning under inflation. *J. Construction Div. ASCE*, **104** (C04), 624–38.

Winkler, R. J. and W. L. Hays (1970) *Statistics: Probability Inference and Decision.* Second edition, Holt, Rinehart and Winston, New York.

Wyman, H. E. (1973) Financial lease evaluation under conditions of uncertainty. *Accounting Review*, **48**(3), 489–93.

CIM models for independent risks

Summary

This chapter introduces controlled interval and memory (CIM) models, in the context of combining independent risks. The CIM framework will be extended in later chapters throughout the book. A histogram representation of probability distributions is used. The combination of independent distributions is interpreted as a probability tree, and 'collapsed' calculation patterns are derived. Computational efficiency and precision, distribution specification flexibility and precision, and other combination methods are discussed.

INTRODUCTION

Combining probability distributions involves operations fundamental to most risk analysis. One of the simplest and most common of these operations is the addition of independent probabilistic variables, but many other operations are important, including multiplication, division and 'greatest' operations, with a variety of dependence forms. Many well-established approaches are available, as discussed in the previous chapter. This chapter describes a 'controlled interval' (CI) approach to the addition of independent probabilistic variables, as a first step in the elaboration of a 'controlled interval and memory' (CIM) approach to more general probabilistic modelling.

The choice of an approach depends on a number of considerations:

Its computational efficiency;
The precision of its calculation processes;
The flexibility it allows in specifying probability distributions, and the size of the errors associated with the specification;
The flexibility it allows in specifying dependence structures and the inter-relationships between probability distributions;

Loss of information, in both the specification and the computation processes;

The flexibility it allows in combining probability distributions, in terms of the combination operations that are possible;

The flexibility it allows in specifying combination structures when dealing with a large number of probability distributions.

Some blend of all seven of these should be the basis of a choice of approach, the blend varying with the circumstances. The advantages of the CI approach with respect to the first four of these considerations are examined in this chapter; the other three are dealt with in later chapters.

The next two sections of this chapter provide a simple common interval example of the controlled interval (CI) approach. This example is used throughout to illustrate and explain the major points. The following section considers CI computation error, ways to reduce or eliminate it, and associated generalizations of the CI computation process. Ways of specifying distributions so as to control distribution specification error are then considered. The next section briefly compares the generalized CI approach with alternative approaches, in the context of independent addition, in terms of computational efficiency and precision, errors in the specification of distributions and loss of information. The final section considers the impact of a requirement for operations other than sequential independent addition on the topics of the preceding sections.

The flexibility of computation operations and the flexibility in specifying dependence structures were key factors in the development of the CIM approach, and perhaps key areas of its comparative advantage. However, adequate treatment would need a detailed discussion of other operations and dependence forms, and thus it is beyond the scope of this chapter. The very important impact of the flexibility of computation operations on the associated modelling methodology is discussed later. Treatment of dependence and distribution combination structures at an elementary level is also discussed later.

AN OFFSHORE PIPELINE PROJECT

The controlled interval approach is illustrated by its application to an example concerned with the analysis of risks associated with the time schedule for constructing an offshore pipeline. The problem is fictitious, for expository convenience, but it is a composite of features of real problems experienced many times in a variety of environments.

A project team have a base plan for a 200 km offshore pipeline. The base plan includes a target schedule (programme or timetable) and associated contingency plans. Five activities are central to the plan: design of the

Table 3.1   Offshore pipeline activity list

Activity	Description
1	Design
2	Procurement
3	Delivery
4	Coating
5	Laying

pipeline, procurement of pipe suppliers, delivery of the pipe, coating the pipe and laying the pipe (Table 3.1).

Design is straightforward, but the project team must compete with other projects for staff. Procurement has a predictable duration, if it is known which of two suppliers will be chosen for reasons of corporate policy. Pipe delivery has a reasonably predictable short duration for one supplier, and an equally predictable longer duration for the other.

The pipe is steel, 32 inches in diameter. Before it can be laid, it must be coated with six inches of concrete and anti-corrosive materials. Coating involves three main sources of uncertainty: when a coating yard will be available, how productive the yard will prove on a normal shift basis, and whether or not overtime or second-shift working will be required.

Laying involves a number of sources of uncertainty because of the nature of the task and its physical environment. Pipe sections are welded together on a lay barge and strung over the back of the barge, maintaining a smooth *S* curve, even in several hundred metres of water, via tension on a large number of leading anchor lines. As the barge approaches an anchor, a tug lifts the anchor and carries it out in front again. There is a nominal maximum wave height for laying which may be from 1.6 m up to 5 m depending upon the barge and the anchor handling tugs. In March a 1.6 m barge may be unable to lay any pipe, or it may achieve 31 lay days, with an expectation of about 5 days, depending upon the sea area. Conditions improve to midsummer, with an expectation of about 25 lay days, then decline to a November low comparable to March. As 1.6 m barges and associated equipment can cost about £100 000 per day, the shoulder seasons are expensive per kilometre of pipe laid, and the winter is non-viable. The latest generation of barges are significantly more productive during the shoulder seasons, and such barges have been used during the winter, but their daily rate can be closer to £200 000, including support facilities.

During laying, a single pipe buckle is likely, and two or more are possible. When the pipe buckles, it drops to the ocean floor and fills with water, sucking in mud and other debris. Repair usually takes 20–30 days.

Although starting again used to be the only alternative in these circumstances, submarine repair and hookup is now feasible.

New barges involve uncertain lay rates, in the 1–5 km per day range. If a barge gets into trouble on a prior contract, it may not be available on the planned start date. Unless substantial retainers are paid, a barge may not be available for unplanned additional seasons, and replacements may not be easy to find. If a pipeline is completed a season earlier than necessary, the opportunity cost of the idle capital is about £400 000. If a pipeline is a season late, the opportunity cost of non-productive platforms and wells may be very much greater.

The nominal (and rather restricted) objective of the risk analysis in this example is to determine the probability of completing the five sequential activities on time. The first two activities are examined in detail in this chapter. The others will be considered in subsequent chapters as new features of the controlled interval approach are introduced.

COMMON INTERVAL ADDITION

The first of the sequence of activities is 'design', associated with uncertainty largely related to competition for project design staff. A simple CI (common interval) definition of this uncertainty uses three durations D_1 for the activity in months, with associated probabilities, $P(D_1)$, as indicated in Table 3.2.

Table 3.2   Design distribution, D_1 months

D_1	$P(D_1)$
5	0.2
6	0.5
7	0.3

Two alternative interpretations of this tabular representation are possible, both useful on occasion. One is the discrete probability tree of Figure 3.1. The other is the rectangular histogram of Figure 3.2, or the equivalent cumulative form of Figure 3.3, where the durations are central classmarks for values over the intervals 4.5–5.5 months, 5.5–6.5 months and 6.5–7.5 months. Smooth curves can be used in Figures 3.2 and 3.3, but for most purposes the simplicity employed here is preferable.

Only three cells were used for this example, but computer software can allow distributions to be specified in this form using any number of D_1 values. A graphical approach using a smooth curve version of Figure 3.3 can be convenient in this context. Computer software can also generate

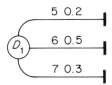

Figure 3.1   Discrete probability tree for the design distribution D_1

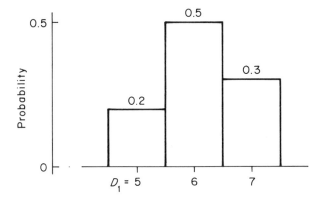

Figure 3.2   Rectangular histogram for the design distribution in density form

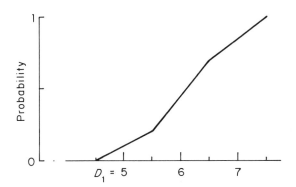

Figure 3.3   Cumulative design distribution

Table 3.3   Procurement distribution, D_2 months

D_2	$P(D_2)$
3	0.2
4	0.1
5	0.7

distributions in this form from conventional distributions specified in terms of parameters, like the minimum, maximum and most likely values used to define PERT Beta distributions.

Experience in a project planning context suggests this flexibility and generality is occasionally invaluable and never unwelcome.

The next activity is 'procurement', associated with uncertainty largely related to a choice between two pipe suppliers for reasons of corporate policy. The simple CI definition is provided by Table 3.3.

The bimodal form of $P(D_2)$ is a clear indication of two quite different underlying situations. Project planning experience suggests a single probability distribution associated with more than one underlying situation is quite common, but not always obvious, and it is useful to initially estimate the separate distributions, as illustrated by Figure 3.4. Computer software which allows them to be combined, weighting by associated probabilities, is useful in such cases.

Design and procurement are independent activities. Adding their duration distributions, to determine the duration distribution for the combination of 'design' followed by 'procurement', can be performed using a two-level probability tree.

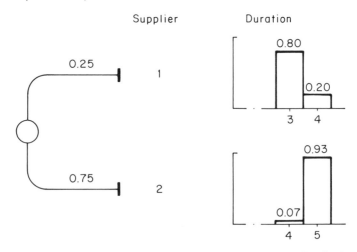

Figure 3.4   Situations underlying the bimodal procurement distribution D_2

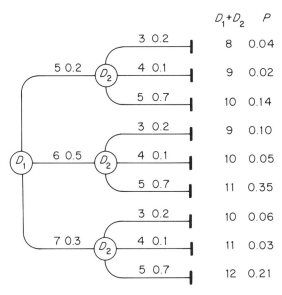

Figure 3.5 Two level probability tree for the independent addition of design plus procurement

A simple representation of the probability tree is provided in Figure 3.5, D_1 defining three branches, each of which is associated with three D_2 branches. Table 3.4 provides a tabular form of this tree. Implied values of $P(D_a)$, $D_a = D_1 + D_2$, the joint distribution of design plus procurement, may be obtained from the probability tree in the normal way, as shown in Figure 3.5 and Table 3.4. However, the common interval form allows the

Table 3.4 Two level probability tree for design plus procurement

Design		Procurement		Design plus procurement	
D_1	$P(D_1)$	D_2	$P(D_2)$	D_a	$P(D_a)$
5	0.2	3	0.2	$5 + 3 = 8$	$0.2 \times 0.2 = 0.04$
		4	0.1	$5 + 4 = 9$	$0.2 \times 0.1 = 0.02$
		5	0.7	$5 + 5 = 10$	$0.2 \times 0.7 = 0.14$
6	0.5	3	0.2	$6 + 3 = 9$	$0.5 \times 0.2 = 0.10$
		4	0.1	$6 + 4 = 10$	$0.5 \times 0.1 = 0.05$
		5	0.7	$6 + 5 = 11$	$0.5 \times 0.7 = 0.35$
7	0.3	3	0.2	$7 + 3 = 10$	$0.3 \times 0.2 = 0.06$
		4	0.1	$7 + 4 = 11$	$0.3 \times 0.1 = 0.03$
		5	0.7	$7 + 5 = 12$	$0.3 \times 0.7 = 0.21$

Table 3.5 The simplified computation for design plus procurement, in the case where the individual design and procurement intervals do not need to be remembered

D_a	Design plus procurement Computation	$P(D_a)$
8	0.2×0.2	0.04
9	$0.2 \times 0.1 + 0.5 \times 0.2$	0.12
10	$0.2 \times 0.7 + 0.5 \times 0.1 + 0.3 \times 0.2$	0.25
11	$0.5 \times 0.7 + 0.3 \times 0.7$	0.38
12	0.3×0.7	0.21

simplified approach illustrated in Table 3.5. Each possible combination of D_1 and D_2 is considered, the joint probabilities producing the computation entries, and the entries associated with the same D_a value are summed. If we do not need to remember D_1 or D_2 individually, we can choose to remember only their sum D_a.

For illustrative simplicity, the same interval widths have been used for both distributions and only three classes. In practice, more intervals are normally used, with different interval widths for each component distribution and the result, but a constant interval within each distribution. The procedures used here are very basic special cases, but they are important as a basis of understanding for all those involved in actual studies.

COMPUTATION ERROR AND COMPUTATION GENERALIZATION

Had we chosen to interpret the D_i values of Tables 3.2 and 3.3 as integer values, we could interpret the D_a values of Table 3.5 as integers, and the $P(D_a)$ computation of Table 3.5 would be precise and error free.

Alternatively, had we chosen to interpret the D_i and $P(D_i)$ of Tables 3.2 and 3.3 as doublets which represented the limits of our state of knowledge in the Discrete Probability Distribution (DPD) sense, the D_a and $P(D_a)$ of Table 3.5 would represent the limits of our state of knowledge, implicitly admitting but explicitly ignoring any computation error associated with 'knowledge' not available.

Having interpreted the D_i as classmarks with associated class boundaries, representing very large sets of integer values, classified or grouped, with continuous variable D_i being a special limiting case, we must recognise a source of computation error.

Some of this computation error arises because values in the top half of one class together with values in the top half of another class may be associated with a joint classmark value which is one class too low. For example, in Table 3.5, the probability associated with $D_1 = 6.4$ and $D_2 = 4.4$ is associated with a joint duration $D_a = 6 + 4 = 10$. As $6.4 + 4.4 = 10.8$, it should be associated with a joint duration $D_a = 11$.

A corresponding computation error arises because values in the bottom half of one class together with values in the bottom half of another class may be associated with a joint classmark value which is one class too high. For example, in Table 3.5, the probability associated with $D_1 = 5.6$ and $D_2 = 3.6$ is associated with a joint duration $D_a = 6 + 4 = 10$. As $5.6 + 3.6 = 9.2$, it should be associated with a joint duration $D_a = 9$.

If the original classes for $D_1 = 6$ and $D_2 = 4$ are interpreted as rectangular histograms, functional integration shows that the joint distribution D_a is a triangle (Figure 3.6).

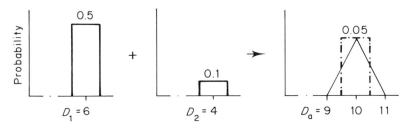

Figure 3.6 **The independent addition of two rectangular intervals yields a triangular distribution, using functional integration. The histogram interpretation is also shown, indicating the errors involved**

Most of the misallocation of probabilities cancels out, but some residual remains. In particular, modal probability values are over-estimated, and extreme values are ignored. In this sense the joint distribution of Table 3.5 under-estimates risk, a distribution in density form free from computation error being slightly wider and flatter.

Complete elimination or partial reduction of this computation error within the CI framework can be achieved via one or more of five approaches:

derived correction factors;
interpolated correction factors;
more classes;
empirically determined correction factors; or
more allocations.

Derived correction factors

This approach involves assuming specific within-class probability distributions for any two component items or item groups, and deriving

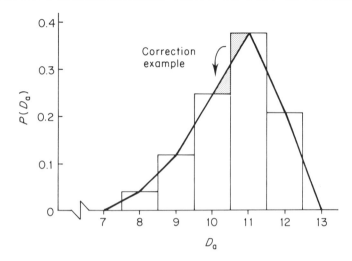

Figure 3.7   **Probability density distributions for design plus procurement. The rectangular distribution comes from Table 3.5; the trapezoidal form is obtained by functional integration of the rectangular components from Tables 3.2 and 3.3**

correction factors based upon the associated probability distribution function for the within-class distributions associated with the result. For example, if the distributions of Tables 3.2 and 3.3 are associated with a rectangular density form, the joint distribution has the trapezoidal density form illustrated in Figure 3.7, as can be proved using functional integration or finite difference techniques (illustrated in Figure 3.6). Associating the joint distribution of Table 3.5 with a rectangular density form introduces error, the necessary net corrections involving a transfer from higher probability classes to adjacent lower probability classes equal to one eighth of the difference between adjacent probability values, also illustrated in Figure 3.7. The necessary correction is equivalent to cutting off the corners of the rectangular density form and relocating them as indicated.

In this case the key errors are a probability of 0.005 which should be allocated to the classmark 7, and a probability of 0.026 25 which should be allocated to the classmark 13. More generally, 0.01 is the order of magnitude of the errors associated with extreme classmarks, other errors being comparatively trivial, if only three classes are used for component distributions as for this example. Adding successive distributions will lead to smoother and smoother joint distribution curves, involving smaller and smaller corrections.

One difficulty with this approach is the more and more complex form of the corrections required as more and more items are considered, or if smoother curves are used to begin with. Continual application of corrections based on rectangular histograms is inconsistent. It over-states risk, because it over-corrects relative to the smoother distributions which must result from successive distribution combinations. However, as most other sources of bias under-state risk, a compensating bias can be attractive, if it can be justified.

Interpolated correction factors

This approach involves using the correction procedure derived above as an upper bound, in relation to a lower bound provided by the uncorrected procedure of Table 3.5. This yields a modified correction procedure which might be interpreted as an unbiased interpolation between these bounds. The difficulty with this approach is defining and justifying the interpolation point. However, it provides more flexibility than the first on its own.

More classes

This approach involves recognizing that computation error decreases in proportion to the difference in adjacent class probability values, as illustrated by Figure 3.7. This means computation error decreases as the number of classes increases. In principle it does not disappear entirely until each class contains a single integer, a special limiting form of within-class distribution which is error free. In practice it decreases to zero very rapidly, for whatever degree of precision is required. Direct specification of a finer class width structure is possible, but not necessary. Any convenient class for specification purposes can be used to define a narrower width version of Tables 3.2 and 3.3 for computation purposes, using a suitable interpretation of the distribution shape. For example, the classes associated with D_1 and D_2 in Tables 3.2 and 3.3 might be separated into five sub-classes, defined assuming uniform within-class distributions, as indicated by Table 3.6 and Figure 3.8.

Table 3.6 A finer interval structure for D_1 and D_2, assuming uniform within-class distributions in the original specifications in Tables 3.2 and 3.3

Design		Procurement	
D_1	$P(D_1)$	D_2	$P(D_2)$
4.6	0.04	2.6	0.04
4.8	0.04	2.8	0.04
5.0	0.04	3.0	0.04
5.2	0.04	3.2	0.04
5.4	0.04	3.4	0.04
5.6	0.10	3.6	0.02
⋮		⋮	

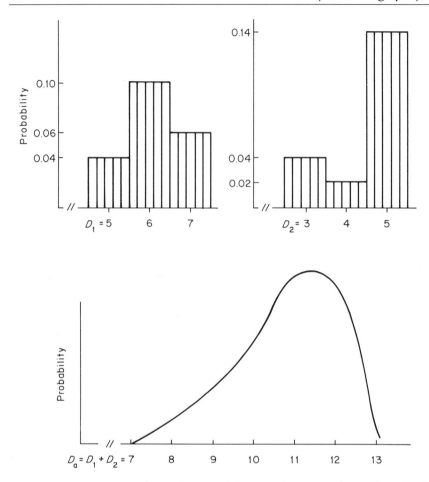

Figure 3.8   Addition using finer sub-intervals for D_1 and D_2, assuming uniform distributions within the classes in Tables 3.2 and 3.3

The $P(D_1) = 0.04$ associated with $D_1 = 4.6$ in Table 3.6 was obtained via 0.2/5, the $P(D_1) = 0.2$ for $D_1 = 5$ of Table 3.2 providing the 0.2, and so on for the $3 \times 5 = 15$ classes of each distribution. If the distributions associated with Table 3.6 were combined using the procedure of Table 3.4, the result would be as indicated by Table 3.7 and Figure 3.8.

This clearly provides a result much closer to the trapezoidal cumulative form illustrated by Figure 3.7 than Table 3.5. Indeed, the $0.0016 + 0.0032 = 0.0048$ probability allocated to 7.2 and 7.4 is very close to the 0.005 which should have been allocated to $D_a = 7$ in Table 3.5, as noted earlier. More generally, 0.001 is the order of magnitude of the errors associated with

Table 3.7 The simplified probability-tree computation for $D_a = D_1 + D_2$ using the finer interval structure of Table 3.6

	Design plus procurement	
D_a	Computation	$P(D_a)$
7.2	0.04×0.04	0.0016
7.4	$0.04 \times 0.04 + 0.04 \times 0.04$	0.0032
7.6	$0.04 \times 0.04 + 0.04 \times 0.04 + 0.04 \times 0.04$	0.0048
7.8	$0.04 \times 0.04 + 0.04 \times 0.04 + 0.04 \times 0.04 \ldots$	0.0064
8.0	$0.04 \times 0.04 + 0.04 \times 0.04 + 0.04 \times 0.04 \ldots$	0.0080
8.2	$0.04 \times 0.02 + 0.04 \times 0.04 + 0.04 \times 0.04 \ldots$	0.0112
8.4	$0.04 \times 0.02 + 0.04 \times 0.02 + 0.04 \times 0.04 \ldots$	0.0144
8.6	$0.04 \times 0.02 + 0.04 \times 0.02 + 0.04 \times 0.02 \ldots$	0.0176
$\vdots$		$\vdots$

extreme classmarks, other errors being comparatively trivial. All such errors decrease as a function of n^2, where n is the number of classes. The availability of this approach makes the procedure of Table 3.5 and extensions like that illustrated by Table 3.7 inherently error free. Computation error is simply an option, which can be accepted if it is not worth the effort to reduce or eliminate it, at any appropriate level.

Empirically determined correction factors

This approach involves empirical experiments to assess correction factors akin to those associated with the first and second approaches. Any pair of distributions can be combined using a very fine class structure, so fine it can be treated as error free to the level of precision required. The result can then be summarized in a variety of simple frameworks, which can be treated as error-free results. Simplified versions of the component distributions can then be combined, and compared to the error-free equivalent. Error measured in this way can be related to the class width, the number of classes, the difference in adjacent probability values, or other parameters suggested by the first or second approaches. This approach demands extensive experimentation, but it lends further flexibility to the first three.

More allocations

This approach to computation error involves allocating each joint probability component in a manner which reduces error to an acceptable level. For example, instead of redefining Tables 3.2 and 3.3 in the form of Table 3.6 with 5 times as many classes, and then combining the results as illustrated by Table 3.7, the same result could be obtained more directly.

The factor set

$$0.04 \quad 0.08 \quad 0.12 \quad 0.16 \quad 0.20 \quad 0.16 \quad 0.12 \quad 0.08 \quad 0.04$$

could be applied directly to the $0.2 \times 0.2 = 0.04$, $0.2 \times 0.1 = 0.02$, $0.5 \times 0.2 = 0.10$ and subsequent entries of Table 3.5 to generate the entries of Table 3.8.

The factor set thus serves to integrate each pair of component distribution class intervals, allocating the associated probability to a joint probability distribution with a different class structure. The chosen factor set sums to one and spans twice the class width of Table 3.5, using a triangular pattern conforming to the result class width as for Table 3.7. For independent component distributions based on equal intervals, a triangular factor set provides a simple and attractive allocation pattern, but any of the first three approaches to reducing computation error can be applied to the definition of alternative factor set shapes. The triangular shape is based upon integrating two within class distributions which are both uniform (constant probability) and both the same width. Its validity given these assumptions is illustrated by Table 3.7.

An obvious advantage of using more allocations in comparison to using more classes is the considerable gain in computational efficiency. Apart from avoiding the need to refine the component distribution scales as the number of intervals is increased for the result, computation effort increases in a linear manner, whereas the approach of Tables 3.6 and 3.7 involves an increase in computation effort which is proportional to the square of the increase in the number of intervals.

Table 3.8   The computation of $D_a = D_1 + D_2$ using the factor set 0.04, 0.08, 0.12, 0.16, 0.20, 0.16, 0.12, 0.08, 0.04

	Design plus procurement	
D_a	Computation	$P(D_a)$
7.2	0.04×0.04	0.0016
7.4	0.08×0.04	0.0032
7.6	0.12×0.04	0.0048
7.8	0.16×0.04	0.0064
8.0	0.20×0.04	0.0080
8.2	$0.16 \times 0.04 + 0.04 \times 0.02 + 0.04 \times 0.10$	0.0112
8.4	$0.12 \times 0.04 + 0.08 \times 0.02 + 0.08 \times 0.10$	0.0176
8.6	$0.08 \times 0.04 + 0.12 \times 0.02 + 0.12 \times 0.10$	0.0208
8.8	$0.04 \times 0.04 + 0.16 \times 0.02 + 0.16 \times 0.10$	0.0240
$\vdots$		$\vdots$

A further advantage of the more allocations approach is that it generalizes easily to component item and result classes which are not the same size, an obvious advantage when the items are of different magnitudes, allowing a controlled number of classes for all component and result distributions. As with Table 3.8, each class interval combination involves a form of integration of the associated within-class distributions. The minimum value of the resulting distribution is the sum of the component class distribution minima. The maximum value of the resulting distribution is the sum of the component class distribution maxima. The shape of the allocation defined by the functional equivalent of the factors can reflect specific within-class distribution assumptions, adjustments based on bounds, or adjustments based on empirical experiments, including adjustments designed to balance the effects of truncating unwanted distribution tails. Each component distribution and the resulting sum distribution can use different interval widths.

Another advantage of the more allocations approach is the ability to drop common intervals within each distribution, if precision within one particular region is more important than precision in other regions, as may occur when very long distribution tails are of interest.

A final advantage of the more allocations approach is that it generalizes easily to other distribution combination operations.

Generalized CI approaches

Detailed treatment of generalized CI approaches, embedding the first four approaches as necessary in the fifth, is beyond the scope of this book. However, the examples chosen should clarify the principles involved, and illustrate the order of magnitude of the computation effort and error. The initial simple example of Table 3.5 provides errors of the order of 0.01, which the example of Table 3.8 reduces to the order of 0.001. Computation error of the order of 0.01 is acceptable for simple examples. Computation error of the order of 0.001 may not be acceptable for analysis purposes, but it is easily reduced by further orders of magnitude, at negligible cost in modern computing terms. Computation cost and error balancing can be an explicit part of CI computer software, either automatically or through manual intervention.

Generalizing the addition of two independent probabilistic variables to three or more poses no new problems.

SPECIFICATION ERROR AND SPECIFICATION GENERALIZATION

Computation error of the order of 0.01 for the joint distribution of Table 3.5 should be considered in the context of errors in specifying the probability distribution which may be of the order of 0.1, ten times as large. Controlling specification error is much more important than controlling computation error. Two kinds of specification error are worth distinguishing, although they are not independent: approximation error and residual error. There are a number of ways of reducing or eliminating specification approximation error:

direct use of more classes;
maximum order polynomials for input distributions;
less than maximum order polynomials for output distributions;
standard probability level specifications;
other input distribution functions.

Direct use of more classes

The use of one month class intervals for the distributions of Tables 3.2 and 3.3 involves a specification approximation error which the smaller class interval of Table 3.6 could reduce by using a smoother curve specification like that of Table 3.9 and Figure 3.9. The probability allocations of Table 3.9 are quite different from those of Table 3.6, and differences of this kind could be argued to be a specification approximation error associated with Tables 3.2 and 3.3, corrected by Table 3.9.

Sometimes it is convenient to reduce specification approximation error to an acceptable level by the direct use of more classes, as illustrated by Table 3.9. Flexibility and simplicity are maximized. Any distribution shape can be used, to any degree of specification precision. The existence of this approach makes the CI approach inherently free from specification approximation error. Approximation is simply an option, to be accepted if the saving in specification effort is worthwhile.

Table 3.9 A finer interval structure for D_1 and D_2, assuming a smooth-curve specification

Design		Procurement	
D_1	$P(D_1)$	D_2	$P(D_2)$
4.2	0.01	2.2	0.01
4.4	0.01	2.4	0.01
4.6	0.01	2.6	0.02
4.8	0.01	2.8	0.02
5.0	0.03	3.0	0.05
5.2	0.05	3.2	0.06
5.4	0.08	3.4	0.03
5.6	0.08	3.6	0.02
⋮		⋮	

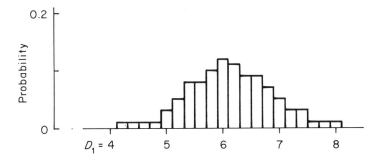

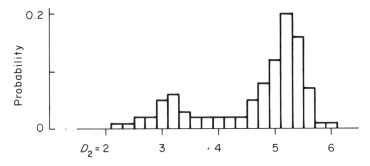

Figure 3.9 A smooth-curve specification for D_1 and D_2

Maximum order polynominals for input distributions

This approach involves fitting a smooth curve to a specification which is cruder than that used for computation purposes, and interpreting the curve choice as part of the specification. For example, the three classes of $P(D_1)$ in Table 3.2 could be associated with a cumulative distribution shape defined by the third-order polynomial

$$b_0 + b_1 X + b_2 X^2 + b_3 X^3 = p,$$

where for $X = 4.5, 5.5, 6.5$ and 7.5, $p = 0, 0.2, 0.7$ and 1.0 (Figure 3.10). Solving the associated four linear equations for the b_i and using them to allocate probabilities to classmarks $4.6, 4.8, 5.0 \ldots 7.4$ will yield a shape more like Table 3.9 than Table 3.6. Using still finer classes would involve no additional specification effort, and computation effort could be balanced against both specification approximation error and computation error.

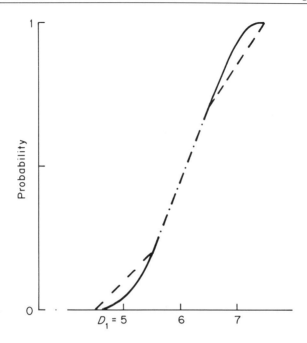

Figure 3.10   Polynomial cumulative distribution for D_1

More generally, nth-order polynomials with n classes, given an n greater than 3, provide a useful complement to direct specification of more intervals.

Less than maximum order polynomials for output distributions

In addition to, or instead of, smoothing input or component distributions, result or output distributions could be smoothed using regression analysis and polynomials of lower order than the number of classes would permit.

Standard probability level specifications

An alternative involves using standard probability levels, like quartiles or deciles, and fitting a polynomial in a manner akin to that just discussed.

Other input distribution functions

A final alternative involves using distribution functions other than polynomials, specified in terms of suitable parameters. For example, Normal (Gaussian) distributions can be specified in terms of mean and variance, and Beta distributions can be specified in terms of optimistic (minimum), pessimisstic (maximum) and most likely (modal) values. Hybrids are also useful. For example, Normal distribution tails can be used in conjunction with a Beta distribution between confidence limits associated with optimistic and pessimistic values.

Specifications like this may be used for reasons of convenience, or they may be based on theoretical results. For example, in the next chapter, distributions of times between failures are specified as negative exponential distributions, defined by the appropriate failure rates or mean times between failures, making the reasonable assumption of random failures. Many other examples will be seen in subsequent chapters.

Computer software which facilitates user choices with all these options makes a CI approach very flexible, and associated specification approximation error is easy to control. Adequate treatment of this source of error will often provide more than sufficient freedom from computation error as an indirect spinoff.

Specification residual error

Specification residual error, all other forms of specification error, is the most important kind of error, because it is the most difficult to control. No approach can fully resolve these difficulties, including the CI approach. However, three characteristics not shared by most other approaches make the CI approach comparatively attractive.

First, computer software which allows a flexible approach to specification approximation error as just discussed also allows the user to select a means of specifying any particular distribution which is the most comfortable for the circumstances. The specification method can be adjusted to the user and the problem, rather than forcing the user to conform to a rigid model.

Second, given such software, it is an easy matter to extend it to allow comparisons of different approaches to specifying a distribution as a means of checking consistency.

Third, if n distributions are summed, the computation procedure automatically provides $n - 2$ intermediate sums, a useful basis for further consistency tests, including representations showing the relative contribution to uncertainty of each source distribution. The usefulness of this facility has been demonstrated in many case studies. It will be seen frequently in subsequent chapters.

COMPARISON WITH ALTERNATIVE APPROACHES

The CI approach is closely related to the DPD approach. If component and joint distributions are associated with rectangular histograms, a convenient convention, class mark values are also conditional expectations, expected values within each interval. This means Tables 3.2 to 3.5 can be given a DPD interpretation. However, the DPD approach ignores computation error, making it impossible to control explicitly, and limiting implicit control to the use of more D_i and $P(D_i)$ doublets, or different doublet patterns. Further, it lacks the specification flexibility of the CI approach, with implications for specification approximation error and residual error. Finally, it involves a loss of information if large numbers of doublets are summarized. Its use may be preferable in some cases, but it would seem such circumstances must be very limited.

The CI approach is also related to a functional integration approach. If the errors indicated by Figure 3.7 are corrected, using the allocations approach to computation errors and the factor set

     0.125   0.750   0.125,

assuming rectangular histogram components and a trapezoidal histogram joint distribution, the resulting distribution is the same as a functional integration approach would provide. However, the CI approach is clearly much simpler in its basic forms, as illustrated by Tables 3.2 and 3.5, and much more flexible in general. Functional integration is only preferable when simple special cases are involved, as in basic random arrival and departure queueing systems.

The CI approach is also related to a numerical integration approach. If the rectangular histogram assumption for component distributions is interpreted as an approximation to an underlying smooth curve, the results are the same. However, the CI approach is simpler in its basic forms, and much more flexible in general. Numerical integration has no apparent advantage, although in some respects it is the alternative to CI which is closest conceptually.

Given a large number of distributions to sum, with none dominating because of size or variability, summing distribution means and variances to define a joint distribution mean and variance is an attractive approach. However, when these conditions do not hold, moment based approaches become complex by comparison to Table 3.5 and generalizations of it, without any guarantee of a decrease in computation cost or error. Further, a serious loss of information associated with component and resulting distributions is involved. Using such approaches to replace Table 3.5 should make this clear.

Monte Carlo approaches offer computational simplicity and flexibility when complex non-sequential distribution combination structures are involved. However, specification flexibility is not greater in the present context, and computation (sampling) error is much greater for comparable levels of computation effort. To provide a single sample, many random number generation processes would involve a computational effort comparable to that employed by Table 3.5, and computational precision of the same order would involve an increase in computational effort of several orders of magnitude.

OPERATION FLEXIBILITY AND OPERATION GENERALIZATION

As illustrated in Chapter 7, the basic common interval independent addition operation of Table 3.5 will generalize easily to accommodate dependent distributions using conditional specifications, and simplified percentage dependence specifications (akin to coefficient of correlation specifications) are also possible. Subtraction and 'greatest' operations involve equally simple generalizations. However, the basic common interval approach will not generalize directly to multiplication and division. These operations in independent and dependent forms require the generalized controlled interval (CI) approach with allocation factor sets as illustrated by Table 3.8, or functional equivalents, which reflect the operation in question. For example, multiplication of two within-class distributions must be related to maximum and minimum values defined by products of component class maxima and minima.

However, it should be clear that within the context of a generalized CI approach incorporating the multiple allocation concept illustrated by Table 3.8, many other operations, involving dependence if required, pose no new special difficulties in terms of distribution specification effort, computational effort, or computational error. This is not true of the functional integration, numerical integration, or moment-based approaches to combining distributions. Monte Carlo approaches have no new advantages relative to the CI approach, unless complex non-sequential distribution combination patterns are involved, as in some PERT networks.

The DPD approach has some new comparative advantages, but only if precision is not very important and a basic distribution specification approach is acceptable.

COMPUTER SOFTWARE

BP International have developed a second generation of computer software to perform CIM calculations on a mainframe computer, incorporating many of the features noted above, after taking a first generation of software through nine revisions incorporating developments suggested by one of the authors of this book and their experience. The authors have developed software for Acres International for CIM computations within several analysis structures, described in Chapters 5 and 6. K & H Project Systems Limited have worked with the authors to produce a commercially available CIM software package PERK for use on microcomputers, including the IBM PC family. This package contains a number of the features discussed in this chapter, although the emphasis is on ease of specification of distributions and computation structures. As in the case of Monte Carlo simulation, CIM procedures are conceptually simple enough for anyone to write their own computer software, but good commercially available software is cost effective because of the investment in easy-to-use input and output facilities and procedures which balance computation speed and precision in an appropriate manner.

CONCLUSION

The controlled interval (CI) approach to adding independent probabilistic variables is simple in its basic common interval form, and very flexible in its generalized forms. It allows specification effort, specification error, computation error, and computation effort to be controlled in an integrated, effective, and efficient manner. Moment-based, DPD and functional integration approaches may be preferred in some cases, but only in very special circumstances, and numerical integration and Monte Carlo approaches offer no advantages.

Chapter 4

Case study: reliability analysis of an LNG facility

Summary

This chapter introduces the risk engineering _method_, as distinct from the _models_ which have been discussed so far. This is done in the context of a case study of a risk engineering reliability analysis of a proposed liquefied natural gas (LNG) production and delivery system to be located in the high Arctic. The case study illustrates:

(a) the concept of the risk engineering method;
(b) an analysis structured on system components;
(c) the combination of independent risks, with different combination methods corresponding to different engineering procedures;
(d) analysis with a single criterion;
(e) forms of presentation of results;
(f) the importance of non-numerical aspects of risk analysis.

INTRODUCTION

Model, method, and method design distinctions

A simple but useful textbook characterization of the operational or operations research (OR) method is a sequence of steps: describe the problem, formulate a model, derive a solution, test the model and evaluate the solution, implement and maintain the solution.

Some people view the 'problem' which underlies this method as too constraining in a world full of 'messes'. However, even if the problems presented are embedded in messes requiring resolution, the authors have found it useful to employ what some might regard as an even more constrained version of the OR method, in that it is specific to the problem situation and to the proposed family of models.

A simple well known example of such a method/model/situation combination, not always considered in these terms, is provided by critical path

47

analysis (CPA). The model is the activity network, with its graphical and mathematical forms. The method is the sequence of steps used to apply CPA to project planning: list the activities, estimate activity durations, diagram the activities, compute the project duration and activity float, identify the critical path, adjust for timetable restrictions and cost tradeoffs, adjust for resource restrictions and cost tradeoffs, implement the plan, and keep it updated (Table 4.1). The first three steps combine problem description with model formulation, greatly increasing the effectiveness and efficiency of the problem description and model formulation process by prejudging the model form to be used. The ready availability of CPA computer software makes the fourth 'derive a solution' step straight-forward. The fifth and sixth steps make testing the model and evaluating the solution more specific to similar ends, as does the final step. Using the CPA model and method to plan and control a project is one form of project planning. The design of new techniques involving a model and method which is specific to the model and the situation, like CPA, is the concern of this chapter.

An initial method design exercise

In 1976 the second author undertook the design of a project planning method incorporating risk analysis for offshore North Sea projects for BP International. It was based on the synthesis of a range of models and methods used for earlier studies. It was tested by the author and BP engineers, revised in the process of testing, and documented over the 1976–7 period. Its initial testing and its first use on a live project in 1977–8 employed pocket calculators, to avoid restricting model formulation to pre-judged computer software. After the first live project, computer software development began. It has been used by BP on more than 20 major projects to date. Details of the method, models, computer software, and context of use are provided elsewhere. Chapter 1 used it to illustrate the method concept, and it will be referred to in later chapters, but not discussed in detail, for expository reasons. For present purposes it will be referred to as the SCERT method (synergistic contingency evaluation and review technique).

A further method design exercise

In 1980 the second author undertook the design of a reliability assessment method for a study of the reliability of a liquid natural gas (LNG) facility in the Canadian Arctic assisted by the first author, who undertook necessary software modifications, both assisting with implementation. In this case a

Table 4.1 Models and methods for project planning
(The links shown assume a particular network-based perspective of project planning models. Other interpretations are possible and would lead to different linkages. Iterative loops have been omitted.)

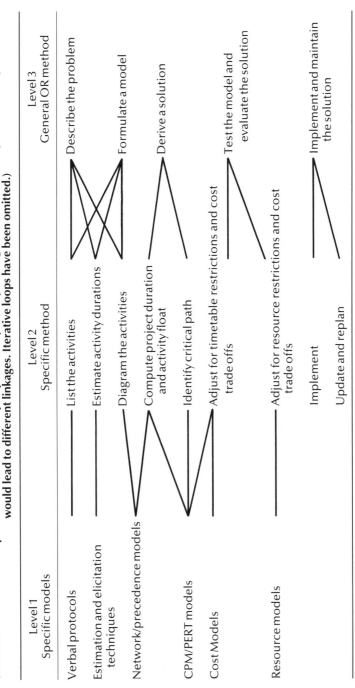

Level 1 Specific models	Level 2 Specific method	Level 3 General OR method
Verbal protocols	List the activities	Describe the problem
Estimation and elicitation techniques	Estimate activity durations	
Network/precedence models	Diagram the activities	Formulate a model
	Compute project duration and activity float	
CPM/PERT models	Identify critical path	Derive a solution
Cost Models	Adjust for timetable restrictions and cost trade offs	
		Test the model and evaluate the solution
Resource models	Adjust for resource restrictions and cost trade offs	
	Implement	Implement and maintain the solution
	Update and replan	

two week period was set aside at the beginning of the study for methodology design. It was a busy two weeks, but a detailed procedure with examples was available at the end of that period, and the study proceeded based upon that method with few difficulties. With half a dozen engineers working on the study to coordinate, a tight budget and a tight timetable, the explicit method design phase proved very worthwhile.

This chapter discusses the specific risk engineering method developed for the reliability analysis of the Arctic LNG facility: reliability analysis, evaluation and review (RAER). The emphasis here is on methodological issues in the context of a particular case study. Although sample results are presented, it is not intended to discuss specific models in any detail; these are treated elsewhere both in general terms, and in relation of the present reliability analysis example.

DECISION SITUATION

The proposed LNG facility was part of a proposed means of recovering natural gas from the Arctic and transporting it to appropriate markets. The gas gathering, processing, liquefaction and storage facilities would consist of a conventional wellhead and gas-gathering system, a pipeline buried in permafrost, a single-train gas-processing plant, and barge-mounted storage tanks. Delivery of LNG would be made to ships berthed nearby, using a pipeline system and loading arms. Heat from the liquefaction process would keep the berthed ships free of ice, and once in motion, the ships would have substantial ice-breaking capability.

Only nine LNG liquefaction plants had been constructed in the world at the time of the study. None had experienced the severe climatic conditions and geographical isolation of the proposed site. All existing systems were multiple-train systems, as opposed to the single-train system under consideration. None of the existing systems required integration with the complex delivery considerations imposed by long distance and year-round navigation in ice-covered waters to satisfy a base load demand. For these reasons, and others, it was essential to investigate the reliability of the proposed LNG facility. The overall concern of this particular study was the sizing of the storage facilities: was the proposed capacity large enough to cushion the shipping operation from most LNG production outages? This chapter concentrates on the reliability aspects of this study.

An external consultant was required. The consulting firm selected to perform the study had considerable expertise with respect to Arctic engineering and risk analysis, and LNG-related expertise. However, detailed LNG experience and information was clearly going to be hard to find, in part because of the limited and geographically diverse existing plants, and in part for reasons of confidentiality.

Computer software developed for SCERT was available to the consultant in Canada. The SCERT specific OR method had been developed over some years and was now the basis of the approach taken to all offshore operations by BP International using a full-time risk analysis study group. The same family of mathematical models was clearly relevant, but the nature of the model structure was very different, as was the structure of the study team and other decision situation characteristics.

A limited budget and a limited amount of time was available.

METHOD OUTLINE

The RAER method was defined in terms of four phases and a number of steps, as outlined in Table 4.2. This phase/step structure was developed by modifying the SCERT method to accommodate the perceived differences in the decision context. About two man-weeks were involved, most of it being complete before the study began. Notes discussing each step formed the basis of the study plan and an associated study schedule. The method provided the framework and the direction for the study team (including large groups of 'non-OR' people), and it formed the basis for individual tasks and models.

The importance of this framework cannot be overemphasized. As will be seen from the detailed description of the method which follows, the study required input from a large number of specialists from a variety of disciplines, each with its own perspective and its own technical language: civil, structural, mechanical and hydraulic engineers, geologists, computer scientists, OR personnel and managers, amongst others. The method, in the form of a 'Procedure Manual', provided the unifying focus for this diverse team. It gave the essential information structure which allowed the study team to communicate across disciplinary boundaries, and which enabled a large volume of mainly verbal information to be collected from a wide range of sources and integrated coherently.

SCOPE PHASE

The scope phase provided an outline definition of the reliability analysis task. It involved three steps, started sequentially but substantially overlapped.

Engineering review familiarized the study team with the proposed plans. In some areas these plans were detailed; in others they were still at a conceptual level.

Subsystem/element identification defined the system in terms of twenty system elements, grouped in seven subsystems (Table 4.3). Two forms of documentation were used. A system element details list expanded each

Table 4.2   The RAER method in relation to the general OR method

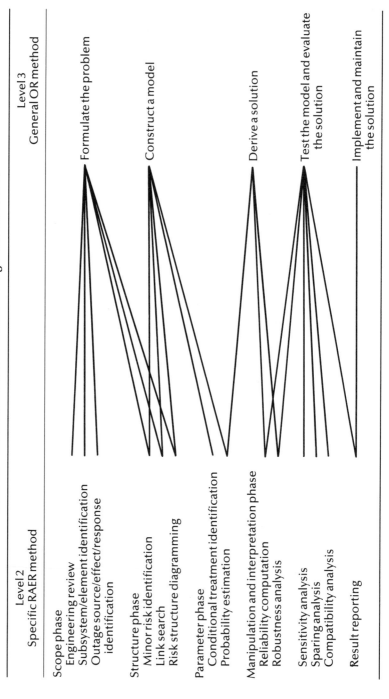

Table 4.3 Subsystems and system elements

Subsystem	System element
10. Gathering system	11. Wellhead
	12. Dehydration plant
20. Pipeline delivery system	21. Pipeline
30. LNG plant	31. CO_2 removal
	32. Dehydration
	33. Liquefaction
	34. Make-up refrigeration and storage
	35. Hazard detection
40. Utilities	41. Generating plant and distribution system
	42. Fuel gas
	43. Water supplies
	44. Miscellaneous utilities
	45. Venting, flare stack and burn pit
	46. Nitrogen plant
50. LNG storage system	51. Plant barges
	52. Storage barges
	53. Containment system
60. General outage sources	61. Common site outages
100. Delivery system	101. LNG piping and pipeways
	102. Loading system

element label with several pages of elaboration, including a paragraph of description, an equipment list, a drawing, when available, and notes on levels of duplication, dependencies, key assumptions, sources of information, and the date of the latest revision or addition. The level of the breakdown into elements was based on a target at the lower end of the 5–50 range, to keep the basic analysis framework simple. The form of the breakdown was chosen within the first few days of the study, and it remained stable throughout the study, apart from a few redefinitions and additions.

Outage source/effect/response identification defined outages in relation to each system element. Again two forms of documentation were used. An outage source labels list provided a summary using simple labels and extending the nested numbering scheme. For example, element 12, the 'dehydration plant', was associated with 12.1, 'power failure', 12.2 'pump failure', and so on. An outage source details list expanded each source label, with a pre-formatted page of information. At this stage it included a discussion of what was involved, possible reasons for the outage, effects in terms of lost production, possible responses to an outage, potential problems associated with responses, the assumed response, and the date of the latest revision or addition. Outage sources like 'major fire' and 'minor fire' were distinguished because the effects and responses were different. Most outage sources were linked to components and identified by scanning the equipment list. Outage sources like 'power failure' were defined in terms of a specific element failure, the generation plant and the power distribution system being separate elements. Outage sources like 'human error' and 'sabotage' were treated in relation to the system as a whole and associated with a dummy element, 'common site outages'.

The scope phase produced some 300 pages of carefully structured information, largely verbal. It was generated by engineers with LNG related experience and reviewed by existing LNG plant operators, engineers conducting LNG literature searches, and the client, with a view to completeness, accuracy, and current status. The first iteration took about a month; the last was not completed until just before the study finished, some three months later. Storing all the text in a structured computer file available to subsequent phases and linked to word processing capabilities made the iterative nature of the analysis as a whole comparatively easy to deal with.

STRUCTURE PHASE

The structure phase clarified the outline definition of the reliability analysis task provided by the scope phase and refined and tested the implicit analysis structure. It involved three steps, each deliberately isolated from the other two steps to the maximum extent possible.

Minor risk identification excluded from further consideration those outage source/effect/response chains which involved a negligible probability of occurrence or a negligible effect on production, on the grounds that their inclusion would not significantly affect the results. For example, dehydration plant 'filter failure' was deemed easily remedied, and 'minor fires' were defined as those which could be controlled without interrupting production. Risks so identified were associated with an 'M' in a 'class' column of the outage source labels list. The 'M' class plus verbal justification was noted on the outage source details list. The minor/major fire distinction in the scope phase noted earlier anticipated this step, and other examples of possible anticipation could be cited. However, it was thought important to avoid prejudging minor risks until a complete set of outage source/effect/response chains was available to minimize the risk of misclassification. Further, it was thought important to document all risks classified as minor, incorporating a defendable justification. Had a large number of minor risks been identified, they would have been treated as a single composite outage source. Major risks were identified as a residual.

Link search examined the outage source lists, looking for any form of linkages. In part, completeness was the aim: was an outage source identified in relation to one element also an outage source for another? The main concern was possible dependencies, in relation to all possible pairs of outage sources, of three kinds: common-mode relationships, involving a common reason for the outage; propagation or cascade relationships, involving an increased possibility or an increased effect for one outage source if another is realized; and statistical dependencies, involving either of the earlier two or some other form of causal dependency in an unspecified form. During the scope phase, common-mode relationships were avoided as far as possible by defining common services as separate elements: electric power systems, air systems, and so on. During the scope phase, propagation or cascade relationships were embodied directly into outage source/effect/response chains, as part of the sequence resulting from the initial fault.

During the link search phase, no evidence of further significant common-mode propagation or cascade effects was identified. It became obvious that weather would induce some dependence, unless different seasons were assessed separately, but it was agreed that an average season view was more in keeping with available data and manpower, and associated dependence should be minimal. It also became obvious that system age would induce some dependence unless different age periods were assessed separately, but it was agreed that an average age view was appropriate, and it should not induce significant dependence. Had significant dependence been found, which could not be avoided or subsumed, dependence would have been treated directly, as discussed in later chapters.

Risk structure diagramming was planned as a final step in the structure phase to provide a summary picture of key dependencies, using a format appropriate to their structure. As no significant dependencies were observed, this step was omitted, and conventional fault tree representations were adopted for report purposes.

PARAMETER PHASE

The parameter phase provided probability distributions for those outage source/effect/response chains to be assessed probabilistically. With respect to each outage source not given an 'M' classification in the last phase, two steps were followed, in sequence with respect to each outage source. Different people pursued different outage sources in parallel.

Conditional treatment identification excluded from data search and probabilistic analysis those outage sources which were to be treated as conditions, because the LNG storage was not meant to cater for their occurrence. For example, sabotage and major fires fell into this category, identified by a 'C'. Had a large probability been associated with any of these

Table 4.4   Sample outage source/effect/response distribution

Time between incidents	2 years				
Production cutback per incident (per cent)	0	25	50	75	100
Probability	0.4	0.2	0.1	0.1	0.2
Duration of responses: minimum	1.0 days				
most likely	3.0 days				
maximum	7.0 days				

outage sources, or a large number of 'C' sources been identified, the role of the LNG storage would have been reassessed. 'P' sources, those to be given a probabilistic treatment, were identified as a residual.

Probability estimation involved three distributions for each outage source/effect/response chain, each with a pre-specified form (Table 4.4).

The first distribution was defined by the mean time between incidents, in years. The associated distribution could be viewed in two ways: as a negative exponential distribution of times between incidents; or as a Poisson distribution of incidents in a given time period. Both views were used as feedback to the estimators. Each view involved the standard assumption of random incidents: the probability of an incident is independent of the time since the last incident. The randomness of incidents for a given outage source implies an 'average age' and an 'average season' view of the process, as noted earlier. It also requires the embedding of all start-up problems in each outage source/effect/response chain.

The second distribution was defined in terms of the probability of a 0, 25, 50, 75 or 100 per cent cutback in production per incident until the response has been completed. The associated distribution was given a discrete approximation interpretation, a crude but simple way to capture a wide range of possibilities, including bimodal situations when either 0 or 100 are probable but intermediate positions are unlikely.

The third distribution was defined in terms of optimistic, most likely and pessimistic response durations, in days. The associated distribution was assumed to be triangular, although a variety of more sophisticated interpretations might have been used.

Most estimates originated as engineering judgements, based on LNG related experience. However, these original estimates were cross-checked as far as possible with operators of LNG plant, other LNG experts, unpublished reports, published literature on LNG operations, other risk analyses and standard reliability texts.

All this information was assembled in standard format on hard copy current versions of the outage source details lists, as provided by word processing facilities linked to the computer file. It was then added to the computer file.

COMPUTATION AND INTERPRETATION PHASE

As soon as some probability distributions were available, computation and interpretation began. Five steps involved considerable iteration and feedback to earlier phases, prior to a final result-reporting step.

Reliability computations combined the three distributions associated with each outage source to define a 'days of lost production' distribution, given one day of attempted operation. It then combined these distributions, first within elements, then across elements, to define a 'days of lost production' distribution for the system as a whole, given 1 day of attempted operation. Next, it used this result in a semi-Markovian process to define a steady state distribution for the system as a whole, given 1 day's operation. Finally, it used the steady state distribution to compute a set of distributions for 'production achieved' (days) given 1–20 days of attempted operation. Details of the procedures involved, associated assumptions, and intermediate and final output formats are discussed in the rest of this section and in following sections.

Robustness analysis compared intermediate and final level outputs, given different assumptions and associated procedures with respect to the first step. For example, the adopted approach used an independent additive relationship when combining outage sources. This implies that overlapping incidents require sequential responses because of repair crew limitations. An alternative was tested, using an independent 'exclusive or', 'maximum', or 'greatest' relationship. This implies that responses can overlap, using more than one repair crew. In general, conservative assumptions were adopted, but it was important to confirm that they were not excessively conservative by testing alternatives.

Sensitivity analysis compared intermediate and final level outputs, given different probability distributions. For example, as the compressor was the most significant source of potential outage, its estimated interval between incidents was halved and doubled for comparative purposes.

Sparing analysis compared single and two train compression systems and looked for other potential system plan improvements.

Compatibility analysis compared overall system reliability and availability results in a variety of forms with all available information on the overall reliability of other LNG plants.

Results reporting involved the preparation of a variety of tabular and graphical representations of the reliability of the LNG delivery system. These had to satisfy a number of purposes. First, they had to serve as communications devices between the various members of the consultant's study team, and between the consultant and the client. For example, Figure 4.1 illustrates clearly the importance of the liquefaction subsystem in determining the overall system reliability, a result which led to the

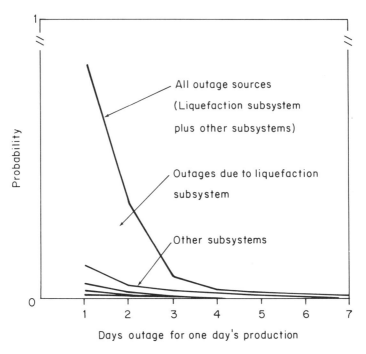

Figure 4.1   Sequential combination of subsystems for the original engineering design

consideration of alternative engineering designs for this subsystem. Second, the results had to interface with the study of the operating schedules of the LNG tankers.

RELIABILITY CALCULATIONS

Individual outage source summary distributions

For each production system outage source, three estimates were provided:

(a) the mean time between occurrences of the outage source, in years;
(b) the production cutback distribution if there is an outage, as a percent production loss; and
(c) the response time distribution if there is an outage, in days.

Shiploading system outage sources used loading operation units instead of years for (a) and omitted (b).

The distribution of response times, including any subsequent startup problems, was estimated as a triangular distribution, in which the minimum, most likely, and maximum response times are specified. Given the

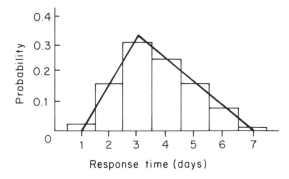

Figure 4.2   Response time distribution for the outage source example

nature of the estimates, the use of a more complicated distributional form did not seem warranted. The triangle was scaled and transformed to a histogram with one-day intervals. Figure 4.2 shows the daily distribution for the outage source example of Table 4.4.

If there is an outage, a production cutback may occur. Production cutback was defined as a percentage reduction in production; allowed values were 0, 25, 50, 75 and 100 per cent. The production cutback distribution associates a probability with each of these levels of reduction.

The production cutback distribution was combined with the response time distribution to form a conditional distribution of days of lost production given that an outage incident has occurred, $p(d \mid i)$. It was assumed that production is cut back by the same amount over the entire time required to respond to the outage.

The expected time interval between incidents in years was used to derive the probability of an incident on any day. The major assumption here is that incidents occur randomly: the probability of an outage occurring on any day is independent of the time since the last outage of this kind. This is something of a simplification, as engineering experience indicates that outages may be more frequent shortly after system start-up than they are after the system has been operating for some time. However, there was insufficient engineering information available to allow separate treatment of the start-up phase. Seasonal and age of plant variations were omitted for similar reasons.

If t is the expected time between incidents in years, then the daily incident rate is $r = 1/(365\ t)$. The number of incidents in a one-day interval is a Poisson distribution (due to the randomness assumption), with the probability of n incidents in a day given by $p(n) = \exp(-r)\ r^n/n!$.

With rare incidents it is reasonable to assume that no more than one incident can occur within a one-day period for any particular outage source, or if more than one occurs, it will not add to the response time. The probability of an incident is $p(i) = 1 - p(0) = 1 - \exp(-r)$.

The conditional distribution of lost production given that an incident has occurred, $p(d \mid i)$, is combined with the probability of an incident, $p(i)$, to obtain the unconditional lost production distribution, $p(d)$. This represents the production loss which may be expected, due to this outage source, over a one-day interval. The probability of no production loss is the probability that no incident occurs plus the probability that one occurs but no production is lost: $p(d) = p(0) + p(i)p(d \mid i)$, for $d = 0$. The probability of a loss of d days is $p(d) = p(i)p(d \mid i)$, for $d \neq 0$.

Outage dependencies

The assumption of random incidents has a number of implications:

(a) the LNG system is at 'average age'.
(b) climatic effects are 'average season' effects.
(c) response time distributions include start-up problems.
(d) there are no common mode sources of outage. Common services like electric power were analysed separately.
(e) there are no 'cascade' or induced-effect dependencies between outage sources which are not embedded in mean time between failure estimates.

An implication of the random incidents assumption which goes beyond those noted above is dependent response time distributions. Response time distributions, as well as outage probabilities, may be weather dependent. This implies two simultaneous outages may display correlated response times: when one is long because of climatic effects, the other will tend to be long for the same reason. There are other reasons to anticipate such correlation. For example, if repair crew performance is poor for any reasons other than climatic conditions, simultaneous outages might display correlated response time distributions in a given season. In the context of subsequent analysis for other purposes it might be important to consider such sources of correlation, and they could be handled within the same basic approach. However, significant sources were not identified, and so what little correlation might exist was balanced with a somewhat conservative approach within the independence assumptions.

System element summary distribution

The unconditional production loss distributions for all the outage sources associated with a particular system element were combined in pairs to form a production loss summary distribution for the system element itself. Two relationships are available, representing series and parallel response methods.

Series response.
The 'ADD' effect associates the duration of one outage D_1 and another D_2 with a combined effect defined by the sum of the durations, $D_{1,2} = D_1 + D_2$. This corresponds to the case where outage responses are activities in series, where, for example, the same personnel or equipment are required for the response. This is a conservative or pessimistic combination method, as it represents a 'worst case' response regime.

Parallel response
The 'MAX' effect associates the duration of one outage D_1 and another D_2 with a combined effect defined by the maximum of the durations, $D_{1,2} =$ Maximum (D_1, D_2). This corresponds to the case where outage responses are activities in parallel, where separate personnel and equipment are available to deal with each response. This is an optimistic combination method, as it assumes unlimited resources and a 'best case' response regime.

In practice, the difference between these two combination methods is small, provided that the probability of either outage is small and the outages are independent. Sample calculations are shown in Table 4.5. In the analysis, the more conservative series combination method was used for reasons already discussed.

A system element will generally contain a number of outage sources. These are combined in a systematic way to build up a production loss summary distribution for the system element. This results in the sequence of distributions R_1, $R_1 + R_2$, $R_1 + R_2 + R_3$ and so on. The final distribution $R_1 + R_2 + R_3 + \ldots$ represents the production loss which may be expected due to this particular system element operating over a one-day period. It is often more useful to examine a cumulative form of the distribution which indicates the probability of losing at least the designated amount of production. When the intermediate distributions in the cumulative process are plotted on the same axes it is possible to visualize the contributions of the individual outage sources to the overall reliability of the system element. Figure 4.1 shows an example of this process, based on the original engineering design.

Sparing of components

Frequently an outage source corresponds to the failure of a specific component within a system element. When it seemed appropriate, particularly where individual outage sources appeared to lead to high risks of production loss, the analysis examined the effects of providing spares or

Table 4.5 Series and parallel response examples

			Probabilities	
Days	R_1	R_2	Series response, $R_1 + R_2$	Parallel response, Max (R_1, R_2)
0	0.6	0.5	$(0.6)(0.5)$ = 0.30	$(0.6)(0.5)$ = 0.30
1	0.2	0.3	$(0.2)(0.5) + (0.6)(0.3)$ = 0.28	$(0.2)(0.3 + 0.5) + (0.6)(0.3)$ = 0.34
2	0.1	0.2	$(0.1)(0.5) + (0.2)(0.3) + (0.6)(0.2)$ = 0.23	$(0.1)(0.2 + 0.3 + 0.5) + (0.2 + 0.6)(0.2)$ = 0.26
3	0.1		$(0.1)(0.5) + (0.1)(0.3) + (0.2)(0.2)$ = 0.12	$(0.1)(0.2 + 0.3 + 0.5)$ = 0.10
4			$(0.1)(0.3) + (0.1)(0.2)$ = 0.05	
5			$(0.1)(0.2)$ = 0.02	

Table 4.6 Combination method for sparing

		Probabilities	
Days	Main component	Standby	Spared combination
0	0.5	0.4	$(0.5)(0.4 + 0.2 + 0.2 + 0.1 + 0.1) + (0.3 + 0.2)(0.4)$ = 0.70
1	0.3	0.2	$(0.3)(0.2 + 0.2 + 0.1 + 0.1) + (0.2)(0.2)$ = 0.22
2	0.2	0.2	$(0.2)(0.2 + 0.1 + 0.1)$ = 0.08
3		0.1	
4		0.1	

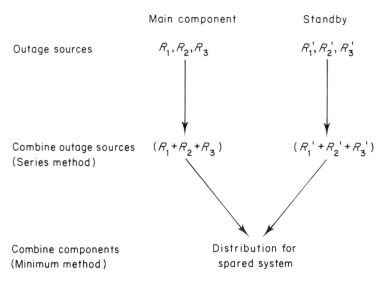

Figure 4.3 Calculation scheme for component sparing (main component with standby). Outage sources are first combined using the 'AND' method (series response), and these component distributions are combined using the 'MIN' method (sparing)

standbys for critical components of subsystems, additional to any allowed on the original engineering description.

Sparing involves placing two components in parallel; production will not be affected unless both components fail at the same time. The components in parallel need not have the same reliabilities. In general, sparing uses the 'MIN' effect, which associates the duration of one outage D_1 and another D_2 with a combined effect defined by the minimum, $D_{1,2} =$ Minimum (D_1, D_2). An example is given in Table 4.6.

In some cases a single component may be subject to different failure modes which may lead to different kinds of responses and different production losses. In such cases there will be several outage sources relating to the component. If the component is spared, then it is the distribution corresponding to the appropriate combination of the relevant outage sources which must be used (Figure 4.3).

System summary distributions

The previous sections described how individual outage source distributions were combined to produce a distribution for each system element. The same methods were used to combine system element distributions, to derive a production loss summary distribution for the complete production system and for the ship loading system.

Either the series or the parallel response methods may be assumed when combining system elements. The more conservative series approach was used in the initial analysis, although a good case could be made for the parallel approach at this level within the system. Within a system element there are likely to be constraints on the availability of skilled personnel, specialist equipment, or simply physical space in which to work, that will require a series response mode. System elements, however, may involve different technical skills and equipment, and are more likely to be physically separated, and so a parallel response assumption may be appropriate.

Sparing of entire system elements was treated in the same way as sparing of components within a system element. Graphs similar to Figure 4.1 were used to display the combination process and aid in identifying critical system elements.

Dynamic analysis

The summary distribution of the production system is a transition distribution for an underlying Markov process. It defines the outage probability as a consequence of operating the production system for one day, given the system began that day in an operational state. A proper understanding of the system's reliability must consider the implication of the production system's dynamics, and its relationship with the ship loading summary distribution.

A Markov process defining the production system's dynamics involves starting the system in an operational state and considering the effect of transitions for successive days. A state distribution for the start of day 1 and a transition distribution for day 1 are combined to define a state distribution for the start of day 2, this state distribution and a transition distribution for day 2 are combined to define a state distribution for the start of day 3, and so on. The transition distributions may be dependent on the associated state distribution and other factors, but the 'memory' of the process is not total, this limited memory being the Markovian property. When the production process is in a shutdown state for more than 1 day, it was assumed that further sources of outage cannot be realized after the first day. The approach adopted was comparatively optimistic, consistent with operating experience.

Using the production system summary distribution in a Markov process formulation to simulate operation of the production system over a number of days, a steady-state distribution was generated, similar in form to the system summary distribution except that it is not dependent on the system starting in an operational state. The production system summary distribution can be applied in the same Markov process formulation to define the relationship between days of operation, production achieved, and probability. Iso-curve representations for each of the three factors were

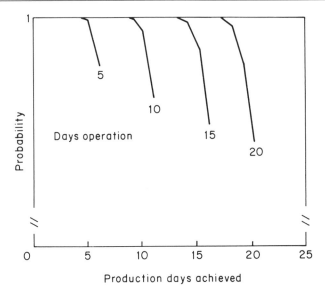

Figure 4.4   Iso-operation curves

used to provide slightly different views of the system for different purposes; Figure 4.4 shows iso-operation curves which are related to traditional concepts of system reliability, while the iso-production curves of Figure 4.5 were more relevant to the storage capacity aspects.

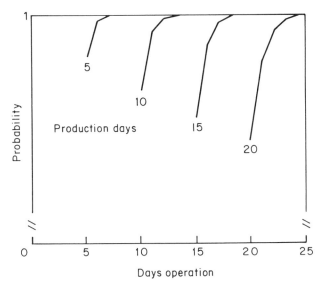

Figure 4.5   Iso-production curves

RESULTS

For reasons of commercial confidentiality, it is not possible to give details of the numerical results obtained in the analysis. The results which are presented below have thus been adjusted and distorted, and scales have been omitted from the graphs. Nevertheless the main features have been preserved.

The unconditional distributions for the lost production attributable to each outage source as a result of one day's operation were calculated, and they were combined, assuming series response, to derive summary distributions for the seven subsystems. Figure 4.1 shows these summary distributions. The most obvious feature of Figure 4.1 is the large production loss associated with the liquefaction subsystem in comparison to the rest of the system. Examination of the individual outage sources indicated that this was due to a single outage source, a major failure in a compressor-turbine package, which accounted for more than ten times the production loss attributable to the next most important outage source.

Because the compressor–turbine package plays such a dominant role compared to other individual outage sources, the effect of providing a spare liquefaction compressor was examined. As might be expected, sparing the liquefaction compressor has a dramatic impact on the reliability of the system (Figure 4.6). Over one year's operation (less scheduled downtime for maintenance), sparing this compressor is expected to reduce the unscheduled downtime by a factor of 3.

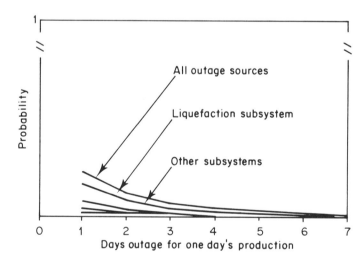

Figure 4.6   Sequential combination of subsystems with sparing of the liquefaction compressor-turbine package

The iso-curves in Figures 4.4 and 4.5 have been used in conjunction with a simulation model of ship arrivals to assess the LNG storage provision at the pipeline terminal. Details of this analysis are beyond the scope of this chapter.

Overall, the CIM based methods described above proved to be flexible and easily communicated. Within the broad framework of the study, they were readily accepted by a diverse group of engineers, operations researchers, and computer scientists from both the consultant and the client organizations. More importantly, they provided results which the client could understand and use.

CONCLUSIONS

As a case study indicating how reliability analysis might be approached, an important reservation needs to be noted. The preceding study does not illustrate mainstream reliability analysis practice. It illustrates a risk engineering approach brought to bear on reliability analysis for the first time, with no serious defects apparent to the authors or others involved in this study.

As a case study illustrating the extent to which the main characteristics of a specific method may be worth preserving in the face of a significant change, a more positive note is needed. Time risk analysis of North Sea offshore projects involves very different considerations from reliability analysis of an Arctic LNG facility. However, the RAER method outlined here was heavily based upon the SCERT method. Some important differences were involved. For example, attempting to operate the complete LNG system is analogous to a single activity like attempting to lay pipe in the North Sea, but the latter typically involved a dozen interdependent risks with complex interdependent responses, while the former involved some 200 independent outage sources. This difference had effects on the documentation, diagrams, computer software and method steps. However, most differences were minor, or purely changes in terminology, as comparison will verify.

It would clearly be unwise to assume that very different kinds of decisions would lend themselves to very similar specific OR methods. The advantage of a specific OR method relative to the general OR method is the increase in efficiency based on specific characteristics of the decision situation. Differences in the decision situation sufficient to require different models raise particular difficulties. However, if the same general family of models is clearly applicable, it would seem reasonable to assume that similar specific OR methods are applicable. This premise was tested in another very different context described in the next chapter, and in a range of further studies, some of which are described in Chapter 13.

As a case study demonstrating how the specific OR method concept can be used to increase decision efficiency in any context, a still more positive position is possible. In the authors' experience large-scale risk analysis studies involving many 'non-OR' people have been heavily dependent upon the development of a suitable specific method as a first priority. Usually a very limited amount of time and money were available. As many as 20 or 30 people had to provide input of many different kinds. Without a specific method, such studies would have failed or proved much less satisfactory. A large number of studies involving a variety of specific method development levels over nearly a decade are the basis of this view. It would seem that such an approach must have relevance to other OR-based studies. No doubt others do the same thing but conceive of it in a different way, or describe it in different terms.

REFERENCES

Frondeville, B. (1977) Reliability and safety of LNG shipping: lessons from experience. *Transactions, Society of Naval Architects and Marine Engineers* **85**, 459–80.
Green, A. E. and A. J. Bourne (1972) *Reliability Technology*, Wiley, New York.
Phillipson, L. (1978) Operational reliability of LNG systems. *Proceedings 1978 Annual Reliability and Maintainability Symposium.*
Science Application Inc (1975) *LNG Terminal Risk Assessment Study for Oxnard, California.* Report prepared for Western LNG Terminal Co., Los Angeles, CA.
Smith, W. A. and W. W. Bodle (1980) Reliability of base-load LNG delivery. *International Conference on LNG, Japan.*
Technigaz (nd) Operating Experience of Mark 1 LNG Carriers. Confidential Reports.
Welker, J. R. and H. P. Schorr (1979) *LNG plant experience data base.* American Gas Association Transmission Conference, New Orleans, L.A.

Chapter 5

Case study: choosing a river crossing method

Summary

This chapter examines a risk analysis structure rather different from that discussed in Chapter 4. It considers a case study involving a choice amongst alternative engineering options for a gas pipeline river crossing in the vicinity of a strategic bridge. The case study illustrates:

(a) the risk engineering method and method design concepts;
(b) an analysis structured on risks, rather than on system components;
(c) the combination of independent risks;
(d) the use of impact/response scenarios;
(e) analysis with multiple criteria, including a method for combining criteria and an introduction to dependent risks.

The chapter stresses methodology design as a way of developing an organizational framework for large risk analysis teams.

INTRODUCTION

Chapter 4 discussed a case study which demonstrated how the simple risk engineering models of Chapter 3 and modest extensions could be used in practice. It demonstrated the role of a risk engineering method, and it indicated the importance of a number of practical considerations, like the form of presentation of the results and the need to be concerned with non-numerical aspects of the risk analysis.

This chapter also demonstrates how the simple risk engineering models of Chapter 3 and modest extensions can be used in practice, and the role of a risk engineering method. However, a somewhat different problem and analysis structure is involved, and a different set of practical considerations are addressed. In particular, the analysis is structured by system configurations, rather than system components, and impact/response scenarios are considered in terms of a formal model which develops considerable detail by comparison to the approach of Chapter 4, including multiple criterion treatment of associated consequences. In addition, methodology design as a way of developing an organizational framework for large risk analysis studies is emphasized.

DECISION SITUATION

A substantial oil and gas field located in a remote region had been developed commercially for some time, but exploitation of the natural gas reserves was just beginning. Oil was transported by a large diameter pipeline to a coastal town where terminal and port facilities are sited.

Between the coastal town and the oilfield, the oil pipeline crossed a large river. It did this on a bridge, which also carried the only major road in the region. The bridge had a central road deck, with pipeways located on either side. One of these pipeways carried the oil line; the other was vacant.

As an integral part of the development of the gas reserves, a gas pipeline had been proposed, following the same alignment as the oil pipeline, where access was assured and the geology was known. How, though, should the gas pipeline cross the river?

Placing the new pipe on the bridge, in the vacant pipeway, seemed the obvious solution, but there were complications. A variety of government, commercial and financial organizations were involved with different aspects of the bridge structure, the road, the oil pipeline and the oil which flowed through it, and they were all wary of anything which might jeopardize their interests. Placing a gas pipeline on the bridge would necessarily create some additional risk to these interests, and in extreme circumstances the financial consequences might be large, so there were pressures from several quarters for a comprehensive risk analysis study.

In the spring of 1981 the contractor responsible for engineering planning for the gas pipeline commissioned a separate engineering consulting company to undertake a risk analysis. Its purpose was to recommend a river crossing method, with a credible case for the recommendation.

This task was to be completed during the summer of 1981, in a three month timeframe. Virtually all the resources of one office of the consultant were available for the project, with several additional people brought in from other offices. Only broad consideration of method design issues had been possible during the proposal stage of the project. The study as a whole started with the arrival of the authors, simultaneously mobilizing about 30 people.

PROJECT TEAM

The project team was headed by an experienced senior engineer, and another experienced engineer was responsible for day-to-day coordination. The first author was responsible for software development and coordinating computing. The second author was responsible for method design and coordination of its use, but both authors and the two managing engineers participated in the method development process. Several junior engineers were primarily concerned with computing aspects of the project. Several economists were primarily concerned with the valuation of lost production of oil or gas, social cost implications of oil spills and similar issues. A large team of engineers with a range of backgrounds and levels of experience made up the rest of the team. It included several very experienced engineers whose role was technical review in a quality control or audit sense rather than performance of the task directly.

SCOPE PHASE

A common feature of the SCERT method mentioned in Chapters 1 and 4 and the RAER method described in some detail in Chapter 4 was an initial 'scope' phase. This scope phase corresponds roughly to the CPA step 'list the activities'. A number of steps were anticipated in this phase, involving concepts similar to other methods, but with a different structure and terminology. In general terms these expectations were realized, with a few interesting surprises.

Configurations

The first step of the scope phase determined alternative ways the gas lines could cross the river, referred to as 'configurations'.

The existing bridge carried road traffic and a single oil line. This study was concerned with the implications of alternative means of getting gas across the river, with and without the future need for a second oil line. In all, seven configurations were analysed in detail, and many more were considered. This chapter concentrates on the four most important initial configurations. Each was given a descriptive letter designation.

Configuration OXG

In this configuration, there was an oil pipeline in one of the two pipe-racks on the bridge as was currently the case (O), and nothing new was added below the bridge deck (X). The proposed gas pipeline (G) was placed in the existing vacant pipeway. From the point of view of low initial cost and ease of construction and maintenance, this crossing method appeared the most attractive. It was the risk analysis 'base case'.

Configuration OGX

This configuration, like all others considered, maintained the existing oil line (O). It placed the proposed gas pipeline below the bridge deck (G). The other pipeway remained vacant (X), as a provision for a contingent second oil line.

Configuration OXX-G

This configuration used an aerial river crossing method for the gas pipeline, with the vacant pipeway on the bridge left as a contingency for future expansion. Of the several alternative forms of aerial crossing mode, this study assumed the preferred alternative as determined by an independent engineering design assessment.

Configuration OXX-S

This configuration involved a submarine below-ground pipeline crossing. The risk analysis concentrated on the submarine crossing mode recommended by an independent engineering design study.

   Engineering review of these options began immediately, developing detailed descriptions of each, and documenting technical and financial considerations, in a free format word processed mode suitable for direct incorporation in report appendices where possible.

States

The next step of the scope phase defined the 'states' of interest for each configuration. Construction, testing and operating states were identified. Initially, summer and winter distinctions were made, yielding six states for each configuration. Subsequently, the summer and winter distinctions were dropped as a complication beyond study resources and data availability, and most of the effort focused on the operating state. This focus was important in relation to the engineering review of configurations just discussed, and all subsequent steps in the scope phase. Arguably it should have preceded the configuration step, but some attention had to be paid to risks associated with construction and testing before a focus on the operating state was justifiable, and some understanding of summer and winter operating differences was equally important when justifying an 'average season' approach.

Risks

Identification and technical evaluation of 'risks' was the next step in principle, although in practice it started in parallel with the first two.

Separate groups of 'riskateers' tackled the engineering review of configurations and each of the categories of risk, with further divisions of labour on a configuration and source of risk basis, to get everyone busy as soon as possible and to make most effective use of available specialist expertise. However, team discussions were used to consider the completeness of the list of risks, and senior engineering review started very early in the process.

The technical evaluation defined each potential source of risk in terms of its nature and magnitude. Primary and secondary risks were distinguished. Sources of risk which are self-initiating were identified for direct treatment as primary risks. Examples are flood, lightning, sabotage, and the like. Sources of risk which are consequences of primary risks, or which are potential sources of damage when a response to a primary risk is undertaken, were identified for indirect treatment as secondary risks. An example is a leak in the gas line, as a consequence of weld failure, corrosion, or vehicle collision. It was important to make these distinctions in order to understand the failure mechanisms, and to avoid introducing dependence of a statistical or causal nature which could not be handled easily and effectively. In general, care was taken to define primary risks so that they could be treated as independent: realising one risk would not increase the probability of another. This was done by incorporating dependent secondary risks in this independent initiating set.

Four categories of risks were considered: natural risks, structural/mechanical risks, maintenance/construction risks, and postulated risks. A partial list is given in Table 5.1.

Initially, risks were identified in the context of specific configurations and states. Subsequently, all other configurations and states were considered in relation to each risk, and risks which were exclusive to particular configurations and states confirmed as such, using a matrix format to identify feasible configuration/risk combinations for the operating state. This dual approach is arguably inefficient, but it is more likely to provide exhaustive lists.

Table 5.1   Primary risks (sample only)

Natural risks	Maintenance/construction risks
Flood	Gas line construction
Wind	Pipeline maintenance
Lightning	Bridge maintenance
Earthquake	Postulated risks
Structural/mechanical risks	Vehicle collision
Weld failure	Marine collision
Oil line corrosion	Vandalism
Gas line corrosion	Sabotage

Identification and technical evaluation of risks proceeded in parallel to some extent, although in principle these two might be better approached sequentially. Technical evaluation included preliminary estimation of associated probabilities.

SCERT and RAER methods deliberately delay estimating probabilities until the third phase. Estimating probabilities at this stage was not just a question of trying to do everything in parallel to keep everyone busy. The way in which the analysis was structured for each risk depended upon developing a feel for associated probabilities. This can be interpreted as a movement back to a more general method, describing or formulating the problem in more detail before constructing a model. However, it is consistent with the CPA method, in that estimating activity durations usually precedes diagramming the activities.

Primary risks were assessed directly in probabilistic terms. In most cases this assessment was independent of the configuration. For example, the probabilities of different wind speeds and levels of flood were assumed to be independent of the configurations. However, lightning was considered in terms of the extent to which single or double crossing configurations might attract different numbers of strikes, and gas pipeline related risks clearly do not apply to the existing bridge and oil line.

Natural risks (like flood) were assessed objectively in relation to available data, with subjective input limited to adjustments. The data base for natural risks was generally more complete than for other risk categories. Through a variety of agencies, considerable data collection and research had been undertaken in areas such as hydrology, meteorology, and seismology. Most was not site-specific, but it did relate to the general vicinity of the bridge. For example, wind data was not available for the bridge site, and nearby sites involve differences which cannot be directly estimated in an objective manner, but nearby site data provided a good objective basis for risk assessment.

Structural/mechanical risks (like oil line corrosion) were assessed both objectively and subjectively, using engineering experience plus all available data and literature. This generally included a review of the specifications for the material properties of various components, and pipeline industry experience of the incidence of failure events for similarly specified items. The direct use of pipeline industry experience was recognized as a conservative approach, since it takes into account problems encountered on older pipelines, where technological advances in inspection capability, uniformity of product, and construction techniques had not yet occurred.

The first two risk categories dealt primarily with the forces of nature or the properties of materials. The second two considered risks associated with inadvertent and deliberate human failures, as well as with malfunctions of equipment not integral to the crossing system itself. Maintenance/

construction risks such as damage caused by pipeline maintenance were assessed subjectively using engineering experience, as data in this area was limited. Although there is a finite probability that some damage will occur as the result of maintenance risks, the associated damage scenarios generally do not lead to the likelihood of catastrophic failures or long production losses, so they were not pursued in depth.

The most difficult area for determining the probabilities that particular events will occur in a given year was in the postulated events category. While some data was available, there were problems associated with extrapolating it, and a variety of subjective approaches were used to estimate annual occurrence probabilities.

Extensive information for each risk produced by this technical evaluation was documented in a free format using word processing, as for the engineering reviews of the configurations.

STRUCTURE PHASE

While the scope phase proceeded, method design for the three other phases anticipated on the basis of SCERT and RAER methods was completed, and software development began. The 'structure' phase defines the model used.

Risk events

The first step of the structure phase was the definition of a set of credible risk events which represented all reasonable possibilities associated with the realization of each primary risk. For example, floods were associated with the maximum credible flood as defined by hydrological data, and a range of more likely, less extreme cases. Up to ten risk events represented all reasonable possibilities associated with each primary risk. They did not have to be ordered in terms of severity, although most were. Some risks, like lightning, were simply associated with occurrence or not.

With the exception of risks realized in a discrete manner like lightning, a discrete approximation to continuous distributions was involved. Associated conditional distributions (like the height of a flood given a flood occurs) were used to assist in the definition of appropriate representative scenarios, as well as providing initial estimates of associated probabilities.

Damage scenarios

Given the realization of a risk event, a number of very different consequences can follow. For example, in the case of an earthquake, if a ground acceleration above the design level for the bridge is experienced, the bridge may collapse or it may survive almost undamaged, and there is a range of intermediate possibilities. Moreover, intermediate possibilities may not be amenable to ordering: one may be worse than another in some respects, better in others. Up to ten different damage scenarios were associated with the realization of each risk. Each damage scenario was described in terms of the physical characteristics of the situation.

The damage scenario set was common to all risk events associated with each risk, although it was assumed some damage scenarios would be associated with a conditional probability of zero. This simplified the associated tree structure for estimation and computation purposes. Identifying the need to make this simplification was a key aspect of the model building process.

Responses

Given the realization of a risk event, consequences may vary because of the nature and level of the damage experienced. Consequences may also vary as a result of the chosen response. It is important to ensure that responses are appropriate. For example, a separate submarine gas line crossing might fail in a manner requiring six months to repair, but it might be possible, and preferable, to install a gas line on the empty pipe-racks of the existing bridge in one or two months. In this case, the latter response would be the appropriate one.

A single response, assumed to be appropriate, was associated with each risk event/damage scenario combination. However, alternatives were considered. To the extent possible in the time available, an attempt was made to ensure all choices were appropriate.

Primary responses may not work as planned, leading to secondary risks and responses. For example, a minor repair to a gas line could lead to an explosion during the purging process following the repair. Such secondary risks were not modelled separately, but subsumed in the assessment of associated risk event/damage scenario/response combinations.

These assumptions meant that the potentially very complex tree structure associated with each damage event was simplified to a single branch. If a more detailed assessment of risk were required, this is a key area for more sophisticated modelling.

Consequences and natural criteria

Describing the consequences of an action or event solely in terms of a single monetary value criterion is often convenient. In this study doing so would have been very misleading. Several different perspectives were possible and relevant, and the use of common money units alone would

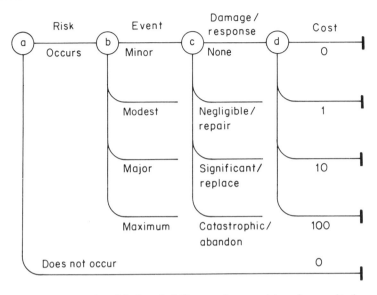

Figure 5.1 Simplified probability tree for one risk and one criterion

have obscured important considerations. The study employed separate specifications of six natural criteria: duration of lost oil production, duration of lost gas production, duration of lost road use, volume of oil spill, volume of gas leak, and cost of repairs.

Given the realization of a risk event/damage scenario/response combination, each natural criterion was associated with a triangular probability distribution. This provided a simple but flexible way to assess the uncertainty associated with the outcome being considered. More sophisticated distribution assumptions were not judged necessary for this study, although they have been used for similar subsequent studies, like the one described in Chapter 8.

Discrete probability trees could have been used here too. Had this been done, Figure 5.1 provides a simple picture of the probability tree for one risk and one criterion given a particular configuration state. The 'modest event' branch involves the same damage response branches as the 'minor event' branch, and so on for all other branches not terminating in a vertical bar at the right-hand side. Figure 5.2 provides a somewhat clearer picture than Figure 5.1 for some purposes, not used at the time but used for subsequent studies. In particular, Figure 5.2 shows clearly how the four-level tree collapses to a single-level tree, associated with cost in this case. In a SCERT context, diagrams constructed by the end of the structure phase are very important communication devices. In the RAER case study

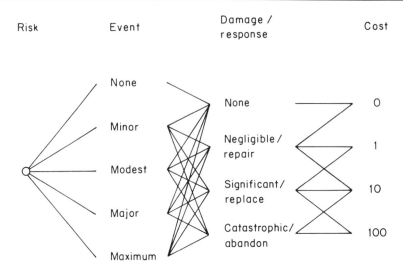

Figure 5.2   Event-on-node form for Figure 5.1

described in Chapter 4, the model structure was simple enough to allow the use of conventional fault tree diagrams. In this study there was no time to get beyond representations like Figure 5.1.

Structure phase documentation

The risk event, damage scenario, response, secondary risks, and natural criterion information was documented in predesigned and preformatted data lists. An important aspect of the methodology was the way this extensive and diverse body of information produced by a large number of different people became an integrated basis for analysis. Regular review and the use of word processing storage and computer data files to keep the documentation up to date were important contributors to this process.

PARAMETER PHASE

By the time the structure phase finished, the software was ready, and probability estimates and other parameters could be input as and when they were available.

Probabilities

Probabilities associated with each risk involved four components: a probability the risk would occur; a vector of probabilities defining the chance of each risk event given a risk occurs; a matrix defining the probability of each damage/response scenario given each risk event; a set of distributions of natural criterion consequences for each damage/response scenario. Although considerable probability information was developed prior to the structure phase and used to assist structuring, in formal terms the probability parameters were not estimated until this third phase, using pre-designed formats.

Uncertainty with respect to the assessments of probabilities was explicitly recognized. The concern was developing unbiased estimates of the correct order of magnitude, with consistency between risks and configurations. The importance of potential bias was tested later by means of sensitivity analysis.

Dollar transformations

Transformation of natural criteria into present worth dollar equivalents was undertaken to allow order of magnitude assessments of relative importance. Work began on these transformations at the outset of the study. However, total dollar valuations were viewed with care. Important interdependencies between criteria and risks were considered in outline, and dollar valuations reflected an 'average' perspective with scope for large departures in practice. For example, the relative importance of loss of oil production and volume of oil spill resulting from an act of sabotage during a time of war and shortage is very different from that associated with a similar loss in production and spill caused by a flood during a time of peace and plenty, in addition to different perspectives for oil producers and local fishermen, different implications for different times of year, and so on. Any such average figures are themselves exposed to risk of significant proportions. Some of the valuations were also the source of very considerable differences in value judgements. For example, the value of lost oil production to the producer is heavily influenced by a range of conditions and perspectives which suggested a range between zero and full market price, with grounds go outside even this very broad range in some special circumstances.

COMPUTATION AND INTERPRETATION PHASE

As soon as some probability distributions were available, computation began, using the software interactively. In summary, the tree structures of Figure 5.2 were collapsed for each risk, having first applied the dollar transformations to obtain a separate seventh criterion distribution in dollars for each damage/response scenario. Each natural and dollar criterion distribution was then added separately for successive risks within

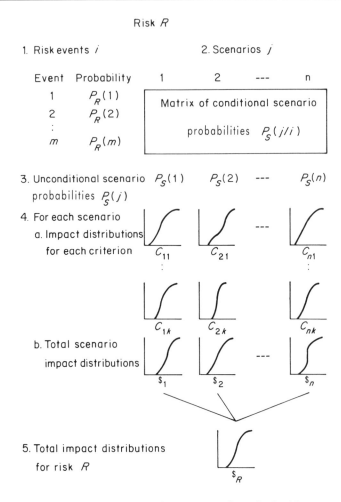

Figure 5.3   Computation structure for a single risk

each category, then across categories, for each configuration. Figure 5.3 shows the computation structure for a single risk.

This section explains how the methodology was applied in the form of a detailed exposition of the calculation processes. The calculation example used here was not taken from the case study for confidentiality reasons, but it shows the essential features.

Risks

Risks (more formally, sources of risk) are the basic elements which drove the analysis. As noted above, risks were defined such that they were independent of one another. There are two different kinds of risks: those which may occur as one of a set of discrete events (for example, collision risks), and those which arise on a more or less continuous scale (for example, flood risks). Continuous risks were reformulated in a discrete event structure by dividing the scales into suitable intervals and defining the risks being associated with representative values within the intervals. This process varied in its detailed implementation from risk to risk.

Given this reformulation, there are various levels at which a risk may arise, each level corresponding to a distinct event or a scale interval. The levels were defined so that they were jointly inclusive but mutually exclusive, covering all possibilities but not overlapping. Associated with each level of a risk, i, was the probability that this risk level will occur, $PR(i)$ for risk R. Because the risk levels provided an inclusive set, the sum over i of the $PR(i)$ equals 1 for each risk R. An example is shown in Table 5.2.

Table 5.2   Risk levels and probabilities for example risk

Risk levels i	Probability $PR(i)$
Small	0.7
Large	0.2
Enormous	0.1
	1.0

Scenarios

When a risk acts on a configuration, there may be a range of effects, responses and secondary risks. These were simplified to a set of scenarios which were consequent on the level of the risk. Scenarios were defined so that they were jointly inclusive but mutually exclusive.

Associated with each scenario j was a set of conditional probabilities of the scenario being realized given that level i of the risk arises, $PS(j \mid i)$. Because the scenarios were jointly inclusive, the sum over j of the $PS(j \mid i)$ equals 1 for each risk level i. An example of a scenario set and its matrix of conditional probabilities is shown in Table 5.3.

The $PS(j \mid i)$ conditional probabilities for scenarios and the $PR(i)$ probabilities of risk levels were used to calculate the unconditional probabilities of scenario j arising, $PS(j)$, independent of the risk level. $PS(j)$ equals the sum over i of the products $PS(j \mid i)*PR(i)$. The sum over j of the $PS(j)$ equals 1 for each scenario set S.

Table 5.3   Conditional probability matrix for example risk

	Conditional probabilities $PS(j \mid i)$		
	Risk level i		
Scenario j	Small	Large	Enormous
No damage	0.9	0.2	0.1
Minor damage	0.1	0.6	0.3
Major damage	0.0	0.2	0.6
	1.0	1.0	1.0

An example is shown in Table 5.4. The 0.63 entry is obtained by combining the 'small' risk level probability (0.7) and the 'no damage' probability given a small risk level is realized (0.9), taking the product ($0.7 \times 0.9 = 0.63$), and so on for each possible risk level/scenario combination.

Consequences

Scenario consequences were evaluated in terms of a set of criteria. For each criterion and each scenario, three values were provided; a minimum or optimistic estimate, a modal or most likely estimate, and a maximum or pessimistic estimate. These were interpreted as defining a triangular distribution (Figure 5.4). The distributions of criterion values reflected true uncertainty about the consequences of the scenario, lack of knowledge about it, and the uncertain scope of a broadly defined scenario.

For calculation purposes, an interval base was defined for each criterion, and each triangular distribution was converted to histogram form on this

Table 5.4   Example unconditional probability calculation

Scenario j	$PS(j \mid i) * PR(i)$		Unconditional probability $PS(j)$
No damage	0.63 + 0.04 + 0.01	=	0.68
Minor damage	0.07 + 0.12 + 0.03	=	0.22
Major damage	0.00 + 0.04 + 0.06	=	0.10
			1.00

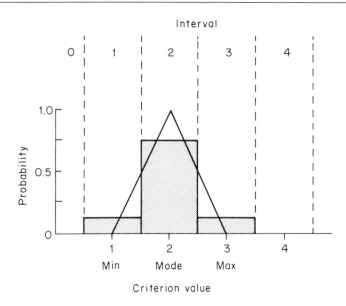

Figure 5.4   Triangular distribution and corresponding histogram

base. For example, the probability of 1/8 associated with the triangle of
Figure 5.4 in the interval 1.0 to 1.5 was redistributed as a rectangle in the
interval 0.5 to 1.5, a slightly conservative assumption. This provided a
consequence distribution which was conditional on the scenario arising.
This distribution was then scaled by multiplying by the unconditional
probability of the scenario arising, to form an unconditional consequence
distribution for the scenario, independent of the risk level. An example is
shown in Table 5.5. The conditional $PC(k \mid j)$ was taken from Figure 5.4: the
0.68 is the 'No Damage' $PS(j)$ from Table 5.4.

**Table 5.5   Conditional and unconditional consequence distributions for the
no damage scenario, criterion k: (min, mode, max) = (1, 2, 3)**

Interval	Conditional $P(k \mid j)$		$P(j)$		Unconditional $PC(k)$
0: 0–0.5	0	×	0.68	=	0.000
1: 0.5–1.5	1/8	×	0.68	=	0.085
2: 1.5–2.5	3/4	×	0.68	=	0.510
3: 2.5–3.5	1/8	×	0.68	=	0.085
4: 3.5–4.5	0	×	0.68	=	0.000
	1.0				0.680

Table 5.6   Unconditional consequence distributions

Interval	No damage (1, 2, 3)		Minor damage (2, 4, 6)		Major damage (2, 4, 6)		Combined
0: 0.0–0.5	0.000	+	0.0000	+	0.0000	=	0.000
1: 0.5–1.5	0.085	+	0.0000	+	0.0000	=	0.085
2: 1.5–2.5	0.510	+	0.0069	+	0.0031	=	0.520
3: 2.5–3.5	0.085	+	0.0550	+	0.0250	=	0.165
4: 3.5–4.5	0.000	+	0.0962	+	0.0438	=	0.140
5: 4.5–5.5	0.000	+	0.0550	+	0.0250	=	0.080
6: 5.5–6.5	0.000	+	0.0069	+	0.0031	=	0.010
7: 6.5–7.5	0.000	+	0.0000	+	0.0000	=	0.000
	0.680		0.2200		0.1000		1.000

For a particular risk, scenarios are independent. The unconditional consequence distributions were added by intervals across scenarios, for each criterion, to form a combined consequence distribution for the scenario set associated with the particular risk. An example is shown in Table 5.6, assuming 'minor' and 'major' criterion distributions of 2, 4 and 6. The first column of the Table 5.6 computation comes directly from the Table 5.5 result. The other columns are obtained using the procedure illustrated by Table 5.5 for 'minor' and 'major' scenarios.

Dollar consequences

For most criteria, criterion values were defined in terms of natural units: for example, production loss in months, oil spill in barrels, and repair cost in dollars. However, all criterion values were transformed to a common scale of equivalent dollars to allow more direct comparison across criteria. This transformation was done at the level of individual scenarios.

For a particular scenario and a particular natural criterion, the minimum, modal and maximum values 'a', 'b', 'c', were transformed to dollar values $a, $b, $c, and these dollar values were interpreted as defining a triangular distribution in the same manner as the natural values. This interpretation was precise so long as the transformation from natural values to equivalent dollars was linear in the range from 'a' to 'c'. If the transformation was non-linear, the true dollar distribution was distorted from the triangular form assumed here, but these errors were not significant relative to the errors associated with the averaging effect of dollar transformations noted in the last section.

Conditional consequence distributions of equivalent dollars for a particular criterion were scaled and combined across scenarios in a scenario set in the same way as the distributions of natural criterion values.

Total dollars

The conditional consequence distribution of total dollars for an individual scenario was also a triangular distribution. The minimum, modal and maximum values of this distribution were defined as the sums of the minimum, modal and maximum values respectively of the equivalent dollars across all criteria. For example, if 'a' was the minimum value for criterion k and $\$a$ was its dollar equivalent, the minimum $\$A$ of the total dollar distribution was defined by the sum over k of all such $\$a$. This 'direct sum method' of calculation reflects the correlation and interdependence between the consequences in terms of different criteria within a particular scenario.

Table 5.7   Effect of combination method on total dollar distribution

Direct sum method

Interval	Criterion 1 ($1, $2, $3)	Criterion 2 ($1, $2, $3)	Sum ($2, $4, $6)	Cumulative
1	1/8	1/8	0	0
2	3/4	3/4	1/32	1/32
3	1/8	1/8	1/4	9/32
4	0	0	7/16	23/32
5	0	0	1/4	31/32
6	0	0	1/32	32/32
7	0	0	0	1
	1	1	1	

Independent add method

Interval	($1, $2, $3) + ($1, $2, $3)		Cumulative
1		0	0
2	(1/8)(1/8)	= 1/64	1/64
3	(1/8)(3/4) + (3/4)(1/8)	= 3/16	3/16
4	(1/8)(1/8) + (3/4)(3/4) + (1/8)(1/8) = 19/32		51/64
5	(3/4)(1/8) + (1/8)(3/4)	= 3/16	63/64
6	(1/8)(1/8)	= 1/64	64/64
7		0	1
		1	

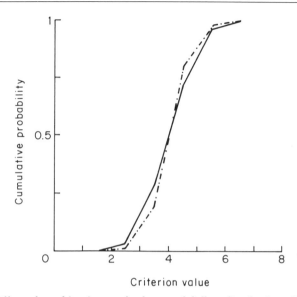

Figure 5.5   **Effect of combination method on total dollars distribution (direct sum, solid curve; independent add, chain curve)**

The example in Table 5.7 and Figure 5.5 compares this procedure with a combination method based on the assumption of independence between criteria. Both use the Figure 5.4 distribution for the criteria. The 'independent add method' considers all possible combinations, taking products to obtain joint probabilities, and adding probabilities associated with common joint criterion intervals. For example, the (1/8) (3/4) entry associated with a joint interval value of 3 involves the first criterion at level 1, the second at level 2, while the (3/4) (1/8) entry involves the first at level 2, the second at level 1. The direct sum method in effect re-defined the minimum, modal, and maximum values of Figure 5.4 as 2, 4, and 6, having added minimum, modal and maximum values for the two component distributions. On this new scale, a probability of 1/8 is associated with the interval 2 to 3, instead of 1 to 1.5: a quarter of it, 1/32, is allocated to the interval 1.5 to 2.5, while the rest, 3/32, is part of the allocation to the interval 2.5 to 3.5; the rectangular histogram approximation to the triangle is twice as precise, because of the scale changes.

The direct sum approach used here is clearly more conservative than the independent add procedure. It is not as conservative as a perfect positive correlation assumption, which could have been used. Its degree of conservatism was assumed to be appropriate, reflecting the level of dependence to be expected in practice, obtained by direct modelling of the dependence structure which would operate in practice.

The conditional consequence distributions of total dollars was scaled and combined across scenarios in a scenario set in the same way as the corresponding distributions of natural criteria and equivalent dollars.

Combination across risks

The unconditional criterion distributions for the scenario sets associated with particular risks were combined in pairs using an independent add method, as illustrated in Table 5.7. This was the appropriate combination method since the risks were independent (by definition) and it was assumed that the consequences of multiple risk occurrences were cumulative.

By successively accumulating risks in this way, distributions corresponding to groups of risks were constructed. By plotting these distributions, a pictorial representation of the importance of the risk or group of risks was obtained. Figure 5.6 is an example. Curve 'a' corresponds to the group of natural event risks (wind, lightning, flood, earthquake, and so on). Curve 'b' corresponds to curve 'a' plus the structural-mechanical risks. Curve 'c' adds maintenance risks. Curve 'd' was plotted from the distribution of all natural and all structural-mechanical risks combined. Successive areas between the curves indicate the size of the risk contribution. The example is for total dollar cost. Similar graphs were formed for each of the criteria, both in natural value and in equivalent dollar terms.

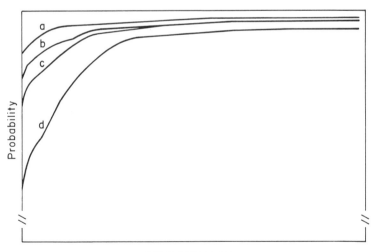

Figure 5.6　Cumulative risks by category, for configuration OGX (curve a, natural risks; curve b, a + structural/mechanical; curve c, b + construction/maintenance; curve d, c + postulated risks = total)

Output

Output was provided in two basic forms, illustrated by Figures 5.6 and 5.7. Both these figures are based on early trial plots which do not use real information for reasons of commercial confidentiality, but they are representative of the main features of the final results.

Figure 5.6 allowed a direct form of sensitivity analysis for the different categories of risk. The same format showing different risks within a category provided a similar direct sensitivity analysis. The same format showing different natural criterion contributions to dollar value assessment at any risk level were also used to a similar end. Where these pictures suggested a risk or natural criterion was more important or less important than had been anticipated, re-assessment was undertaken, and further sensitivity analysis. These diagrams were central to the initiation of feedback communication between the coordinating group and individual riskateers.

The Figure 5.7 format allowed comparison and tests for dominance or tradeoffs using dollar criteria and all individual natural criteria. Sensitivity analysis in relation to important areas of sensitivity identified in the Figure 5.6 format were tested in the Figure 5.7 format. These diagrams were central to the discussion and development of engineering judgements about the relative advantages of each configuration by the senior engineers

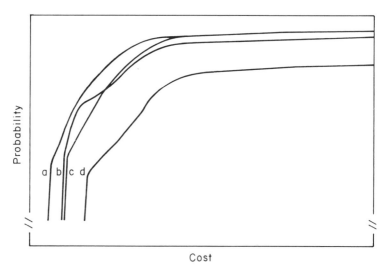

Figure 5.7   **Comparison of configurations (curve a, OXG (base case); curve b, OGX; curve c, OXX-S; curve d, OXX-G). Criterion: Total dollar cost plus annualized capital plus operation and maintenance**

involved. They indicate how complex procedures can be used to produce outputs which are readily comprehended by senior managers.

Although dollar transformations were used to illustrate the relative importance of risk sources and their different effects upon different configurations, limited effort was devoted to the measurement of 'average' or 'expected' cost transformations. The emphasis was on the senior engineers gaining an understanding of what was involved, and using this information to present a balanced case for and against each alternative in graphic and verbal terms.

The report written for the client used some of these diagrams in the main text. However, the key aspect of the report was discussion of engineering judgements based upon insights gained by the senior engineers in the process of this phase. No doubt the considerable weight of appendices providing structured and accessible backup to these judgements were an important source of credibility for the report. However, it was the strength of the argument in engineering terms which made the process valuable to the senior consulting engineers and the client.

SOFTWARE ASPECTS

The formal computation procedures and display options discussed above easily lend themselves to computerization. Modifications were made to previously developed computer software to accommodate the special nature of the assessment structure used for this study. This software allowed large volumes of input data to be assembled and maintained efficiently, and allowed computations to proceed in a flexible manner with minimal intervention. Further, a wide range of presentation forms, formats and levels of detail for results were specified.

The risk analysis program had two main functions, data handling and risk calculations. In its data handling mode, the program allowed users to enter and remove data from the file structures, to change data, and to display it. This could be done at several levels, related to risks, configurations, or damage/response scenarios within a particular configuration. The calculation and plot modes produced probability distributions and generated plot files respectively.

The program was interactive, providing the user with a series of prompts or questions at each stage. The program detected most illegal or meaningless input. A set of HELP messages gave more detail about each prompt and the kinds of responses expected. Since the program was interactive, a standard flow chart is not applicable. However, a simplified structure outline is shown in Figure 5.8.

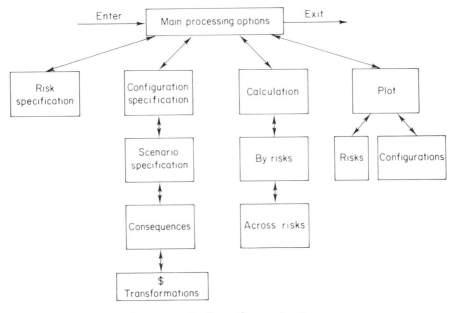

Figure 5.8   Outline software structure

A user could enter the program and perform any or all of the main processing options as follows:

(1) Specify risk probabilities.
(2) Specify (or change) scenarios and consequences for each configuration. This level also performs the cost function transformation from natural value criteria to equivalent dollar costs.
(3) Calculate probability distributions in terms of natural values, equivalent dollar costs and total dollar costs for each risk, and combine these distributions across risks.
(4) For any or all natural values, equivalent dollars or total dollars, plot results to:
 (a) Compare risks within a configuration (for example, Figure 5.6);
 (b) Compare configurations (for example, Figure 5.7).

Plots could be done either on a line printer or a Cal Comp (pen-type) plotter.

Program verification

Each routine of the program was tested to check for proper data base handling. The calculation portion of the program was verified by using a number of simplified examples (similar to the one outlined above) and hand computing the results.

CONCLUSION

Some aspects of this study have been revised when faced with a similar context. For example, the triangular probability distributions used for natural criterion assessments, in conjunction with the limited number of scenarios for some risk and damage/response sequences, made some of the lower level natural criterion probability curves 'lumpy'. Once a user of the curves understood why, this was not a problem in modelling terms. However, it was a minor source of irritation, and at least one similar subsequent study has used 'smooth' distributions of natural criteria instead of triangular distributions (described in Chapter 8).

Others would no doubt wish to handle some modelling aspects differently. For example, multiple criteria decision analysis might seem the only obvious way to approach this problem for some. In this particular case we would strongly disagree, but on other aspects the strength of feeling would be limited. A wish for a more sophisticated treatment of responses falls into this category.

Of prime concern here is our view that attempting the design of a method for an analysis like this, that design being specific to a model and the situation, makes sense. Some might argue this approach preconditions things too much. It smacks of deciding upon the solution before the problem is understood. We would argue that a more flexible approach is simply not viable if a large group of people must be involved at the same time, and an organization-based approach to the problem must be considered. The only realistic alternative is to take an existing method and model off the shelf without any method design flexibility. That is what most people do most of the time, and in our experience there is good reason to believe that when it doesn't work, it is often because of a mismatch between the situation and the technique. This can frequently be avoided if *method design* is addressed rather than *technique selection*.

This should be coloured by one provision. If method design can take place well in advance, success may be evasive but there is good reason to believe it can be ensured. When method design is a pre-study phase with a limited timescale as in the RAER case in Chapter 4, success is exposed to some risk. When method design is integrated with the problem solving process, the risks can lead to a loss of sleep. To ensure viability in this context it is very important to keep the model set as general as possible, and to approach method design with the full force of a general management science methodology.

Many important decisions involve a choice between alternatives, each of which involves significant uncertainty. The approach described here was developed for the specific task. However, it was based upon concepts which have been used in a wide range of quite different contexts, and the particular version discussed here has been adapted with equal flexibility to risk analysis for offshore oil production platforms. An extension of the same approach to a hydroelectric project is described in Chapter 8.

Notation

a, b, c	Minimum, modal, maximum criterion values, natural units
$\$a, \$b, \$c$	Minimum, modal, maximum criterion values, dollar units
$\$A$	Minimum of total dollar distribution
i	Risk level
j	Scenario
k	Consequence level
K	Consequence
OGX	Configuration, gas line below bridge
OXG	Configuration, base case
OXX-G	Configuration with separate aerial crossing
OXX-S	Configuration with submarine crossing
$PC(k)$	Unconditional probability of criterion level k
$PC(k \mid j)$	Probability of criterion level k, conditional on scenario j
$PR(i)$	Unconditional probability of risk level i
$PS(j)$	Unconditional probability of scenario j
$PS(j \mid i)$	Probability of scenario j, conditional on risk level i
R	Risk
S	Scenario set

Eliciting subjective probabilities for risk analysis

Summary

This chapter identifies the kinds of subjective judgements that specialists may be required to make to provide input to a risk analysis study. It briefly surveys the problems associated with these kinds of judgements, and indicates how probability elicitation is conducted in practice.

INTRODUCTION

Risk analysis can require three different types of probabilistic information:

(1) Probabilities particular sources of risk will occur;
(2) Conditional probabilities particular scenarios will arise given the occurrence of a particular source of risk;
(3) Consequence distributions, conditional on the occurrence of a particular risk.

Frequently these different types of information are considered jointly, as when estimating an activity duration or cost distribution without explicit reference to sources of risk. It is generally easier to estimate risk probabilities in a decomposed form. However, even in a decomposed form, and sometimes because of it, appropriate data for 'objective' probability estimation may not be available.

Much of the information necessary to product probabilities must be provided by individuals who are specialists in the risk area being assessed. This information may involve interpretation and adjustment of objective data, or judgements based on experience with no directly relevant data. The information is therefore highly subjective, and it could be highly unreliable. Since the objective of risk analysis is to create a basis upon which effective decisions are made, it is important that the information is as reliable as possible, and that the sources of unreliability are well understood.

One of the main sources of unreliability comes from biases present in the mind of the specialist providing the data. A secondary source of unreliability comes from violations of the probability calculus. This is due to the fact that many specialists may not be experienced in the use of probability calculus in their normal activities, and may not know how to use it.

This chapter discusses some of the most common biases in subjective data, and common violations of the probability calculus. Guidelines are presented to enable estimators to provide information for risk analyses which are, as far as possible, free from major biases or probability calculus violations. This should make the risk analysis more accurate and more useful for those who must base decisions upon the outcome. These guidelines are not difficult or time consuming to use.

HEURISTICS AND BIASES

The literature on human judgement and decision making (for example, see Kahneman, Slovic, and Tversky 1982; Slovic, Fischoff, and Lichtenstein 1977; Peterson and Beach 1967; Tversky and Kahneman 1974) indicates that judgements are based upon limited processing of a subset of the available evidence. This means that tasks which may or do call for complex analysis are reduced to short-cut or heuristic procedures. These heuristics are used mainly to simplify cognitive processing requirements.

Short-cut procedures may result in efficient information processing. They may also lead to systematic biases, which could in turn produce costly errors in the judgements made when using the information. This section discusses the most common heuristics and the biases which they cause. It also considers in outline some other kinds of biases which may occur in the analysis, such as motivational bias.

Heuristic information processing procedures

When assessing probabilities of uncertain events it has been shown that people rely upon a limited number of heuristic principles (Tversky and Kahneman, 1974). The three most common heuristics are representativeness, availability, and anchoring and adjustment.

Representativness

Representativeness heuristics are judgemental procedures whereby some properties of the available data are over-emphasized when subjective probabilities are generated. There may be an over-reliance on some characteristics of evidence and a corresponding neglect of other available information on the problem. This approach to decision making can lead to serious errors because similarity or representativeness may not be influenced by factors which should be taken into account in a rational decision process.

The bias which Tversky and Kahneman (1974) call the 'illusion of validity' provides a striking example of the representativeness heuristic. This bias occurs because people often predict by selecting the outcome that is most representative of the input. They show great confidence in predictions which match their stereotypes or expectations, even when the available evidence is unreliable, sparse or out of date. The degree of confidence they have in their prediction depends primarily upon the degree of representativeness, with little or no regard for the factors which limit the predictive accuracy. Other biases due to representativeness which are important in risk analyses are outlined below.

Insensitivity to the prior probability of outcomes (or base rate frequency): Kahneman and Tversky (1973) found that when using the representativeness heuristic to evaluate probabilities people did not take prior probabilities fully into account.

Insensitivity to sample size: when using samples of different sizes in order to assess probabilities, people ignore the sample size and give roughly the same probabilities for each sample. They should be more wary of the smaller samples, which are likely to be more inaccurate.

Insensitivity to predictability: if predictions are made using other predictions or evaluations then there may be insensitivity to the reliability of the evidence given. Tversky and Kahneman found that the degree to which the description is favourable is insensitive to the reliability of the (original) description and to the degree to which it permits accurate prediction.

Availability

Wright (1980) described the availability heuristic as 'a cognitive procedure in which the subjective probability of an event is based on mental recall of past occurrences of events or the ability to generate possible scenarios leading to event outcomes'.

Tversky and Kahnemann (1974) noted that this can be useful when assessing frequencies or probabilities because instances of large classes are usually recalled much better and faster than instances of rare or infrequent classes. They also noted that availability is not only affected by the frequency and probability of an event, but there are other factors which should be taken into account. When they are not, biases may occur.

Biases caused by the retrievability of information about instances: a class whose instances of occurrence are easily retrieved appears to be more numerous than a class with an equal probability of occurrence but whose instances are less retrievable. This would seem to be caused by familiarity, but other factors such as salience and the time span of occurrences also play their part.

Biases due to the effectiveness of a search set: people tend to assess the frequency of occurrence by the ease with which the various events come to mind.

Biases of imaginability: when assessing frequencies of classes whose instances are not readily available people tend to generate several feasible classes. They then evaluate the frequency or probability depending upon the ease with which the relevant classes can be constructed.

Illusory correlation: this is a bias caused by thinking about how frequently two events co-occur, and then basing a judgement on this illusion.

Adjustment and anchoring

Slovic and Lichtenstein (1971) found that in many situations people generate estimates of events by starting from an initial value and then *adjusting* it to yield the final answer. The initial value may be suggested by the formulation of the problem or it may be the result of a partial computation. In both cases they found that the adjustments were typically insufficient. They also found that for a single problem different starting points may lead to different final estimates which are biased towards the starting values. This is known as *anchoring*.

Over-estimation of conjunctive ('and') events and under-estimation of disjunctive ('or') events is one important source of bias. The probability for any elementary event provides a natural starting point for the estimation of the probability of a conjunctive or disjunctive event. Anchoring on this value typically causes an adjustment to be insufficient and the final estimate for the events to remain too close to that of the elementary event. Since the overall probability of a conjunctive event is lower than the probability of an elementary event it causes the probability of that event to be over-estimated. For disjunctive events, the probability tends to be under-estimated.

This can be a serious source of bias in risk analysis applications. For example, where a project involves a series of events which typically follow a conjunctive structure, the probabilities of the events may individually be fairly high, but the overall probability of success of the project may be low, especially if the number of events is large. Thus the probabilities of completing individual activities in a project on time may all be high, yet there may be a large probability that the project itself will be delayed, because *all* the activities must be finished before it is complete. This bias will lead to an over-optimistic estimate that the project will be successful.

Conversely, the evaluation of risk may have a disjunctive structure in a complex system where the whole system will malfunction if any of its essential components fails. The likelihood of failure may be low for each of the components, yet the probability of an overall failure may be quite high due to the large number of components. People tend to underestimate the probabilities of failure in this case due to the anchoring heuristic.

Overconfident judgement is another important source of bias. When assessing subjective probabilities, people state overly narrow confidence intervals which reflect more certainty than is justified given their knowledge about the quantity. This occurs for experts as well as less experienced assessors. If given a starting point, people will adjust from there to find the values for the confidence limits X_{10} or X_{90}. Anchoring will cause this adjustment to be too small and consequently the confidence interval between X_{10} and X_{90} will be too narrow (that is the assessed probability distribution will be too tight) given the available information.

Other heuristics and biases

The biases listed above are all concerned with cognitive information processing, and they may be explained in terms of a few common heuristics. Other biases may occur due to the nature and assessment of the problem. Some of the more common ones are outlined below.

Incorrect intuition concerning sampling theory: Tversky and Kahneman (1971) state that 'Our thesis is that people have strong intuitions about random sampling; that these intuitions are wrong in fundamental respects; that these intuitions are shared by naive subjects and by trained scientists alike; and that they are applied with unfortunate consequences in the course of scientific enquiry'. The most typically used intuitions are: insensitivity to prior probabilities, which can be explained by the representativeness heuristic; insensitivity to sample size, which can also be explained by the representativeness heuristic; and lack of comprehension of regression to a central tendency. An extreme outcome at some time period will generally be followed by a less extreme outcome during the next time period. According to Tversky and Kahneman (1973) people tend not to expect this regression and in order to overcome this they invent spurious 'causal' explanations.

Cue-response mode effect: when using data for estimation of probabilities, the relative importance of the datum (cue) has been shown to depend upon the consistency of the measurement or scaling of the cue with respect to the scaling of the judgement variable (Slovic and Lichtenstein, 1968). If data is given in the same units as the judgement variable, people tend to weight the cue more heavily than other data given in different units.

Overconfidence: people tend to be overconfident when they make judgements. This occurs due to the anchoring heuristic and the hindsight bias. Fischoff and Beyth (1975) found that when people were asked to recall their own predictions about past events, they remembered having assigned higher probabilities to events which actually occurred than was actually the case. Similarly, they tended to suppress their estimates when the events did not take place. People have inordinately high opinions of their own predictive ability when estimating single events.

Cascaded inference: in the case of single judgements it has been shown that people tend to be conservative, whereas in problems that have several stages, with inferences at each stage relying upon the previous inferences, the opposite is true. Youssef and Peterson (1973) found that cascaded inferences tend to be systematically over-estimated in comparison with corresponding non-cascaded inferences.

Motivation bias: these are 'conscious or subconscious adjustments to probability assessments motivated by the assessor's perception of the personal rewards that will result from the various uses of their probability assessments' (Spetzler and Stael von Holstein, 1975). These biases may not be relevant to risk analysis studies undertaken by independent professionals. However, one bias which may be relevant is the suppression of uncertainty: an 'expert' in a particular field may express confidence in his judgements because he feels that he should know the answer better than he actually does.

This section has dealt with the biases which could occur in risk analysis probability assessment and the reasons for their occurrence. The next section deals with ways and means of eliciting the necessary information without the biases.

RESPONSE ELICITATION

Identification of risks

The identification of risks can be done in two basic ways: using a panel group, or individual experts.

Panel group
A number of specialists gather for a session to conduct a 'brainstorming' exercise. Each member of the panel suggests risks which could, theoretically, occur. Once all possibilities have been exhausted, the group then decides which risks should be included in the analysis. It is hoped that by using this process all plausible risks will be identified and included in the analysis.

Individual experts
When using this method as a means of identifying risks, individual specialists are asked to provide all the relevant risks which they can think of in

their areas of expertise. This has disadvantages, in that a risk could be ignored because of the way in which the expert was thinking at the time, or an improbable risk could 'slip through the net' because a single individual did not have all the relevant information. This would be less likely to happen in the panel group where a wider range of information should be available.

If there have been similar projects completed before, it may be possible to use the risks identified for earlier projects as a base for later ones, with slight modifications for any special features.

Identification of risk events and scenarios

This identification process can be undertaken by the specialist who is responsible for providing the data. He may be asked to identify a number of events or levels for each risk, or a number of scenarios for each event. It is essential that the specialist understands the need to justify the choices and provide reasons for including or not including each specific event and scenario. This also makes it easier for estimators to relate to each event and scenario, if they know why each has been included.

Structure and formulation of events, scenarios and responses

Once the identification stage has been carried out it is necessary to structure and formulate the questions to elicit the quantitative data required. Spetzler and Stael von Holstein (1975) and Selvidge (1975) give general guidelines for this. The relevant ones for risk analysis applications are as follows:

(1) Choose only uncertain quantities that are important to the decision making process, and be prepared to explain why specific quantities are omitted.
(2) Structure the quantity carefully. The specialist may think of a specific quantity as being conditional upon other quantities. If he or she does it is important that these conditions are considered consciously and incorporated into the analysis so that mental acrobatics are minimized.
(3) Clearly define the quantity to be assessed, so that no further information is needed by the specialist in order to make a judgement.
(4) Describe the quantity using a meaningful scale. It is very important that the specialist be comfortable using a specific unit, so he will be able to concentrate on the assessment without any distractions. As a general rule, let the individual specialist choose the scale to be used; after the encoding process the scale can be changed in order to fit the analysis models.

Encoding methodology

In the assessment process, specialists are asked to provide different kinds of estimates. They can be assessed with two different answering modes.

(1) The assignment of probabilities to an event, whilst the values remain fixed (P method). For example, an engineer might be asked to give the probability of a response time to an equipment breakdown being a week or less.
(2) The assignment of values to an event whilst the probabilities remain fixed (V method). For example, an economist might be asked to give the cost of a response which he would not expect to be exceeded 90% of the time.

The answers can be provided by the use of two different modes of judgement.

(1) Direct response modes. Here the specialist is asked questions which require numbers as answers. Depending upon the methods being used, the numbers will be either probabilities or values.
(2) Indirect response modes. Here the specialist is asked to choose between two or more bets (or alternatives), and these are adjusted until he is indifferent between the two. This indifference can then be translated into the necessary probabilities or values.

This last response mode is only available in interviews, or if interactive man/machine programmes are developed to help the decision maker in his task.

Indirect response techniques

There are four important indirect methods for eliciting responses.

Probability wheel
This is a disc, with two adjustable sectors of different colours, which has a fixed pointer in the centre. When spun the disc comes to a stop with the pointer in one of the sectors. The sector sizes can be adjusted simply and quickly. The method used is to ask the specialist which of the two events he considers most likely, the event that the pointer ends up in the orange sector of the disc, or the event relating to the uncertain quantity. The size of the orange sector of the disc is then varied until the specialist is indifferent between the two questions. The amount of orange in the disc corresponds to the probability of the event occurring. This method is mainly used for probability assessment, rather than for assessing values. It is only useful for the evaluation of probabilities between 0.1 and 0.9,

because difficulty is encountered when discriminating between the sizes of small sectors. Other alternatives based on the same principle use a horizontal bar with a movable marker, instead of a disc, or an urn containing balls of two different colours.

Fixed probability events
This method is useful when assessing low probability events. It is a value-oriented method. It involves comparing an event which has a fixed probability of occurring, such as tossing a coin to show 10 heads in a row, to the event which is being decided. Then the specialist is asked to provide a value for an event which has the same probability as the fixed probability event.

Interval technique
The specialist is given a range of values split into two parts. He is then asked which of the two parts he would bet on as the one most likely to occur. The relative sizes of the parts are then altered until the specialist is indifferent between them. This gives the median point. The process can be done again with the two intervals to find the quartiles. This can be done many times in principle, but in practice it is rarely meaningful to continue with the analysis past the quartile stage.

Relative likelihoods
Here the specialist is asked to assign relative likelihoods to two well defined events. For example, a sales manager might be asked whether he or she considered next year's sales to be above or below 5000 units. She or he might then be asked how many more times likely it was, followed by more questions designed to elicit these relative likelihoods. It should then be possible to assign values to the events. This method is most useful for the assessment of uncertain quantities which could only have a few possible outcomes.

Direct response techniques

The only applicable direct response technique is to assign a value to an event with a specific probability, or to assign a probability to an event with a specific value. For the assignment of probabilities the specialist can use one of several approaches:

(a) the absolute value, i.e. 0.2,
(b) the percentage value, i.e. 20%,
(c) a fractional value, i.e. one in five,
(d) odds, i.e. four to one against.

It should be left to the specialist to decide with which one he or she feels most at ease.

Rare events

The above techniques are all useful for assessing probabilities within the range 0.1 to 0.9. It is much harder to discriminate values outside this range. This led to the development by Selvidge (1975) of a technique for encoding rare events. She recommends a three step procedure:

(1) Description and decomposition of the event and its setting. The objectives are 'to describe the uncertain event clearly and thoroughly and to try to relate the event in some way to other events with which the assessor is more familiar'.

(2) Expression of uncertainty in relative terms, to give the specialist confidence in his judgements. He or she may not at this stage feel confident enough to give a value for the event, but should be able to rank the events in terms of the most probable event down to the least probable one.

The assessor is led through a series of questions about the events in order to establish conditional statements of uncertainty. Once the initial ranking is completed, the specialist is asked to establish a semi-quantitative relationship between the events, for example by stating how many times more likely A is when compared to B. Once this is done he or she can proceed to more detailed quantification.

(3) Numerical expression of probability. The analyst has a number of 'external calibration' techniques with which to help the specialist assessor relate to rare probabilities.

    (a) the use of reference events, such as plane crashes, floods, or tidal waves, which occur infrequently;

    (b) the use of reference processes;

    (c) the use of 'demonstrative' techniques, in which the specialist is shown various probabilities. For example, a specialist can be provided with a piece of graph paper or a chart which has one million squares on it: the chance of picking out a specific square at random has probability of 10^{-6}.

General rules

When a specialist is asked to provide probabilities or values for rare events, it is important that questions are posed in a way which can be interpreted easily, and which reduces 'mental acrobatics'. Some general guidelines are given below.

Specialists should be given a basic grounding in probability theory, because they often have incorrect intuitions about sampling and other basic theories.

The problems should be structured in such a way that the assessor feels he has no control over the events and that his answers will not change the problem. This should be done to reduce any inherent conservatism.

The problem should be defined in such a way that the assessor can associate with all the events and scenarios upon which judgements must be based.

Descriptions of quantities to be assessed should be given in neutral terms so the assessor cannot infer anything from them.

Assessors should be asked to provide any information on which they have based their projections, so that the analyst can see whether any biases have crept into their judgements.

Let the specialist choose the units in which the answer is to be given. If necessary, change the relevant data so that the same unit is used consistently throughout.

When asking the assessor to assign probabilities or values, the uncertain nature of the event should be emphasized.

When assigning values to a number of scenarios, the assessor should be asked to evaluate the probabilities of the extreme events first, to avoid any tendency to anchor on a particular one.

The analyst should try to stop the assessor from keeping a note of the answers for each scenario. If there are many scenarios the probabilities of which should sum to one, the assessor may try to fit the final one or two answers into the distribution rather than assessing the probabilities.

Methods used for evaluation

There are various methods which can be used for the evaluation of probabilities or values. They can be split into four classes: individual assessments; interviews; groups; and man/machine methods. Each has advantages and disadvantages when used for assessing different types of data.

Man/machine methods

With a few exceptions there has been little development of the compli-cated interactive programmes which are needed for this type of assess-ment. Spetzler and Stael von Holstein (1975) recommended using man/machine methods only when the assessor has had long experience with computer interviews, the assessor has had a number of interviews dealing with similar quantities, the problem is not important enough to justify the cost of an analyst, and the organization concerned uses probabilities regularly and extensively to communicate uncertainty.

Questionnaires
As well as giving the assessor the questionnaire he should be provided with general guidelines on how to answer the questions, and any relevant data for the problem. He should also be asked to provide all the information and assumptions upon which he based his judgement. If he has to estimate the probabilities for rare events he should also be provided with the rules for estimating them, such as the three step procedure developed by Selvidge. Spetzler and Stael von Holstein found that this method suffered due to the lack of interaction between the interviewer and assessor, making it difficult for the answers to be free from bias. They saw this method as being useful only for the first approximation in the encoding process.

Interview techniques
Spetzler and Stael von Holstein have evolved a five phase procedure for conducting interviews. These phases are: Motivating; Structuring; Conditioning; Encoding; and Verification.

(1) *Motivating.* The interviewer should introduce the assessor to the encoding task and explore the possibility of motivational biases. There may be little motivational bias if the analysis is conducted by a team of independent specialists from many disciplines.
(2) *Structuring.* The quantities to be analysed are defined and structured to reduce ambiguity.
(3) *Conditioning.* The aim in this stage is to minimize biases during the encoding process, by making the assessor aware of how he uses his own judgement during the analysis. The interviewer can do this by asking the specialist the main bases for his judgement (to identify anchoring effects), what information is being used (to identify availability effects), and how he is using statistical data, if there is any.
(4) *Encoding.* The techniques used for this procedure depend primarily upon the kinds of answers required for the analysis. The ways of encoding the relevant data for the risk analysis have been discussed earlier.
(5) *Verification.* This stage is used to test the responses with other response techniques. As well as verifying the answers the interviewer should also attempt to cross-check the assumptions used to see if they are the same throughout.

Group techniques
These techniques involve the use of a number of 'experts'. There are two versions, the Panel Group, and the Delphi Group.

The Panel Group is a discussion group where all the participants are in personal contact with one another. Its aim is to facilitate interaction between the participants, to generate a better result than that arrived at by a single subject alone.

The Delphi Group 'replaces direct discussion and debate by a carefully designed programme of sequential interrogation, usually conducted by questionnaires with controlled feedback' (Moskowitz and Kimpel, 1978). The participants are not allowed personal contact with one another. They are only given limited information in the feedback process, which is repeated until there is general agreement.

There are advantages and disadvantages of both group approaches. Panel groups are more effective information transducers, and more efficient in that it takes less time for them to reach a decision than Delphi groups. However, panel groups provide the opportunity for the more forceful participants to influence and sometimes dictate the assessments of the group. In a panel group, the risk analyst should act as 'mediator', guiding the group through a sequence of steps like the interview technique above.

CONCLUSION

The central recurring theme of this chapter is that of personal interaction. The best way to minimize biases is by using interview or group techniques. However, with both of these techniques, the costs involved in eliciting the data are high.

The major fault of single estimation by questionnaire is that biases tend to occur, especially those caused by the anchoring heuristic. Once these biases are introduced they are very difficult to eliminate, even by interview or group techniques.

An effective method of conducting the analysis follows a four stage procedure, with verification being conducted at the end of each stage, between stages, and at the end of the analysis. When describing the methods which can be used to elicit the data it should be assumed that the guidelines given above are followed wherever they are relevant to the type of assessment being used.

The four stages are:

(1) *The identification stage.* This is probably the most important section of the analysis. For the analysis to have any relevance, risk events, scenarios and consequences must be properly defined. This stage involves no quantification: it involves a written description of all events, scenarios and consequences. This information must be presented in the clearest possible terms so that the quantification is made easier.

The next three stages are all concerned with encoding. This is the point where biases emerge and therefore great care should be taken when eliciting the data. In many cases this will mean the presence of an analyst.

(2) *Encoding risk events.* Subjects have little trouble in giving this type of data, except for postulated or special risks, because they have usually a large amount of data or experience upon which they can base their judgements. Much of this encoding can be done by individual experts. For special risks, the encoding should be done using the Panel group approach and the techniques developed by Selvidge (1975).

(3) *Encoding scenario probabilities.* This stage tends to be the stage with which subjects have most difficulty. Therefore it is best that it is conducted using the interview approach developed by Spetzler and Stael von Holstein.

(4) *Encoding consequence distributions.* Due to the large amount of information which must be assessed to give appropriate responses this stage is suited to a questionnaire approach followed by an interview. The subjects should be asked to provide any information from their specialist field which could affect the consequences.

Verification

Most of the encoding processes follow techniques developed by Spetzler and Stael von Holstein. They recommend that verification be used as well. Verification can be conducted using three different techniques: cross checking for consistency between values, verification using different elicitation techniques (where indirect methods have been used), and verification by using the final result.

Cross checking for consistency is a simple method for verification where the interviewer asks the assessor if he feels that the results are consistent across one stage of the elicitation process. For example, if two different risks have roughly the same probabilities of occurrence, the interviewer will ask the assessor if he feels this reflects his view of the risks.

Verification for rare events takes the form of providing new tables for events or representing them in different ways or in different units, and asking the assessor whether his results are a true indication of his thoughts, given this new information. For other values the verification can be done by using different elicitation techniques.

Once the results have been obtained the analyst should ask the assessors whether they give a fair view of the consequences: do they compare to their own ideas about consequences? This is quite easily done and if discrepancies do occur then they can be traced back to the base data.

REFERENCES

Fischoff, B. and R. Beyth (1975) 'I knew it would happen'—remembered probabilities of once future things. *Organisational Behavior and Human Performance*, **13**, 1–16.

Kahneman, D., P. Slovic and A. Tversky (Eds). (1982) *Judgement under Uncertainty: Heuristics and Biases*, Cambridge University Press, Cambridge.

Kahneman, D. and A. Tversky (1973) On the psychology of prediction. *Psychological Review*, **30**, 237–51.

Moskowitz, H. and C. Kimpel (1978) *Prediction of low probability adverse events in panel versus Delphi groups*. Krannert Graduate School of Management, Purdue University, West Lafayette, IN: Reprint 709.

Peterson, C. R. and L. R. Beach (1967) Man as an intuitive statistician. *Psychological Bulletin*, **68**(1), 29–46.

Selvidge, J. (1975) A three step procedure for assigning probabilities to rare events. In D. Wendt and C. A. J. Vlek (Eds) *Utility, Probability and Human Decision Making*, Reidel, Dordrecht, 199–216.

Slovic, P., B. Fischoff and S. Lichtenstein (1977) Behavioral decision theory. *Annual Review of Psychology*, **28**, 1–39.

Slovic, P. and S. Lichtenstein (1968) The relative importance of probabilities and payoffs in risk taking. *J. Experimental Psychology, Monograph Supplement*, **78**(3), Part 2.

Slovic, P. and S. Lichtenstein (1971) Comparison of Bayesian and regression approaches to the study of information processing in judgement. *Organisational Behavior and Human Performance*, **6**, 649–744.

Spetzler, C. S. and C. A. Stael Von Holstein (1975) Probability encoding in decision analysis. *Management Science*, **22**(3), 340–58.

Tversky, A. and D. Kahneman (1971) The belief in the law of small numbers. *Psychological Bulletin*, **76**, 105–10.

Tversky, A. and D. Kahneman (1973) Availability: a heuristic for judging frequency and probability. *Cognitive Psychology*, **5**, 207–32.

Tversky, A. and D. Kahneman (1974) Judgement under uncertainty: heuristics and biases. *Science*, **183**(4157), 1124–31.

Wright, W. F. (1980) Cognitive information processing biases: implications for producers and users of financial information. *Decision Sciences*, **11**(2), 284–98.

Youssef, Z. I. and C. R. Peterson (1973) Intuitive cascaded inferences. *Organisational Behavior and Human Performance*, **10**, 349–58.

CIM models for dependent risks

Summary

This chapter extends the CIM approach, beginning with a conditional probability specification of dependence, and introducing the concept of percent dependence as an alternative specification. Benchmarking of dependence specifications, computational efficiency and accuracy, and specification ease and flexibility are discussed. General decomposition structures are introduced.

A controlled interval (CI) approach to combining probability distributions is illustrated in an addition context involving three ways of treating dependence. In one case the dependence is complex in form, with both positive and negative dependence, and systematic changes in variance, skewness, and kurtosis. In two cases the dependence is simple in form, one calibrating a simplified treatment provided by the other. Specification error and specification effort is treated in some detail, computation error and computation effort to a lesser extent, but in both cases the emphasis is on key concepts which involve significant departures from current practice. It is argued that only in very special circumstances do alternative approaches have advantages, although this chapter demonstrates the rationale of this position only in the context of adding probabilistic variables involving statistical dependence with no restrictive causal dependence structure.

INTRODUCTION

Chapter 3 developed a 'controlled interval' (CI) approach to adding independent probabilistic variables, as the first step in the elaboration of a 'controlled interval and memory' (CIM) approach to probabilistic modelling. This chapter extends the CI treatment to the addition of dependent probabilistic variables. It concentrates on the basic characteristics of the CI approach in the context of the addition of statistically dependent distributions, emphasizing key departures from the treatment of independent addition discussed in Chapter 3.

The next section introduces a simple example problem, and shows one way in which dependence might be specified in terms of conditional distributions. The next two sections re-interpret the conditional specification in terms of percentage dependence, a simple concept comparable to coefficient of correlation for present purposes, and show how such comparison can be used for benchmarking, consistency checking, and simplified specification in some cases. Specification error is discussed next, suggesting that a generalized and refined CI approach to the example problem would be desirable in practice, and illustrating the power of the generalized CI approach in terms of a balanced treatment of specification effort, specification error, and computational effort. A few remarks about alternative approaches follow, providing a modest extension of the treatment in the independent addition context. The final section considers the need to employ other operations, like multiplication and division of probabilistic variables.

EXAMPLE PROBLEM

A cost estimator wants to specify probability distributions for four cost items associated with constructing an oil tankage system: tanks, pipes (and related fittings), equipment and labour. He wants to do so in a way which captures important statistical dependence between these item costs, simply and effectively, such that addition of the item cost probability distributions is efficient and precise.

Unconditional tank distribution

The estimator defines C_i, $i = 1 \ldots 4$, as the costs of the four items (in £ $\times$ 10^5), and provides Table 7.1 for tanks, $i = 1$. The P of Table 7.1 are unconditional probabilities, more formally $P(C_1)$, interpreted as subjective estimates using C_1 classmark values for classes with ranges 3.5 to 4.5, 4.5 to 5.5, and so on. The E of Table 7.1 is the unconditional expected value

Table 7.1   The unconditional cost distribution for tanks, C_1

C_1	=	4	5	6	7	
P	=	0.2	0.3	0.3	0.2	$E = 5.5$

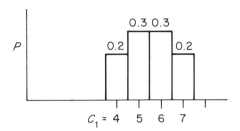

Figure 7.1   The unconditional cost distribution for tanks, C_1

assuming a rectangular density histogram, more formally $E(C_1)$. Figure 7.1 portrays the distribution of Table 7.1 in rectangular histogram form. The symmetric nature of this distribution is associated with symmetric uncertainty with respect to steel prices and fabrication costs.

Conditional pipe distribution

The estimator provides Table 7.2 for pipe, $i = 2$. The P entries are conditional probabilities, more formally $P(C_2 \mid C_1)$, interpreted as subjective estimates using C_1 and C_2 classmarks as for Table 7.1. The E entries are conditional expectations assuming rectangular density histograms for all conditional distributions, more formally $E(C_2 \mid C_1)$. Figure 7.2 portrays the conditional distributions of Table 7.2 in rectangular histogram form. The linear relationship between C_1 and $E(C_2 \mid C_1)$ is associated with common steel and fabrication cost effects upon C_1 and C_2. The common symmetric $P(C_2 \mid C_1)$ distributions are associated with further sources of uncertainty peculiar to the market for pipe and associated fittings.

Unconditional tanks and pipes distribution

The estimator now combines the $P(C_1)$ distribution of Table 7.1 and the $P(C_2 \mid C_1)$ distribution of Table 7.2, defining the unconditional $P(C_a)$ and

Table 7.2   The cost distributions for pipes, C_2, conditional on the tank cost C_1

$C_2 =$	2	3	4	5	6	7	8	
P given C_1 = 4	0.1	0.4	0.4	0.1				$E = 3.5$
5		0.1	0.4	0.4	0.1			4.5
6			0.1	0.4	0.4	0.1		5.5
7				0.1	0.4	0.4	0.1	6.5

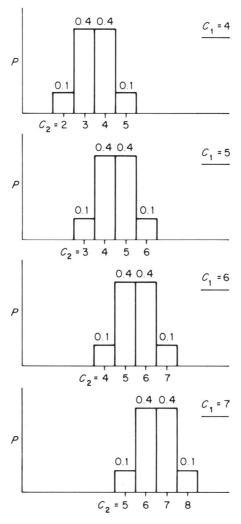

Figure 7.2 The conditional cost distributions for pipes and related fittings, $C_2 \mid C_1$

$CP(C_a)$ of Table 7.3, designated P and CP, $C_a = C_1 + C_2$. The $P(C_a)$ calculation of Table 7.3 collapses the underlying two level conditional probability tree of Figure 7.3 to a single level unconditional tree. It uses a process akin to the common interval integration of two independent distributions discussed in Chapter 3.

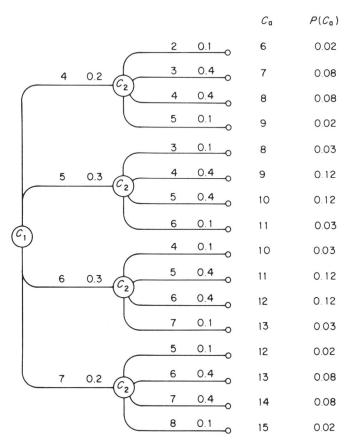

Figure 7.3 The probability tree for $C_a = C_1 + C_2$

Table 7.3 Calculation of the combined cost of the tanks and pipes, $C_a = C_1 + C_2$, based on the specifications in Tables 7.1 and 7.2

C_a	Calculations	CP	P
6	0.2×0.1	0.02	0.02
7	0.2×0.4	0.10	0.08
8	$0.2 \times 0.4 + 0.3 \times 0.1$	0.21	0.11
9	$0.2 \times 0.1 + 0.3 \times 0.4$	0.35	0.14
10	$0.3 \times 0.4 + 0.3 \times 0.1$	0.50	0.15
11	$0.3 \times 0.1 + 0.3 \times 0.4$	0.65	0.15
12	$0.3 \times 0.4 + 0.2 \times 0.1$	0.79	0.14
13	$0.3 \times 0.1 + 0.2 \times 0.4$	0.90	0.11
14	0.2×0.4	0.98	0.08
15	0.2×0.1	1.00	0.02

PERCENTAGE DEPENDENCE INTERPRETATION

Before going on to specify costs for equipment and labour, the estimator might wish to re-examine his first specifications from a slightly different perspective.

Marginal pipe distribution

The estimator recasts the conditional specifications of Table 7.2 in unconditional density form, using $P(C_2) = \Sigma_{C_1} P(C_1) \, P(C_2 \mid C_1)$, and he defines associated cumulative probabilities, $CP(C_2)$, as illustrated by Table 7.4, with $P(C_2)$ denoted P, $CP(C_2)$ denoted CP, and $E(C_2)$ denoted E. Table 7.4 may be viewed as a variant of Table 7.3 or as a simple weighting of the $P(C_2 \mid C_1)$ by the corresponding $P(C_1)$.

Table 7.4 The unconditional distribution for pipe, C_2

C_2	Calculations	P	CP
2	0.2×0.1	0.02	0.02
3	$0.2 \times 0.4 + 0.3 \times 0.1$	0.11	0.13
4	$0.2 \times 0.4 + 0.3 \times 0.4 + 0.3 \times 0.1$	0.23	0.36
5	$0.2 \times 0.1 + 0.3 \times 0.4 + 0.3 \times 0.4 + 0.2 \times 0.1$	0.28	0.64
6	$0.3 \times 0.1 + 0.3 \times 0.4 + 0.2 \times 0.4$	0.23	0.87
7	$0.3 \times 0.1 + 0.2 \times 0.4$	0.11	0.98
8	0.2×0.1	0.02	1.00

$E = 5$

0 per cent dependence bound for tanks and pipes

The estimator combines the $P(C_1)$ of Table 7.1 and the $P(C_2)$ distribution of Table 7.4, defining $P(C_a \mid 0\%)$, $C_a = C_1 + C_2$. Assuming independence, he computes joint probabilities defining a 0 per cent dependence bound illustrated by Table 7.5, with P denoting $P(C_a \mid 0\%)$, and similar more formal meanings for CP and E. The $P(C_a \mid 0\%)$ calculation of Table 7.5 collapses the underlying two level unconditional probability tree as discussed earlier, a process akin to that of Tables 7.3 and 7.4. The column designated '(CP)' misses the row accumulation step of Table 7.4, defining $P(C_a \mid 0\%)$ in this case, to provide $CP(C_a \mid 0\%)$ directly, using all available precision. The column designated 'CP' rounds these values to two places of decimals, to ease interpretation and avoid unwarranted precision. The P column provides $P(C_a \mid 0\%)$ rounded to two decimal places which sum to unity.

Table 7.5   The combined cost of tanks and pipes, $C_a = C_1 + C_2$, assuming independence, producing the 0 per cent dependence bound $P(C_a \mid 0\%)$

C_a	Calculations	(CP)	CP	P
6	0.2×0.02	0.004	0.00	0.00
7	$0.2 \times 0.11 + 0.3 \times 0.02$	0.032	0.03	0.03
8	$0.2 \times 0.23 + 0.3 \times 0.11 + 0.3 \times 0.02$	0.117	0.12	0.09
9	$0.2 \times 0.28 + 0.3 \times 0.23 + 0.3 \times 0.11 + 0.2 \times 0.02$	0.279	0.28	0.16
10	$0.2 \times 0.23 + 0.3 \times 0.28 + 0.3 \times 0.23 + 0.2 \times 0.11$	0.500	0.50	0.22
11	$0.2 \times 0.11 + 0.3 \times 0.23 + 0.3 \times 0.28 + 0.2 \times 0.23$	0.721	0.72	0.22
12	$0.2 \times 0.02 + 0.3 \times 0.11 + 0.3 \times 0.23 + 0.2 \times 0.28$	0.883	0.88	0.16
13	$0.3 \times 0.02 + 0.3 \times 0.11 + 0.2 \times 0.23$	0.968	0.97	0.09
14	$0.3 \times 0.02 + 0.2 \times 0.11$	0.996	1.00	0.03
15	0.2×0.02	1.000	1.00	0.00

$E = 10.5$

100 per cent dependence bound for tank and pipe distribution

The estimator plots the cumulative form of the $P(C_1)$ distribution of Table 7.1, $CP(C_1)$, as illustrated on Figure 7.4 by the 'C_1' curve. The trapezoidal cumulative histogram follows from the rectangular density histogram assumption, as discussed earlier. Each plotted value corresponds to $CP(C_1)$ values from Table 7.1 and associated upper class bounds, apart from the $CP = 0$ point defined by the lowest class bound. He also plots $CP(C_2)$ from Table 7.4, as indicated on Figure 7.4 by the 'C_2' curve. He

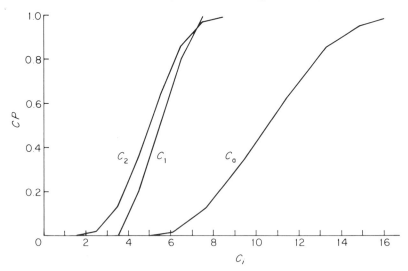

Figure 7.4   Graphical computation of $CP(C_a \mid 100\%)$, shown as the curve 'C_a'

then sums these two curves horizontally to define $CP(C_a \mid 100\%)$, a 100 per cent dependence bound, designated 'C_a' on Figure 7.4. Complete or 100 per cent positive dependence in this sense implies that any percentile value for C_1 will be realized in conjunction with the same percentile value for C_2. Summing the curves horizontally requires a summation operation for each plotted point on the C_1 and C_2 curves, but the trapezoidal shapes imply linear segments joining these points.

Bench-marking and consistency checking

The estimator plots, on a single graph, $CP(C_a \mid 0\%)$, $CP(C_a \mid 100\%)$ and $CP(C_a)$, as illustrated by Figure 7.5. He uses the bounds of Figure 7.5 to bench-mark the approximate level of dependence implied by the conditional distributions of Table 7.2 in percentage dependence terms, defined on a 0–100 per cent dependence scale in terms of horizontal interpolation between 0 and 100 per cent bounds. For example, putting aside the extreme upper end of the curves (for reasons to be discussed later), and allowing for the crudeness of the trapezoidal shapes, he might equate the $P(C_a)$ curve to 90 per cent dependence. He might then commit to memory the equivalence in approximate terms of 90 per cent dependence and a conditional specification like that of Table 7.2, as a basis for a 90 per cent dependence specification in future. Alternatively, he might use the bounds of Figure 7.5 to confirm the level of dependence implied by Table 7.2 in percentage dependence terms: does 90 per cent seem too

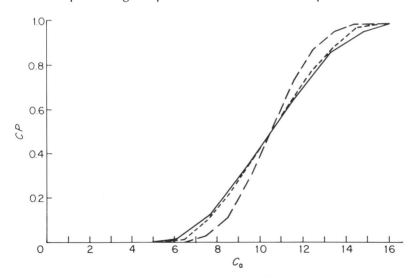

Figure 7.5 *CP(C_a) and associated bounds (CP(C_a), dashed curve; 0 per cent dependence bound, broken curve; 100 per cent dependence bound, solid curve)*

much, or too little? In general an experienced estimator would concentrate on consistency checking, and an inexperienced estimator would concentrate on benchmarking, but both are possible and desirable.

THE EXAMPLE CONTINUED

Unconditional equipment distribution

The estimator provides Table 7.6 for equipment, $i = 3$, using the notation and format of Table 7.1. Figure 7.6 provides a rectangular histogram representation of $P(C_3)$. The wide symmetric spread of this distribution is associated with uncertainty about equipment prices and uncertainty about the approach to be taken: equipment-intensive or labour-intensive. The choice depends upon the need for a quick job, and the availability of the preferred equipment, both considerations involving uncertainty.

Table 7.6   The unconditional cost distribution for equipment, C_3

C_3	=	4	5	6	7	8	9	
P	=	0.1	0.2	0.2	0.2	0.2	0.1	$E = 5.5$

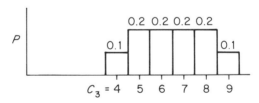

Figure 7.6   The unconditional cost distribution for equipment, C_3

Conditional labour distribution

The estimator provides Table 7.7 for labour, $i = 4$, using the notation and format of Table 7.2. Figure 7.7 portrays these distributions in rectangular histogram format. The $P(C_4 \mid C_3 = 4)$ distribution reflects a high labour cost because of a labour-intensive approach. $P(C_4 \mid C_3 = 5, 6, 7)$ distributions reflect a compensating lowering of labour cost as a more equipment-intensive approach is adopted. They also reflect a declining labour cost saving as more expensive equipment is introduced, because the choice is partially forced by market conditions, involving less desirable equipment and

Table 7.7   The cost distributions for labour, C_4, conditional on the equipment cost C_3

$C_4 =$	4	5	6	7	8	9	
P given $C_3 = 4$			0.1	0.4	0.4	0.1	$E = 7.5$
5		0.1	0.2	0.4	0.2	0.1	7.0
6	0.1	0.1	0.2	0.3	0.2	0.1	6.7
7	0.1	0.1	0.3	0.3	0.1	0.1	6.5
8		0.1	0.2	0.3	0.3	0.1	7.1
9				0.1	0.5	0.4	8.3

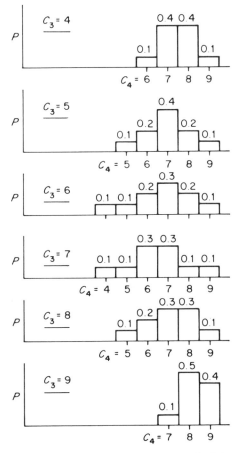

Figure 7.7   The conditional cost distributions for labour, $C_4 \mid C_3$

higher wage rates. The $P(C_4 \mid C_3 = 8)$ distribution reflects an unsuitable equipment choice forced by market conditions, in conjunction with related wage rate effects. The $P(C_4 \mid C_3 = 9)$ distribution reflects the compounding effects of a very serious shortage of suitable equipment and labour. Negative dependence is implied over the lower equipment cost range, positive dependence over the upper cost range, overall a mixed dependence, in addition to changes in distribution variance (spread), skewness (asymmetry) and kurtosis (peakedness).

Unconditional equipment and labour distribution

The estimator uses the notation and format of Table 7.3 to obtain Table 7.8 from Table 7.6 and 7.7, defining unconditional $P(C_b)$ where $C_b = C_3 + C_4$. Entries for $C_b = 8$ and 9 are provided because the sum of the minimum values is used to define the minimum joint value for the basic procedure, although they clearly would be omitted.

Marginal labour distribution

The estimator uses the notation and format of Table 7.4 to obtain Table 7.9 from Tables 7.6 and 7.7, defining the unconditional $P(C_4)$.

Zero per cent dependence curve

The estimator uses the notation and format of Table 7.5 to obtain Table 7.10 from Tables 7.6 and 7.9, defining $P(C_b \mid 0\%)$.

Consistency checking

The estimator plots $CP(C_b)$ and $CP(C_b \mid 0\%)$ on the same graph, as illustrated by Figure 7.8. He also plots a $CP(C_b \mid 100\%)$ curve, as for Figure 7.4. He uses the $CP(C_b \mid 0\%)$ and $CP(C_b \mid 100\%)$ curves to check the consistency of his $CP(C_b)$ result and his specification of Tables 7.6 and 7.7.

For C_b in the range 7 to 10, negative dependence is involved, indicated by the $CP(C_b)$ curve being below the 0 per cent dependence bound over this range in Figure 7.8. Positive dependence is involved in the $C_b = 11$ to 18 range.

The conditional relationship between tanks and pipes could be interpreted in terms of a consistent percentage dependence, but no such interpretation is possible in this case, where the dependence varies to such an extent that it changes sign. Percentage dependence is not suitable for specification purposes here, and neither is any other simple dependence measure such as correlation or covariance. To represent complex interrelationships, there is no alternative to the conditional specification.

Table 7.8 Calculation of the combined cost of equipment and labour, $C_b = C_3 + C_4$, based on the specifications in Tables 7.6 and 7.7

C_b	Calculations	CP	P
8		0	0
9		0	0
10	0.1 × 0.1 + 0.2 × 0.1 + 0.2 × 0.1	0.05	0.05
11	0.1 × 0.4 + 0.2 × 0.2 + 0.2 × 0.1 + 0.2 × 0.1	0.17	0.12
12	0.1 × 0.4 + 0.2 × 0.4 + 0.2 × 0.2 + 0.2 × 0.1	0.35	0.18
13	0.1 × 0.1 + 0.2 × 0.2 + 0.2 × 0.3 + 0.2 × 0.3 + 0.2 × 0.1	0.54	0.19
14	0.2 × 0.1 + 0.2 × 0.2 + 0.2 × 0.3 + 0.2 × 0.2	0.70	0.16
15	0.2 × 0.1 + 0.2 × 0.2 + 0.2 × 0.3 + 0.1 × 0.1	0.80	0.10
16	0.2 × 0.1 + 0.2 × 0.3 + 0.1 × 0.1	0.89	0.09
17	0.2 × 0.1 + 0.1 × 0.5	0.96	0.07
18	0.1 × 0.4	1.00	0.04

$E = 13.54$

Table 7.9 The unconditional distribution of labour, C_4

C_4	Calculations	P	CP
4	0.2 × 0.1 + 0.2 × 0.1	0.04	0.04
5	0.2 × 0.1 + 0.2 × 0.2 + 0.2 × 0.1	0.08	0.12
6	0.1 × 0.1 + 0.2 × 0.2 + 0.2 × 0.2 + 0.2 × 0.3 + 0.2 × 0.2	0.19	0.31
7	0.1 × 0.4 + 0.2 × 0.2 + 0.2 × 0.3 + 0.2 × 0.3 + 0.1 × 0.1	0.31	0.62
8	0.1 × 0.4 + 0.2 × 0.2 + 0.2 × 0.3 + 0.1 × 0.5	0.25	0.87
9	0.1 × 0.1 + 0.2 × 0.1 + 0.2 × 0.1 + 0.2 × 0.4	0.13	1.00

$E = 7.04$

Table 7.10 The combined cost of equipment and labour, $C_b = C_3 + C_4$, assuming independence, producing the 0 per cent dependence bound $P(C_b \mid 0\%)$

C_b	Calculations	(CP)	CP	P
8	0.1×0.04	0.004	0.00	0.00
9	$0.1 \times 0.08 + 0.2 \times 0.04$	0.020	0.02	0.02
10	$0.1 \times 0.19 + 0.2 \times 0.08 + 0.2 \times 0.04$	0.063	0.06	0.04
11	$0.1 \times 0.31 + 0.2 \times 0.19 + 0.2 \times 0.08 + 0.2 \times 0.04$	0.156	0.16	0.10
12	$0.1 \times 0.25 + 0.2 \times 0.31 + 0.2 \times 0.19 + 0.2 \times 0.08 + 0.2 \times 0.04$	0.305	0.31	0.15
13	$0.1 \times 0.13 + 0.2 \times 0.25 + 0.2 \times 0.31 + 0.2 \times 0.19 + 0.2 \times 0.08 + 0.1 \times 0.04$	0.488	0.49	0.18
14	$0.2 \times 0.13 + 0.2 \times 0.25 + 0.2 \times 0.31 + 0.2 \times 0.19 + 0.1 \times 0.08$	0.672	0.67	0.18
15	$0.2 \times 0.13 + 0.2 \times 0.25 + 0.2 \times 0.31 + 0.1 \times 0.19$	0.829	0.83	0.16
16	$0.2 \times 0.13 + 0.2 \times 0.25 + 0.1 \times 0.31$	0.936	0.94	0.11
17	$0.2 \times 0.13 + 0.1 \times 0.25$	0.987	0.99	0.05
18	0.1×0.13	1.000	1.00	0.01

$E = 13.54$

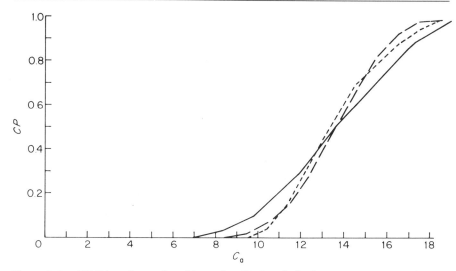

Figure 7.8 $CP(C_b)$ and associated bounds ($CP(C_b)$, dashed curve; 0 per cent dependence bound, broken curve; 100 per cent dependence bound, solid curve)

0 per cent dependence bound for total cost

The estimator defines C_c as $C_a + C_b$, and uses the format of Table 7.5 to obtain Table 7.11 from Tables 7.3 and 7.8, defining the $P(C_c \mid 0\%)$.

Table 7.11 The 0 per cent dependence bound for total cost $C_c = C_a + C_b$, $P(C_c \mid 0\%)$

C_c	Calculations	(CP)	CP	P
16	0.02×0.05	0.0010	0.00	0.00
17	$0.02 \times 0.12 + 0.08 \times 0.05$	0.0074	0.01	0.01
18	$0.02 \times 0.18 + 0.08 \times 0.12 +$ etc	0.0261	0.03	0.02
19	$0.02 \times 0.19 + 0.08 \times 0.18$	0.0645	0.06	0.03
20	$0.02 \times 0.16 + 0.08 \times 0.19$	0.1270	0.13	0.07
21	$0.02 \times 0.10 + 0.08 \times 0.16$	0.2134	0.21	0.08
22	$0.02 \times 0.09 + 0.08 \times 0.10$	0.3194	0.32	0.11
23	$0.02 \times 0.07 + 0.08 \times 0.09$	0.4392	0.44	0.12
24	$0.02 \times 0.04 + 0.08 \times 0.07$	0.5644	0.56	0.12
25	0.08×0.04	0.6839	0.68	0.12
26		0.7867	0.79	0.11
27		0.8667	0.87	0.08
28		0.9234	0.92	0.05
29		0.9603	0.96	0.04
30		0.9828	0.98	0.02
31		0.9946	0.99	0.01
32		0.9992	1.00	0.01
33		1.0000	1.00	0.00

$E = 24.04$

100 per cent dependence bound for total cost

The estimator plots the $CP(C_a)$ distribution of Table 7.3 as illustrated by the 'C_a' curve of Figure 7.9, assuming a trapezoidal form as for Figure 7.1. He also plots $CP(C_b)$ distribution of Table 7.8 as illustrated by the 'C_b' curve of Figure 7.9, assuming a trapezoidal form. He then sums these curves, as for Figure 7.4, defining $CP(C_c \mid 100)$, a 100 per cent dependence bound.

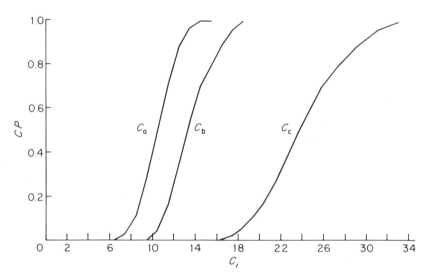

Figure 7.9   Graphical computation of $CP(C_c \mid 100\%)$, shown as the curve 'C_c'

Percentage dependence assessment

The estimator plots $CP(C_c \mid 0\%)$, and $CP(C_c \mid 100\%)$ on the same graph, as illustrated by Figure 7.10. He uses the bounds of Figure 7.5 to assess an approximate percentage level of dependence, 75 per cent. He then plots the 75 per cent dependence curve of Figure 7.10 via interpolation, thus defining $CP(C_c \mid 75\%)$, assumed to be equal to $CP(C_c)$. This reflects a moderately high level of dependence between C_a and C_b because of common market forces, especially at the upper end of both cost ranges, the associated part of the C_c curve in the upper range being of most interest.

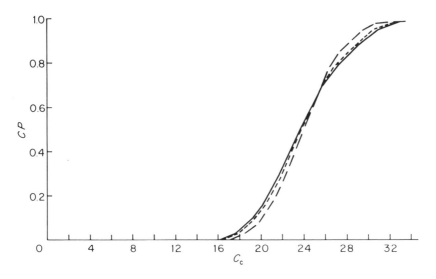

Figure 7.10 *CP(C$_c$)* and associated bounds (*CP(C$_c$)*, dashed curve, 0 per cent dependence bound, broken curve; 100 per cent dependence bound, solid curve)

SPECIFICATION ERROR AND SPECIFICATION GENERALIZATION

Two kinds of specification error are worth distinguishing, although they are not independent: approximation error and residual error. Specification approximation error is defined here as error associated with the deliberate use of a histogram specification structure which does not use an infinite number of classes, or the use of percentage dependence instead of a conditional specification. Specification residual error includes all other forms of error.

Approximation error could be associated with Table 7.1 because C_1 values are on a fairly crude scale. A generalized CI approach can avoid such error in a variety of ways. One is direct specification of more classes, making the CI approach inherently free from specification approximation errors. A second is indirect specification of more classes, fitting a maximum order polynomial to $CP(C_1)$ as defined by Table 7.1, and using this function to allocate probabilities to the finer class structure. A third is indirect specification of more classes using distribution shapes other than a maximum order polynomial, like the Beta distribution used often in CPM/PERT.

Appropriate computer software will allow a flexible approach to distribution specification which facilitates elimination of this kind of error, to whatever level of precision is appropriate, balancing it in relation to specification effort and computation cost. In a bench-marking context like that associated with Figure 7.5, such error is of considerable importance. It is important to avoid any discontinuities and irregularities which confuse the issue, like the change in percentage dependence level around $C_a = 14$. Hence, if a specification like that of Tables 7.1 and 7.2 is used in practice, it would be important to smooth the $CP(C_1)$ and $CP(C_2)$ curves of Figure 7.4 and to use such smoothed versions to compute all the curves of Figure 7.5.

Specification approximation is clearly associated with the use of 75 per cent dependence to define $C_c = C_a + C_b$. However, accepting such error is a choice which can be eliminated via additional specification effort. For example, complete elimination could be achieved by the use of a three-level probability tree, with two levels of conditions, for the specification of C_3, followed by a four-level probability tree, with three levels of conditions, for the specification of C_4. Intermediate levels of specification approximation error are provided by the 'memory' aspects of the CIM approach, but these aspects are beyond the scope of this chapter. They are discussed later in Chapters 9, 10 and 11.

Specification residual error, all other forms of specification error, is usually a much more important kind of error, because it is much more difficult to control. A CI approach cannot fully resolve these difficulties. However, three characteristics noted in the independent addition context are worth a reminder.

First, computer software which allows a flexible approach to specification approximation error allows the user to select a means of specifying any distribution which is most comfortable for the circumstances.

Second, given such software, it is an easy matter to extend it to allow comparisons of different approaches to specifying a distribution as a means of checking consistency.

Third, if n distributions are summed, the computation procedure automatically provides $n - 2$ intermediate sums, a useful basis for further consistency checks, including representations showing the relative contribution to uncertainty of each source distribution.

These characteristics remain important in the context of dependence. However, even more important is the flexibility introduced by the three distinct approaches associated with C_a, C_b and C_c. The approach used for $C_3 + C_4 = C_b$ provides a simple but general way to deal with very complex dependence relationships. This same approach can be used for simple dependence relationships like that associated with $C_1 + C_2 = C_a$, but in this context it also serves to calibrate in the user's mind a simpler approximate representation in percentage dependence terms, or to check a conditional specification against a calibrated perception of percentage dependence. Like similar concepts, and somewhat different single parameter dependence measures such as the coefficient of correlation, percentage dependence implies restrictive assumptions. It only makes sense in a strict manner if both distributions have the same shape, and common forces have a common effect upon both distributions. However, it is a useful simplified representation if properly calibrated in the user's mind, as when applied to $C_a + C_b = C_c$. The availability of all three allows an efficient and effective balancing of specification effort and specification error.

Specification flexibility can be extended within the basic three-prong treatment of dependence outlined earlier. For example, the linear model underlying Tables 7.1 and 7.2 could be specified more directly, and such models could be extended. A -100 per cent dependence bound could be associated with Figure 7.8 as well as a $+100$ per cent dependence bound. The 75 per cent dependence assumption for $CP(C_c)$ could be used to generate a conditional specification for $P(C_4)$. These and many other possibilities are worth pursuing, but they are beyond the scope of this book.

COMPUTATION ERROR AND COMPUTATION GENERALIZATION

A generalized CI computation procedure for the addition of independent probabilistic variables was discussed in some detail earlier. In summary, in relation to the independent addition operation of Table 7.5, it involves recognizing that each P calculation entry is a special form of integration of two within-class distributions, the first 0.2×0.02 entry of Table 7.5 involving C_1 in the range of 3.5 to 4.5 (probability 0.2 from Table 7.1), and C_2 in the range 1.5 to 2.5 (probability 0.02 from Table 7.4). Within this framework, generalization permits the use of different class intervals for each component distribution and the result, and different intervals within a given distribution. Associated computation error can be eliminated, to whatever degree of precision is required, with a modest increase in computation effort.

The conditional specification dependent addition procedure of Table 7.3 is a simple generalization of Table 7.5. A generalized CI approach to Table 7.4 maintains the features and advantages of a generalized CI approach to Table 7.5. However, two further observations are important in the context of conditional specification addition.

First, in the context of a bench-marking exercise like that associated with Figure 7.5, it is important to adopt an approach which eliminates any visible discontinuities or irregularities associated with specification error, as noted earlier. If more classes are used, defined directly or indirectly, to reduce specification error to an acceptable level, computation error will be comparatively negligible. The apparent change in the percentage dependence level on Figure 7.5 around $C_a = 14$ is partly attributable to computation errors associated with the unconditional and 0 per cent dependence curves. However, it is primarily due to specification approximation error associated with the 100 per cent dependence curve. These two sources of error operate in opposition directions, and have their most serious impact in the region of $C_a = 14$.

Second, when obtaining more precision by increasing the number of classes used for computation purposes, interpolation between conditional distributions also needs consideration.

It is worth noting that in the context of a 0 per cent bound, the computation error associated with Table 7.5 is in an appropriate direction, the result being a slight over-statement of risk.

The procedure used to define 100 per cent dependence bounds is most easily visualized in graphical terms. In practice computer software which operates arithmetically in a comparable manner is clearly needed. A directly equivalent procedure to that of Figures 7.4 and 7.9 involves computation error in relation to repeated use of the rectangular density histogram or trapezoidal cumulative histogram assumptions. Figure 7.4 is consistent with earlier assumptions and precise in relation to them, but Figure 7.9 is not consistent with the earlier underlying assumptions, in that successive distribution combinations should lead to smoother and smoother distribution curves. More generally, if the simplification of rectangular density histograms or trapezoidal cumulative histograms is abandoned and smooth curves defined by a polynomial of maximum order are assumed, the use of trapezoidal shapes on both Figures 7.4 and 7.9 involves error. Detailed treatment is beyond this book, but several points require observation.

First, over-estimation of variability is involved, appropriate for a 100 per cent dependence bound.

Second, if specification error is reduced to an appropriate level, as noted earlier, computation error will be negligible.

Generalizing the addition of two dependent probabilistic variables to three or more in the conditional framework used for C_a and C_b poses significant problems. The interpolation approach used for C_a is much more flexible, but it has its limitations and restrictions. These issues are beyond the scope of this chapter.

COMPARISON WITH ALTERNATIVE APPROACHES

The CI approach to the addition of independent probabilistic variables has been compared to alternatives earlier. Dependence makes such comparisons complex, but several assertions follow.

First, the discrete probability distribution (DPD) approach could be generalized to accommodate conditional specifications in a comparable manner, but the lack of specification flexibility, with specification approximation and residual error implications, is even more important. Further, the DPD approach does not generalize readily to accommodate a complementary percentage dependence approach. It is difficult to see any areas of comparative advantage.

Second, functional integration and moment-based approaches retain some specialized areas where they offer comparative advantages, but they are even more limited in a dependence context than they were in an independence context.

Third, numerical integration and Monte Carlo approaches remain comparatively unattractive.

OPERATION FLEXIBILITY AND OPERATION GENERALIZATION

This chapter should illustrate the flexibility and power of the CI approach for addition involving dependence. In the context of a generalized CI approach, it should be clear that this flexibility and power will be preserved for subtraction, multiplication and division operations. Hence, as a general basis for arithmetic operations involving probability distributions, the CI approach compares favourably to all other approaches. However, it should be noted that complex causal dependencies, of the kind involved in a PERT network, may make a Monte Carlo approach attractive. Further, complex statistical dependencies involving large numbers of distributions pose difficulties not considered here.

CONCLUSION

The controlled interval (CI) approach to adding dependent probabilistic variables is flexible and powerful. Specification effort, specification error, computation error and computation effort can be controlled in an integrated, effective and efficient manner. Moment-based and functional integration approaches may be preferable, but only in extremely special circumstances, and no other approach is preferable. This chapter should make these conclusions clear and sustainable. In doing so, it extends the similar conclusions of Chapter 3 in the context of independent addition.

Case study: project costs

Summary

This chapter provides an introduction to the treatment of cost and schedule risks in the context of a hydroelectric development project. The case study illustrates:

Statistical dependence between risks, and decomposition structures;
A similar analysis structure to that seen in Chapter 5, but based on risk-activity combinations;
Simple treatment of a project schedule;
Analysis with multiple criteria which are not all additive in the same way.

INTRODUCTION

This chapter outlines an analysis of the risks associated with the construction costs and schedule of a major hydroelectric development and outages of the associated transmission system when the project becomes operational. It provides an overview of the approach and methodology of the risk analysis study, the major elements of the analysis, the basis for the risk assessment, and the interpretation of the results. The intention is to give a non-technical description of aspects of a large, complex risk analysis project. In particular, the way in which dependence arises, and the way in which it is dealt with, are discussed in detail.

The specific hydroelectric development plan was the result of a vigorous selection process. It took into account multiple criteria and a broad range of potential development schemes. The project which was the subject of this risk analysis was chosen as the apparent best method for meeting a large proportion of the future energy requirements of its region.

Economic analyses indicated that the hydroelectric project would be viable in economic terms despite a broad range of possible deviations from expected values of key parameters. Even so, net project benefits were sensitive to capital cost variations, and alternative financing plans were predicated on the assumption that the proposed project schedule would be met. Every reasonable effort was made to prepare conservative cost estimates and to produce an achievable schedule. Nevertheless, uncertainties were involved, and their potential importance demanded that they be given appropriate consideration at various stages in project development.

A risk analysis was undertaken as the basis for determining the extent to which perceived risks might influence capital costs and schedule. In addition, because a mature project would represent a major portion of the total generation system in the area, a further risk analysis assessed the probability and consequences of a longer-term outage of the proposed transmission system. This chapter outlines the risk analysis procedure.

The purpose of the risk analysis was to identify all relevant risks which, if realized, could impact cost, schedule, project safety, and public confidence; to determine the probable consequences of realizing risks; to assess relevant preventive measures and responses; to estimate the probability that project criteria will be satisfied; and to stimulate documentation of problems and solutions to improve expected risk performance. The risk analysis was conducted by an independent team of senior engineers of various disciplines who provided an objective assessment of the project design, cost estimate and construction schedule. Frequent communication with and between the project groups assured consistency and reasonableness of the underlying assumptions, criteria and methodology.

The next two sections of this chapter describe the general approach that was taken to the risk analysis task, and the major elements of the analysis. Subsequent sections give more detailed discussions of three specific aspects of the study: the assessment of risks; the assessment of dependence relationships; and the interpretation and presentation of results.

In terms of its structure, the analysis is a composite of the LNG case study described in Chapter 4 and the bridge case study described in Chapter 5. Because a schedule is being examined, activities are used as the basis for the analysis, in a manner similar to the use of subsystems and elements in the LNG case; however, it was also convenient to use the scenario approach of the bridge case, structured on risks (sources of risk), and it was important to distinguish construction and operating periods. The methodology described in Chapters 4 and 5 was adapted slightly for this case study, but the structure did not change dramatically. The major differences were an extension of the methodology to consider dependence and the interrelationships between activities and risks, and further changes in terminology to suit the new context.

APPROACH

Any major construction effort is inevitably exposed to a large number of risks. Floods may occur at crucial times. Accidents should not happen, but they sometimes do. Subsurface investigations, no matter how thorough, do not always tell the whole story about what will be found when major excavation work begins. The normal estimation process implicitly accounts for a set of reasonably 'normal' expectations as direct costs are developed, adding a contingency to the directly computed total on the grounds that problems usually do occur even though their specific nature may not be foreseen accurately at the outset. However, contingency allowances do not consider risks explicitly, and this shortcoming can have serious consequences.

The risk analysis took explicit account of 21 different risks, applying them as appropriate to each major construction activity, combining some reasonably precise data with a good deal of relatively subjective judgements. For example, the probability that a particular flood crest will occur in any given year can be determined from analysis of hydrologic records, but until a particular flood crest does occur, it cannot be known with any degree of certainty what havoc it will wreak. The overall methodology is illustrated in Figure 8.1 and described briefly below.

Step 1:   Review base cost and schedule estimate

The base cost and schedule estimation effort was reviewed to determine important underlying assumptions, areas of uncertainty, proposed construction methods and sequence.

Step 2:   Risk list development

A risk list was developed, providing an initial statement of major areas of uncertainty to be considered in the analysis. It was important at this stage to begin to make initial gross assessments of how each risk might affect the project at various stages of completion, as well as to estimate the extent to which dependency existed between one risk and another. In this regard, for example, the risk of a major flood is independent of the risk that geological conditions will differ from those expected. On the other hand, it can be reasonably asserted that the risk that any given contractor will experience a construction accident is at least partially dependent on the risk that the same contractor will have poor construction quality control.

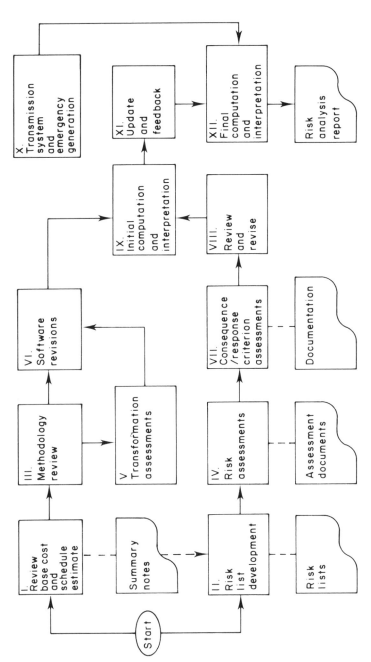

Figure 8.1 Outline of the risk analysis study methodology

Step 3:   Methodology review

Upon completion of the estimate review and concurrent with development of an initial risk list, a review was made of subsequent risk analysis steps as initially proposed. The initial methodology specification was based upon similar methods applied in circumstances which were similar in some respects, different in others. Some methodology revisions were agreed, and related changes to proprietary computer software were approved.

Step 4:   Risk assessments

A data collection effort was accomplished for each identified risk and a determination was made of the probability that each of a selected range of risk magnitudes would be realized in any given year. When data gaps existed, decision analysis and other processes were used to produce the required information.

Step 5:   Transformation assessments

Transformation criteria were developed so that individual risk analysts could more easily view the consequences of realising any single risk in terms of 'natural' values. For example, it is easier to think in terms of the volume of earth involved in a slope failure than to think directly of its cost impact. Transformation criteria can then be used to convert natural values like 'volume of earth' to cost and schedule implications.

Step 6:   Software revisions

Revisions to proprietary computer software were made in accordance with the review noted in Step 3 above, concurrent with the analysis of risks.

Step 7:   Consequence/response criterion assessments

For each major construction activity, the consequences of realizing each possible risk magnitude were assessed and estimated, given an assumed response. The assumed response was an action to be taken if a particular risk is realized, which might mitigate the consequences. Responses were not considered at length, but care was taken to ensure that suitable responses were assumed. Consequences were assessed in terms of all relevant natural criteria.

Step 8:   Review and revise

As the work proceeded, reviews and revisions were made to introduce collective judgements from diverse disciplines into the process.

Step 9: Initial computation and interpretation

The initial probability, consequence and transformation assessments were combined and interpreted. Anomalies were identified and risks emerging as most significant were further reviewed to ensure that their consequences had been accounted for adequately.

Step 10: Transmission system and emergency generation

A separate analysis of the transmission system was undertaken to assess the likelihood and the consequences of a major transmission outage. A similar methodology was followed in this sub-analysis, although it was concerned with an operating phase rather than a construction phase, so significant differences of detail were involved.

Step 11: Update and feedback

All input data was updated based on the results of Steps 9 and 10 above.

Step 12: Final computation and interpretation

A final run was made to compute expected values of costs and completion schedules as well as to create probability distributions for these items. This final output provided the basis for interpretation. Similarly, a run was made to compute expected values for transmission system loss.

ELEMENTS OF THE ANALYSIS

Table 8.1 depicts the most important questions that were addressed

Table 8.1 Elements of the risk analysis

Question	Study element
What major construction projects are involved?	Configurations
What kind of work is going on for a given configuration?	States
What are the possible initiating mechanisms which could influence estimated costs or completion times?	Risks
What major portions of any given configuration are subject to risk realization?	Activities
If a particular risk magnitude is realized, what possible consequences can occur?	Damage scenarios
How can these consequences be measured?	Criteria
What important assumptions and limitations must be established to permit a reasonable analysis and to draw important conclusions?	Boundary conditions

Table 8.2   Main features of the risk analysis for the construction phase

Element	Description
Activities	Construction activities
Risks	Construction related risks
Activity-risks	Risks that apply to certain activities differently
Risk events	Annual probability of construction risk events
Activity-risk event probabilities	Annual probabilities scaled to activity durations
Impact scenarios	Relate various levels of impacts on activities to risk events
Responses	Responses to construction risks in terms of cost and schedule criteria
Secondary risks and responses	Considered in primary responses
Multiple criterion evaluation	Evaluated impact/response in terms of 1. Activity delay (months) 2. Labour increase (%) 3. Additional cost ($M)
Criterion value distributions	Assumed minimum, modal and maximum value distributions for each criterion
Criterion additivity	Like criteria added within activity-risks; cost criterion added across activities
Dependence kinds and types	1. Cause/effect: separable 2. Cause/effect: not separable 3. Common antecedent 4. Compounding consequence 5. Estimation error
Dependence structure	Pairing of activity-risks using per cent dependent addition
Computer software	Interactive risk analysis program (version II)

initially and relates them to the elements of the analysis. Each element is discussed further below, and summarized in Table 8.2.

Configurations and configuration states

The primary configurations that were considered were the hydroelectric project and the transmission system. Two configuration states were considered: the construction period, applicable to the hydroelectric project; and the operation period, applied only to the transmission system configuration.

Activities

A coarse activity structure was used, compared to most PERT/CPM assessments, involving about 20 activities, as indicated in Table 8.3. A simple

Table 8.3   Construction activities

Main access	Intake
Site facilities	Penstock
Diversion tunnels	Powerhouse
Cofferdams	Transformer gallery
Main dam excavations	Tailrace and surge chambers
Main dam fill initial portion	Turbine-generators
Main dam fill final portion	Mechanical/electrical equipment
Relict channel protection	Switchyard
Chute spillway	Transmission
Emergency spillway	Impoundment
Service spillway tunnels	Test and commission

activity structure was used to facilitate a comparatively detailed treatment of the risks associated with each activity. Some large activities, the Main Dam for example, were decomposed to provide useful detail.

Risks

A preliminary list of about 60 risks was condensed to 21 for the construction analysis, as indicated in Table 8.4. The 'estimating variance' risk included all variations due to estimating variations in quantities, unit costs, productivity, and so on: how these can be dealt with at a detailed level will be considered in the next case study in Chapter 9, but such treatment in this

Table 8.4   Risks applying to construction

Natural risks	Flood
	Wind
	Seismic
	Geological conditions
	Low streamflow
Design-controlled risks	Seepage, piping, erosion
	Ground water
Construction risks	Labour, strikes, disputes
	Equipment availability
	Equipment breakdown
	Material availability
	Material deliveries
	Weather
Human risks	Contractor capability
	Construction quality control
	Accidents
	Sabotage, vandalism
Special risks	Regulatory delay
	Estimating variance
	Schedule variance

analysis would have involved too much detail. Most of the other risks are straightforward. Many of these risks also applied in the risk analysis of the operational state, although a separate similar list was prepared.

Activity-risks

Each risk was considered in relation to each construction activity. Not all combinations are logical, and some can be ignored because a negligible impact is involved. The remainder, involving a significant logical combination, are activity-risks: 'cofferdams—flood' for example.

For some risks, the activity-risk concept is, as it suggests, a risk associated with the activity itself. For example, 'main dam excavation—labour disputes' is concerned with the effect of labour disputes during the excavation of the main dam in terms of the main dam excavation labour force. However, with respect to natural risks such as flood, a similar interpretation is not possible. For example, 'main dam excavation—flood' must consider the effects of flood, not just on the main dam excavation, but also on all structures which have been completed to that point: the cofferdam and the diversion tunnels are activities which precede main dam excavation, but a flood during main dam excavation would effect the cofferdam and diversion tunnels.

Risk events

These were specified probabilistically, as in the bridge case study described in Chapter 5.

Activity-risk events

Risk event probabilities were scaled from an annual basis to the duration of the activity.

Damage scenarios

Up to 10 different 'damage' or 'impact' scenarios were associated with each feasible activity-risk combination. While these scenarios varied significantly from one activity-risk combination to another, they generally described a range of possibilities extending from 'no damage' to 'catastrophic loss'. In some cases they were discrete representations from a simple continuum of possibilities. In others quite different kinds of impacts were involved. As was the case for the risk analysis of the bridge, appropriate responses to risk events, and any secondary risks arising from these responses, were embedded in the corresponding impact scenarios.

Criteria

The consequences of realizing particular risk magnitudes for each activity were measured in terms of three construction-phase criteria:

Cost implications;
Schedule implications;
Manpower requirements.

Operational phase criteria were defined as cost implications and days of power lost in the major load centres.

Boundary conditions

Assumptions and limitations were established to permit a reasonable and consistent analysis of the problem. Some examples follow.

All cost estimates were made in terms of base year and month dollars, and results were presented in terms of real potential cost variations, exclusive of inflation.

The analysis was limited to the construction period for the hydroelectric project, since the greatest potential cost and schedule variance would be possible during this period. The risk analysis for the operating period was associated solely with the transmission system since that configuration represents the most likely source of a major system outage during project operation.

The risk analysis was accomplished concurrently with finalization of the total project cost estimate and was necessarily associated with the feasibility level design. There was clearly some potential for design change as the project proceeded, and future risk analyses would have to be undertaken coincident with completion of final detailed design and prior to commitment to major construction activities. Even so, the 'estimating variance' risk took into account the fact that some design changes were likely to appear as detailed design effort proceeded.

A great deal of subjective judgement was necessarily involved in assessing probabilities and in predicting possible damage scenarios. This effort was accomplished initially by individual qualified professionals in the various relevant disciplines, and was subjected to iterative group review and feedback efforts. To the extent that individual biases entered the analysis, their effects were probably mutually offsetting. Even so, sensitivity tests were made for risks which were important contributors to the final results.

The risk list does not include the important possibility of funding delays or of financing problems. These issues were dealt with in a separate financial risk analysis.

RISK ASSESSMENT

For each of the risks identified, the assessment was concerned with a representative range of credible events. For example, as flood was identified as a risk, the magnitudes of floods which could occur were defined and each magnitude was associated with the probability that it would occur. Depending upon the particular risk under consideration, data sources included reasonably accurate scientific data (particularly applicable to the natural risk category), historical experience on water resources projects, and, where data gaps existed, subjective group judgements.

In each case a maximum credible event was identified first: the *most extreme* event, albeit highly unlikely, that could occur. This choice set an upper limit on a scale of possible events which always began with a minimum magnitude corresponding to a 'no damage' situation. Continuing with the flood example, the maximum credible event was considered to be the probable maximum flood which had been computed in the hydrologic studies, corresponding to a return period of more than 10 000 years, an annual probability of occurrence of less than 0.0001. The minimum magnitude 'no damage' event at the lower end of the scale varied from activity to activity. For example, a cofferdam built early in the construction period and designed to withstand a 50 year flood event can be expected to suffer damage if a 100 year event actually occurs. Late in the project, a 100 year flood event would not only cause no damage to structures in place, it might be fortuitous because it improved the reservoir impoundment schedule.

Once risks were defined and feasible activity-risk combinations were reviewed, the consequences of realizing each selected risk magnitude were conceptualized. If this risk magnitude were realized, would a partially completed structure be damaged? Would it fail? If it failed, would some other work in progress be disrupted? Clearly, no-one could know with certainty what precise damage scenario should be associated with a given risk magnitude for a particular activity. To capture this uncertainty, a range of damage scenarios were defined, and a probability of occurrence if a particular risk magnitude were realized was associated with each.

Even if a particular risk level were realized *and* a particular damage scenario were suffered, the cost and time required to restore the activity could not be assessed with certainty. Things go exceedingly well every once in a while, and occasionally they go very badly indeed. Each risk analyst was asked to provide three values for each criterion:

A minimum value, corresponding to the one time in twenty that the weather is particularly good, materials are readily available, no accidents occur, and the like.

A modal value, associated with the most likely expectation of the analyst.

A maximum value, corresponding to the one time in twenty that everything is more difficult than expected.

In the computerized calculation process, the three criterion values supplied by the risk analyst were fitted to a distribution which approximated the Beta distribution illustrated at the bottom of Figure 8.2. In effect, designation of the three criterion values led to generation of a histogram with relatively narrow intervals and a nearly continuous range of possible values over a relatively wide spectrum.

Figure 8.2 illustrates a structural relationship between risk-activity combinations, damage scenarios, and criterion values. While this procedure is

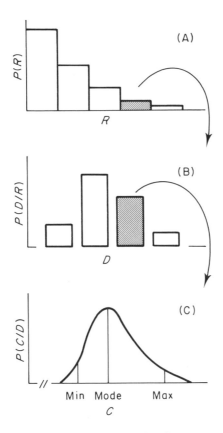

Figure 8.2 Structural relationship for activity-risks, damage scenarios and criterion values. (A) Discrete risk levels exist for each risk-activity combination. The probability $P(R)$ of each risk level R is determined. (B) A risk event can cause a number of possible damage levels. If risk magnitude R occurs, $P(D \mid R)$ is the probability damage scenario D will arise. (C) For each damage scenario D three values define a modified Beta distribution for each criterion C

generally applicable, some commentary on particular aspects of its application and on certain risks is appropriate.

The terminology 'damage' scenario was used for convenience since most identified risks were reasons that the cost would be higher than had been estimated or that the schedule would be exceeded, many of which involved physical damage. However, this structure does permit consideration of 'negative damage' scenarios, sometimes called 'upside risk'. For example, the cost estimate was produced on the basis of estimates of requirements for some concrete lining in the penstocks, extensive grouting, a certain level of rock bolting, and the like. If geological conditions were found to be better than assumed, the costs could be less and the schedule might be accelerated.

Cost variations were assumed to be additive across risks and across activities. Duration variations were assumed to be additive across risks for a particular activity, but not across activities, except to a limited extent on critical paths. It was necessary to allow for possible overlapping of activities, resequencing of subsequent activities, and acceleration of subsequent activities by using more resources, in order to assess the effects of duration variations on the schedule. Manpower variations were assumed to be additive across risks, but not across activities, since activities frequently require different skills and occur at different times.

Estimating variance risk was treated in a special way because it could not be conceptualized easily in physical terms. It accounted for inevitable differences which occur between estimates and actual bids, and between bids and actual activity costs, even in the absence of any other identified risk. Its probability of occurrence and its associated range (fractions or multiples of the basic estimate) were determined from historical data on water resources projects. It included, but was not necessarily limited to, such conditions as:

the influence of competition and market pressures;
estimating discrepancies or errors in unit quantities on the part of both the owner's estimator and the bidder;
particular contract forms and the owner's acceptance or nonacceptance of certain risks;
labour market conditions and the nature of project labour agreements;
productivity and efficiency changes over time;
the cost implications of variances between activity schedules and actual activity durations;
the potential for scope changes over time;
extraordinary escalation of construction costs above the underlying inflation rate.

In addition to estimating variance, a second special risk was associated with regulatory matters. Various legislative controls applied to the project, and it was a relatively simple matter to compute the minimum time in which regulatory requirements could be satisfied. A far more difficult task was estimating the precise nature and duration of possible regulatory delays. It was inappropriate to attempt to apply regulatory risks at the activity level.

Regulatory risk was handled by developing a separate distribution for a range of periods necessary for satisfaction of important licensing and permitting requirements. Data used included recent experiences on other water resources projects, and information obtained from discussions with staff members of the regulatory agency. The effect of applying regulatory risk was primarily one of shifting the starting time for commencement of construction activities, leading to a corresponding change in the projected completion time. A lesser effect of regulatory risk was the introduction of delays during construction.

Each of the various construction risk magnitude probabilities was originally calculated as an annual value. On an activity-risk by activity-risk basis, these annual values were then converted by standard computational procedures to provide a probability of occurrence during the duration of the activity.

The 'response' concept is particularly important in the formal risk analysis process. As the terminology suggests, a response represents the action to be taken *if* a particular event occurs. There are two kinds of response.

One kind of response is a *mitigating response*, an expected reaction to the occurrence of a particular damage level. *If* this damage level is incurred, *then* what actions must be taken to restore the activity to its pre-damage status, and what are the cost, schedule, and manpower implications?

A second kind of response is a *preventive response*. What changes might reasonably be made in the design or construction procedures which would avoid or reduce a particular damage level? Is the cost and schedule change which might ensue worthwhile when compared to the probability and magnitude of the consequences which would otherwise be incurred? A number of preventive responses were identified by the risk analysts during the risk study, and several of these were incorporated into the project design and design criteria. This provided an important link between the risk analysis team and the design team. Preventive responses were not chosen unless they offered a net benefit to the cost or schedule. Hence, as detailed design proceeds and as subsequent risk analysis updates are accomplished, a gradual reduction in the spread of possible values can be expected.

DEPENDENCE AND ITS TREATMENT

The assessment and treatment of dependence was a key feature of this case study. Several different kinds of dependence were considered.

Cause/effect dependence — separable

Consider the pair of risks 'weather' and 'material availability', in the context of the activity 'main dam excavation'. Weather can cause material availability problems. For example, it may be impossible to extract fill materials under some weather conditions. This level of dependence can be avoided by extracting the associated risk from the material availability risk and embedding it in the weather risk, via appropriate definitions. That is, 'weather' can be defined to include the effect of weather on construction progress in direct terms and in terms of associated material supply. Weather effects can be excluded from the material supply risk, except where weather in some location and time frame other than that associated with the activity is involved. Alternatively, a non-separable cause/effect dependence approach may be taken.

Cause/effect dependence — not separable

Consider the pair of risks 'equipment availability' and 'equipment breakdown', in the context of the 'main dam excavation' activity. If equipment is difficult to obtain in the required quantities, less serviceable or less appropriate equipment may have to be accepted, and equipment may have to be used harder and longer. This will contribute to higher breakdown rates. However, it is not very useful to define equipment availability in a manner which embodies induced equipment breakdown effects. In principle, it could be done, but in practice it is not very illuminating. In this study, 'equipment availability' was defined to exclude the breakdown implications of availability problems. Such cost implications were associated with equipment breakdown. Equipment breakdown was associated with a probability distribution which reflected the full range of possible breakdown levels, including those induced by equipment availability problems. When combining the availability and breakdown distributions, dependence reflected the increased chance of higher breakdown cost values if availability problems were realized, and the increased chance of lower breakdown cost values if availability problems were not realized.

Common antecedent dependence

Consider the pair of risks 'construction quality control' and 'construction accidents', in the context of 'main dam excavation'. There is no direct relationship between these two risks in the causal sense discussed above.

However, both are related to the risk 'contractor capability', in the sense that a contractor who tends to be good in cost and duration performance terms tends to be good in quality control and accident terms as well. The relationship between capability and quality, and the relationship between capability and accidents, is based upon underlying common antecedents, the reasons why contractors are good, bad, or indifferent. The relationship between quality and accidents is based upon an explicit antecedent: contractor capability. If the contractor is good, quality tends to be good and accidents tend to be low, which implies that accidents tend to be low when quality tends to be good.

Compounding consequences dependence

Consider the pair of risks 'ice' and 'flood', still in the 'main dam excavation' context. Both pose risks for this activity via their effect on the cofferdam. They have some common antecedent dependence, in the sense that floods tend to occur in the spring when the ice is melting, and the melting of the ice leads to the breakup which causes ice floe problems. In addition to this dependence in terms of their occurrence, they have a compounding effect in terms of damage. If a large floe hits the cofferdam while it is near overtopping, the extent of the damage and its cost implications are very much greater. It is not just that ice and flood problems tend to occur together. When they occur together, the cost consequences are very much greater than a simple sum of their effects when they occur on their own.

Estimation error dependence

Consider two activities which have total costs expected to display a very modest level of dependence in terms of the four types discussed above. Assume they involve very similar design problems, construction problems and contracting considerations. Assume the same person or group of people was responsible for assessing the cost. If the estimators have significantly underestimated or overestimated the cost for one, they have probably made a similar error with respect to the other. If the variation potential associated with the activity costs is heavily influenced by estimate variance and contract variance considerations, a high level of estimation error dependence will be induced. Dependence of this kind has to be associated with risk combinations within activities, and its effects may be very widespread and very important. This case study assumed such effects were modest but significant.

Dependence structures

If all risks or activity-risks and associated criterion distributions are independent, the ordering of distribution combinations can be arbitrary.

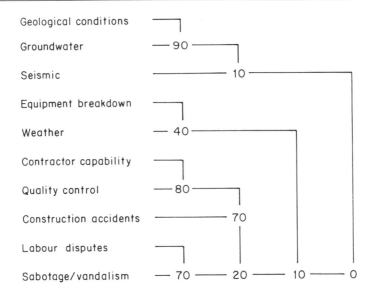

Figure 8.3   Dependence structure for the Penstock activity

However, if dependence is associated with activities or activity-risks, the ordering of distribution combinations is very important.

A pair-wise dependence tree was used to define the computation sequence employed to combine all the construction activity-risks considered, first within activities, then across activities. Each pairwise combination was associated with a percentage level of dependence, from 0 to 100 per cent, as described in Chapter 7.

When choosing pairs within the activity level, initial pairs were chosen on the basis of the strongest or most clearly defined dependence relationship. For example, within the penstock activity, pairs were selected as illustrated by Figure 8.3, for the following reasons.

'Geological condition' risk was linked to 'ground water' risk, at a 90 per cent level of dependence, because ground water problems were assumed to be very heavily dependent upon geological conditions in terms of a direct causal relationship.

'Seismic risk' was linked to the 'geological condition' plus 'ground water' composite risk, at a 10 per cent level of dependence, because these risks are clearly related in terms of the kind of issue involved, but they were assumed to be very weakly related in causal or statistical terms.

'Equipment breakdown' was linked to 'weather' risk, at a 40 per cent level of dependence, because the tendency for equipment to break down as a consequence of working in extreme conditions was thought to be the strongest direct effect of weather not embedded in the weather risk itself, although the level of dependence was thought to be moderate.

'Contractor capability' was linked to 'quality control', at an 80 per cent level, because it was assumed that quality control was a direct responsibility of the contractor.

'Construction accidents' was linked to 'contractor capability' plus 'quality control', at a 70 per cent level, because it was assumed that construction accidents had a weaker link with contractor capability than quality control, but the link was still a strong one.

'Labour disputes' was linked to 'sabotage/vandalism', at a 70 per cent level, because it was assumed that this was the strongest dependence link for either.

'Contractor capability' plus 'quality control' plus 'construction accidents' was linked to 'labour disputes' plus 'sabotage/vandalism', at a 20 per cent level, because a degree of dependence based upon contractor capability skills clearly links all these considerations, although it was assumed to be a weak level of dependence.

'Equipment breakdown' plus 'weather' was linked with 'contractor capability' through 'vandalism', at a 10 per cent level, to capture the last and lowest level of dependence based upon contractor capability skills.

The final link had a zero level of dependence, assuming no linkages between geological conditions and assumptions and other conditions or assumptions.

When choosing pairs across activities, the rationale was similar. In addition, some attention was paid to using groupings which make intermediate results of direct interest.

INTERPRETATION OF RESULTS

Presentation of data

A variety of formats is available for presentation of risk analysis results. Figure 8.4 illustrates three common methods. The choice of a particular graphic display depends on the purpose for which the results are to be used.

The density form illustrated by [A] on Figure 8.4 plots the probability that a particular value will occur against its value. This kind of distribution was used for the input of assessments of risks and damage levels, as may be seen on Figure 8.2. However, for presentation and interpretation purposes, decision makers tend to be primarily concerned about the confidence they can have that a particular value will or will not be exceeded. The reverse cumulative form illustrated by [B] on Figure 8.4 provides a measure of the probability that a particular criterion value will be

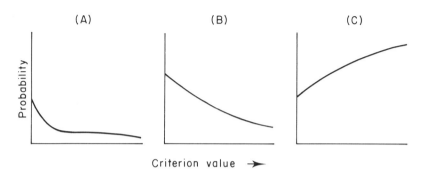

Figure 8.4   Alternative display formats. (A) Density form. (B) Reverse cumulative form. (C) Cumulative form

exceeded. For example, such a distribution might indicate that there is a 10 per cent chance that a particular activity will cost more than $100 million. The cumulative form illustrated by [C] on Figure 8.4 provides a measure of the probability that a particular value will *not* be exceeded. This form was selected for presentation of results since it relates directly to the decision-maker's need to know how confident he can be that total costs will be within certain limits. It also allows him to understand that further exposure may exist.

The expected value is the best estimate of the value which would appear on average if a large number of projects of this type were constructed independently under the same conditions. This value provides useful further information whichever format is used.

Minor variations in activity costs were generated by the estimating team concurrent with development of the risk analysis. In addition, account was taken of the expectation that construction costs will escalate at a faster rate than normal inflation—both in the economic analysis and the risk analysis. To avoid confusion regarding absolute cost values, and for reasons of confidentiality, the results of the risk analysis are presented here as percentages of the estimated project cost or as ratios between actual costs and estimated costs.

Cost distribution

Figure 8.5 presents a sample cumulative probability distribution for the project during construction. The figure may be interpreted as follows

the expected value of the final project cost in base year and month dollars is 90.6 per cent of the project estimate;

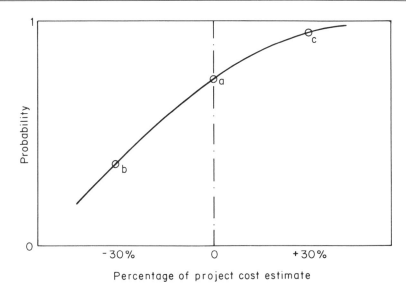

Figure 8.5 Construction cost distribution. (a, project estimate; b, low value; c, high value)

there is a 73 per cent probability that the final project cost will not exceed the project estimate;

there is a 47 per cent probability that the final project cost will not exceed the 'low' value tested in the economic analysis (Point 'b'), and a 90 per cent probability that the 'high' value (Point 'c') will not be exceeded;

there is a small but finite chance that the final project cost will be as much as 140 per cent of the project estimate.

Schedule variations

Figure 8.6 provides an indication of the schedule risks for the project as a whole. It shows a 65 per cent probability that the project will be completed on schedule and a 40 per cent probability that it will be completed a year early. Significant delays, largely introduced by regulatory risks, are possible. There is about a 2 per cent chance that the project will be delayed as much as 40 months. Excluding regulatory risks, whose primary effect is on the starting date for construction, the analysis indicates that there is about a 20 per cent chance that the project will take 15 months longer than the estimated period between commencement and completion.

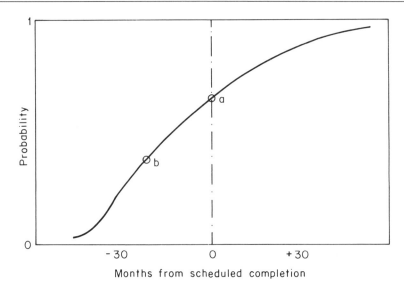

Figure 8.6 Construction schedule distribution, including the effect of regulatory risks. (a, schedule estimate plus contingency; b, schedule estimate without contingency)

Transmission outages

Because the project would represent a large portion of the total generating system in the area, it was important to consider the vulnerability of the transmission system. The most critical period fell in the first decade of the 21st century. After that time, it could reasonably be argued that additional generating resources would be brought on line, gradually reducing the percentage of total energy provided by the project. After an initial shakedown period, the transmission system would mature to a relatively steady state. Because of built-in redundancies, it would not, under normal circumstances, lead to loss of energy delivery capability to major load centres. Extreme risks (major floods, unusually high wind, etc.) would continue to be possible, however. The results of the analysis of an assumed mature transmission system suggested that the expected losses in energy capability were less than one day in ten years.

CONCLUSION

This chapter has described a large risk analysis study in outline. The methodology was similar to that used for the bridge case study in Chapter 5, although the description here used different terminology and concentrated on different aspects of the analysis.

The major difference from the bridge case was the explicit consideration of dependence relationships between risks and activities. This allowed a great deal of engineering judgement to be incorporated in the analysis, using simple per cent dependence specifications. Some preliminary work was necessary to explain the per cent dependence concept, to ensure the engineers were comfortable with it, and a continuous feedback and review process was implemented as initial results were obtained from the risk analysis software. However, the general structure of the analysis, and the specific way in which inter-relationships were assessed, were accepted readily by the engineers involved as being logical and reasonable in a practical engineering sense. The similarities to PERT/CPM processes with which they were familiar were perceived clearly, and the differences imposed by the risk analysis task were interpreted and accepted as an extension of this context.

Similarly, the client was able to accept the approach as a reasonable one, based on logical analysis and sound engineering judgement and common sense. The ability to describe the risk analysis process in engineering terms, and to interpret the results in engineering terms, was a key factor in the acceptability of the study's conclusions by the client.

Case study: construction cost estimate and contingency

Summary

This case study describes an audit of a feasibility-stage cost estimate for a hydroelectric development. One purpose of the risk analysis was to provide an independent check on the reliability of the estimate and to assess whether the contingency allowance in the estimate was adequate. The form of analysis is compared with standard engineering cost estimation procedures. The concepts of structural dependence and memory requirements are introduced. The case study illustrates:

(a) dependent risks;
(b) a similar analysis structure to that seen in Chapter 4, but based on the line item costs in the estimate;
(c) analysis with a single criterion.

INTRODUCTION

This chapter describes a risk analysis of a construction cost estimate prepared during a feasibility study for a proposed hydroelectric development. The purpose of the risk analysis was to provide an independent check on the reliability of the cost estimate, using a different approach from that of the original cost estimate. In particular, the risk analysis used a probabilistic basis to examine the expected cost of the project, and to assess whether the contingency allowance was appropriate. Although discussed here in a hydroelectric context, the approach to risk analysis described here is a general one. It has also been used successfully in a study of the construction costs of large structures for offshore hydrocarbon production.

The next section of this chapter describes the hydroelectric project and indicates why a risk analysis was commissioned. The following sections describe the cost estimate which provided the base case, the risk analysis approach, the risks which might affect the cost estimate, the risk analysis method, implementation of the risk analysis method, and results. A penultimate section considers the relationship between this form of analysis and standard cost estimation procedures in some detail, concluding that an integrated approach may be possible and the benefits could be substantial. The final section draws some general conclusions about the wider applicability of the risk analysis method considered in this chapter.

PROBLEM CONTEXT

Several years ago, a large hydroelectric development was proposed for a region with known hydro potential. Attention was focused on a stretch of river with a number of possible dam sites. At the pre-feasibility stage, preliminary design studies isolated three or four promising alternatives, and provided outline estimates of their construction costs and power generation potential. The risk analysis described here concentrated on the most likely of these alternatives as its base case. It considered the construction costs for the hydroelectric development only; the transmission system was not included.

The risk analysis was commissioned in part because the energy environment had become less certain than it was when the project was conceived. Predictions of the future demand for energy in the region had been scaled down due to the general economic recession, world oil and gas prices were unstable, and the general pattern of future regional energy production was unclear. As a result there was some doubt about the overall economic viability of the development, and a need was seen for the capital costs to be re-examined. This was reinforced by a general feeling on the part of the utilities involved that the original cost estimates may have been optimistic, and that the contingency allowances might be too small.

Base cost estimate

The original estimate was derived from a traditional engineering analysis of the preliminary design plans and drawings. It decomposed the cost of the project into line items representing the major activities or acquisition costs. Each line item showed labour, material, equipment and indirect cost components. Different levels of indirect cost were attributed to different classes of line items according to standard practice: for example, the indirect cost component of a labour-intensive activity was a higher proportion of the cost than that of a line item representing the capital cost of a turbine unit.

Cost variability and uncertainty was acknowledged by incorporating a contingency allowance in the estimate. This was calculated as a proportion of the total construction cost less engineering, management and owner's costs. The contingency proportion reflected past experience with this kind of project, industry practice, and the 'feel' of the cost estimating team.

The original estimate had been through one review process. This was a broad scan to detect obvious anomalies and discrepancies and to escalate the estimate to current costs. The original estimate was revised only where serious differences or errors were detected. Many minor differences were ignored, even if the original appeared, on the surface, to be lacking, on the basis that the original estimators' assumptions and working calculations were not always available to the review team, and at an early stage in the feasibility study one set of assumptions was probably as good as another. The possible variability identified here undoubtedly contributed to the utilities' feeling that the contingency allowances were too small.

The base estimate for the risk analysis was the original cost estimate as revised by the subsequent review. Indirect costs were extracted from the line items in the base estimate and shown as a separate item. Table 9.1 summarizes the relative proportions of major components in the estimate to the whole estimate.

Table 9.1   Summary of base costs, as percentages of the total project cost

Preliminary works	11
Civil works	28
Electrical equipment	18
	57
Indirect	19
Clearing, seepage control	6
Engineering, management and owner's costs	8
	90
Contingency	10
Total project cost	100

RISK ANALYSIS APPROACH

The line items in the revised estimate were used as the basis for risk consideration. These line items were decomposed or consolidated into activity/cost items as required to provide base costs for which common risks could be assessed.

For some line items having a large impact on the total cost of the project, decomposition was required. Alternatively, where several line items had a relatively small impact on the cost, and where risks were similar, consolidation was appropriate. The object was to ensure that sufficient detail was employed to accurately assess the risks, but no more than necessary. Table 9.2 shows the item structure used in the analysis.

A limited number of key risks were identified for each activity/cost item. 'Estimation risk' was used to describe all residual effects not identified specifically. Some risks common to all activity/cost items were distinguished as 'global risks'.

The effect of each risk on an item was assessed as a distribution of proportional variations on the base cost estimate for the item. Proportional variations are usually more convenient to estimate and manipulate than variations expressed in dollar values, they avoid the need to guard against negative dollar values, which can occur when successive absolute reductions to the base cost estimate are used, and they embody a simple multiplicative form of dependence which is usually realistic. Statistical dependence required separate consideration.

Table 9.2   Activity/cost item structure used in the risk analysis

1—Preliminary works
    1.1.—Site development and associated works
    1.2.—Construction camp
    1.3.—Construction camp operation
2—Concrete structures
    2.1.—Common considerations
    2.2.—Spillway
    2.3.—Intake
    2.4.—Powerhouse
    2.5.—Concrete gravity structures
3—Fill structures
    3.1.—Common considerations
    3.2.—Diversion stage I
    3.3.—Diversion stage II
    3.4.—Main dam
    3.5.—Other fill structures
4—Electrical and mechanical equipment
5—Indirect costs
    5.1.—Personnel salaries and expenses, and site expenses
    5.2.—Bonds and insurance
    5.3.—Contractors' financing
    5.4.—Contractors' head office expenses
    5.5.—Contractors' profit and contingency
6—Engineering, management and owner's costs
7—Reservoir clearing
8—Reservoir seepage control
9—Global risks
10—Escalation risks

Risks assessed for each individual activity/cost item were combined into a total risk distribution for combinations of items. Each succeeding combination of risks was added to the aggregation of the preceding combination to generate the total risk distribution, incorporating risks common to all activities last.

An outline of the structure of the basic evaluation is given in Figure 9.1. The risk analysis method is detailed below.

RISKS

The study considered a range of cost variations, due to a variety of causes, referred to as risks. In general, these were variations within the 'normal' range for projects of this kind. The risks that affect individual line item costs can be grouped according to whether or not they affect the quantity estimate, the unit cost estimate, or the schedule. A fourth group of risks which needed consideration act uniformly on all activities; these global risks included labour rates, contractors' profit margins and taxes.

Quantity risks

Design
The engineering design may not have been finalized. This refers to design changes which do not alter the overall concept of the project. For example, changes in concrete slab thickness or pier design were included here, but changes in the relative placement of the powerhouse and spillway were excluded.

Engineering approach
The detailed engineering was not complete and alternative approaches were possible. For example, a different approach might vary the number of construction joints in the concrete structures and thus affect the quantity of formwork required.

Definition
Sometimes it was not clear in the estimate what was included or excluded from a line item cost.

Rock quality
Poor rock and other geological conditions might force excavations to be deeper than planned.

Ground contours
The profile of the river bed was not known in detail.

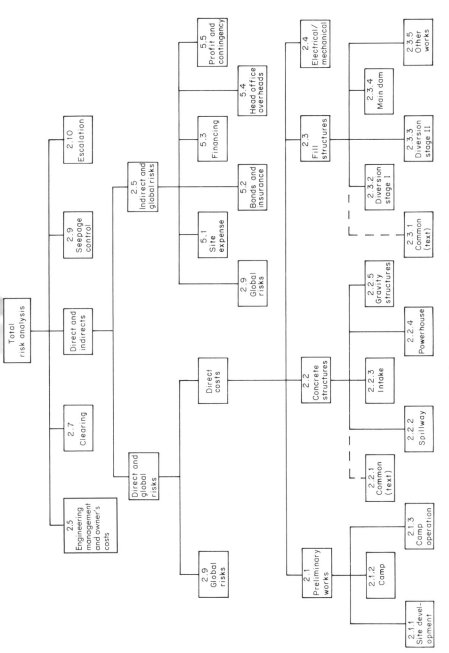

Figure 9.1   Risk analysis structure outline

Overbreak
Significant overbreak during excavation would increase the quantity of excavated material to be removed and additional fill or concrete would be required to compensate.

River bank characteristics
River bank instability might affect the abutments, and the length of the main dam.

Compaction
Compaction variations might affect fill quantities for the dam.

Estimation
Drawings might not be accurate or comprehensive enough for detailed quantity takeoffs, and other considerations like those noted above might not have been identified specifically.

Unit cost risks

Engineering approach
The engineering approach might affect unit costs by varying the mix of labour and equipment. For example, the method for concrete delivery from the batch plant would affect the processing requirements for aggregates.

Weather
Weather conditions might affect labour productivity.

Processing
The cost of processing quarried or borrowed materials might vary according to the availability of suitable materials.

Formwork reuse
The ability to reuse or repair formwork would alter the formwork unit cost. This is related to the engineering approach.

Royalties
Royalties might have to be paid for quarried or borrowed materials.

Placement
Some of the fill structures require material to be placed in flowing water. The risk of loss of fill material was incorporated in the unit costs.

Dewatering
Rock and cofferdam porosity might affect the cost of dewatering the cofferdams.

Engineering and management rates
Variations in contract conditions and in the number and types of contracts might alter the requirements for site engineering, office engineering and management.

Estimation
Unit cost estimation variations arise because of assumptions not considered above about productivity, equipment and labour costs, component costs, embedded materials, and so on.

Schedule risks

It was assumed that if delays occur, or if a likelihood of schedule over-runs was detected, additional resources would be used to maintain the schedule if possible. Schedule recovery risk was included to consider the consequences for the project cost of such changes to the project schedule. Major catastrophes which might cause a whole season to be lost were excluded from the study.

Weather
Adverse weather conditions might cause delays.

Seasons
A late spring or an early fall might reduce the summer construction period.

River levels
High river levels might cause schedule delays if they occur at critical stages of the project. Conversely, lower-than-expected river levels could be beneficial. The river levels throughout the system would be monitored, so that sufficient warning would be given of high river levels for adequate preparation and counter-measures to be implemented.

Equipment delivery
If electrical and mechanical equipment was delivered late, there might be a delay to commissioning.

Global risks

Global risks applied to all construction activities.

Labour related factors
These included possible changes to standard work weeks, labour market effects on the availability of skilled tradespeople, and the existence of an All-Trades Project Labour Agreement.

Bidding environment
Competitive pressures and the state of the heavy construction market would affect contractors' markups.

Risks not assessed

Risks which might be considered as 'normal' variations for projects of this kind were examined. However, 'abnormal' or catastrophic variations which were outside the scope of the study were treated as project conditions: the results of the risks analysis were conditional on these abnormal factors not arising.

Most of the risks that were not assessed could cause large delays to the project, of at least a season. The impact of a long delay would depend on its cause and when it occurred in the project schedule. For example, a six month delay early in the project might be largely recoverable, while the same delay late in the project would almost certainly result in a delay to commissioning. No attempt was made in this study to assess the likelihood of these risks or their possible impacts on the project cost and schedule, although it would certainly be possible to do so. It was felt that identification of extreme risks and their embodyment in the analysis at this stage would not be helpful.

Major design changes
The base case layout and design was examined. Minor design changes within this general concept were assessed, but major changes were not.

Site changes
Rearrangement of the site layout and relocation of the project were not considered.

Water charges
No charges for water were considered.

Labour problems
Major long term strikes were excluded.

Land acquisition
The purchase costs of land were not assessed. The costs of the purchasing

activity (legal costs and so on) were assumed to be included in the owner's costs.

Major floods
Floods which overtop the cofferdam at a critical stage were considered to be unlikely and they were not included. If the main dam were to be washed out, at least one season would be lost.

Jurisdictional and regulatory processes
Jurisdictional and regulatory delays might be caused by problems associated with land ownership, mineral rights, access rights (to fill sites for example), environmental factors, and local community social factors.

RISK ANALYSIS METHOD

The construction cost estimate consisted of a set of major line items which specified the estimated cost of particular construction and acquisition activities. Many of these line items were not related directly to one another, and the areas in which they interfaced or required coordination could be isolated. For this reason the line items provided the basis for the risk analysis approach, and possible sources of cost variation were examined for each one of them. An outline of the approach is shown in Figure 9.2.

The first stage of the analysis was decomposing the estimate of total cost into a set of base costs for analysis (lines 1–4 in Figure 9.2). The initial decomposition was usually into the major line item costs. In some cases the line items were single activities, or composed of relatively similar sub-activities to which a set of risks applied in a uniform way. Here the line item cost was the appropriate base cost. In other cases, the line item referred to a set of cost components of different kinds, with different risk characteristics. Here the line item was decomposed into sub-item costs to determine the base costs. Table 9.2 shows the item structure used in this study. Item 4, electrical and mechanical equipment, was treated as a single composite element, since these acquisitions were broadly similar in nature. On the other hand, the elements of item 2, concrete structures, were sufficiently different to suggest separate treatment.

In general, the analysis was based on as small a set of base costs as was sufficient to give reasonable analysis. Further detail can be added later where an analysis indicates that it is important, but too much detail too early in the process obscures more than it reveals.

The second stage of the analysis was concerned with risks which might affect each base cost (lines 5 and 6 in Figure 9.2). For each base cost a set of

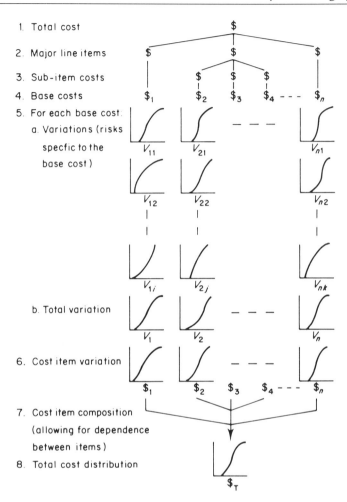

Figure 9.2   Outline of the risk analysis method

risks was identified, and each risk was assessed as a distribution of proportional variation on the cost estimate, as illustrated by Figure 9.3.

The total variation in each base cost, from all the risks which acted on it, was the product of the individual variation distributions. In practice, this product was formed in a series of two-element multiplications: two variations were multiplied together, the product was multiplied by the next variation, and so on. The intermediate variations were plotted on common axes to indicate the relative importance of the individual variations in the total, as illustrated by Figure 9.4.

Figure 9.3 Example quantity estimation risk, shown as a proportional variation on the base value. *P* is the probability of a particular variation or less occurring

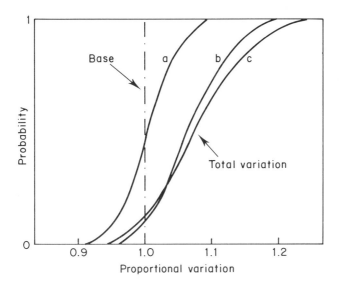

Figure 9.4 Example cost variation due to three risks (curve a, quantity variation; curve b, a + unit cost variation: curve c, b + labour availability variation). The gaps between the lines indicate that the unit cost risk is most important while the labour availability risk is comparatively minor. Curve 'c' is the total variation

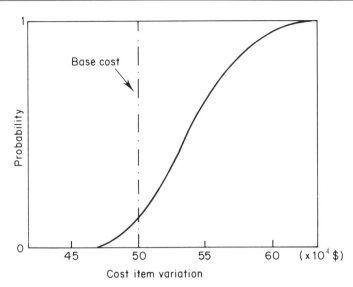

Figure 9.5   Cost item variation for an example with base cost $500 000

Cost item variation in dollars was the product of the base cost and the total variation distribution. This was just a change of scale for the variation distribution, as illustrated by Figure 9.5.

The final stage of the analysis involved the composition of the individual cost item variations to determine the variation in the total cost (lines 7 and 8 in Figure 9.2). This followed a structure which was the reverse of the initial decomposition into the base costs.

Cost item variations were combined by adding pairs of distributions. The assumptions made about the statistical dependence relationships between the distributions were important here. For example, it may be reasonable to assume that the cost variations for site preparation and spillway construction are largely independent, since they involve different labour forces, in different locations, and different risks apply. However, construction of concrete structures involves many common features: they use the same sites, the labour forces may be substantially the same, quantity estimates have been done by the same people, and so on. In this case the combination of variations assumed a substantial level of dependence.

In practice, the total cost distribution was formed in a series of two-element additions: two variations were added, the sum was added to the next variation, and so on. All intermediate sums were plotted on common axes to indicate how the total cost was built up, as illustrated by Figure 9.6. The cost variation curves were also related to the jointly defined minimum (shifted to the right in Figure 9.6 to give a common zero-probability point), to show clearly which cost items contribute most to the cost variation, as illustrated by Figure 9.7.

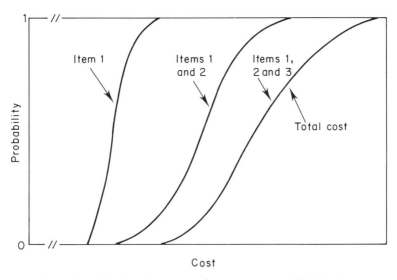

Figure 9.6 Total cost as a sum of component cost distributions

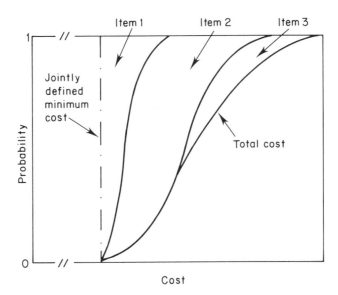

Figure 9.7 Contributions of individual cost items to the total cost variation

The analysis to this point was concerned solely with the effects which risks might have on construction costs. With large-scale construction projects, the effects of risks on the project schedule are also of major importance. Schedule effects could be treated in two ways. First, direct cost variations due to schedule delays could be incorporated in the analysis above, like any other risk variation. Second, delay effects could be extracted for a more detailed time based schedule risk analysis, taking into account weather windows and the 'cascade' effects of losing a season on subsequent activities. This form of schedule risk analysis was not considered in this study, but the direct cost implications of recoverable schedule delays were included.

Table 9.3   Detailed structure of the costs and risks for the intake line item

2.3. Intake
    2.3.1. Excavation quantity
        2.3.1.1. Estimation
        2.3.1.2. Design
        2.3.1.3. Rock quality
        2.3.1.4. Ground contours
        2.3.1.5. Overbreak
    2.3.2. Excavation unit cost
    2.3.3. Excavation schedule recovery
    2.3.4. Foundation preparation and grouting cost
    2.3.5. Concrete quantity
        2.3.5.1. Estimation
        2.3.5.2. Design
        2.3.5.3. Rock quality
        2.3.5.4. Ground contours
        2.3.5.5. Overbreak
    2.3.6. Concrete unit cost
        2.3.6.1. Cement and flyash
        2.3.6.2. Aggregate
        2.3.6.3. Batching
        2.3.6.4. Delivery
    2.3.7. Concrete schedule recovery
    2.3.8. Formwork quantity
        2.3.8.1. Estimation
        2.3.8.2. Design
    2.3.9. Formwork unit cost
    2.3.10. Formwork schedule recovery
    2.3.11. Steel quantity
    2.3.12. Steel unit cost
    2.3.13. Granular fill cost

IMPLEMENTATION OF THE RISK ANALYSIS

The major part of the risk analysis was undertaken by one senior planning and estimating engineer and one risk analyst, over a period of about ten days. A second analyst was involved in the initial design of the risk approach, and other professional engineering and clerical staff provided assistance with computational aspects of the study.

The initial review of the cost estimate revealed about fifteen main activity/cost items, which were later expanded to the list in Table 9.2. For each item, a consideration of possible sources of variation led to a detailed structure of the risks to be assessed, verbal descriptions of the analysts' assumptions about what was meant by each risk and how the variations might arise, and a numerical specification for each variation distribution. A nested numbering scheme was used to summarize and keep track of this information; Table 9.3 provides an example.

Variation distributions were defined as proportional variations on the base estimate. Each distribution was specified initially in terms of most likely, optimistic and pessimistic values, and probabilities of values outside the optimistic and pessimistic bounds. This form of specification was used because the engineer providing the assessments felt comfortable with it; other specification forms have been used in other circumstances. Each distribution was then drawn in the form of a histogram which was used by the engineer to check his initial specification, as illustrated in Figure 9.8.

The histogram representations of the variation distributions were input directly to proprietary computer software. This was an interactive package providing a range of editing and data storage facilities, as well as procedures for combining probability distributions in various ways. The computational procedures were an implementation of a set of simple controlled interval and memory (CIM) models.

Various forms of output were produced by the models as described in the previous section and illustrated in Figures 9.4, 9.6 and 9.7. Presentation of intermediate results in this way as the study progressed allowed the estimator to review his assessments so far. Input specification and coding errors could be detected, specification consistency could be examined across all cost items in the estimate, and specifications could be revised as necessary, in an iterative checking process.

The final results from the risk analysis were summarized in the format of Figure 9.9. Curve 'd' shows the distribution of total project cost, indicating a 54 per cent chance that the project would be completed within the revised estimate *A*, and a 90 per cent chance that it would not exceed the revised estimate plus contingency *B*.

These results indicated that the original estimate (as revised) was a good one, and that the level of contingency allowance was reasonable: the

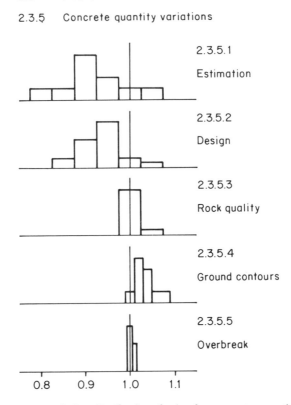

2.3   Intake

2.3.5   Concrete quantity variations

2.3.5.1

Estimation

2.3.5.2

Design

2.3.5.3

Rock quality

2.3.5.4

Ground contours

2.3.5.5

Overbreak

0.8   0.9   1.0   1.1

Figure 9.8   Variation distributions for intake concrete quantity, 2.3.5

utilities' original feelings about the inadequacy of the contingency and the optimism of the estimate were shown to be unwarranted, provided the extreme events excluded from the analysis as indicated earlier ought to be excluded. This was felt to be the case by the utilities for this stage of the feasibility analysis. This view could be debated. The key issue was comparability with other estimates at this stage of feasibility studies versus a less conditional and necessarily more pessimistic view.

The risk analysis provided a review of the original cost estimate, using a different approach. It provided a cheap audit of the reliability of the estimate, and it generated greatly increased confidence on the part of the utilities. It also had a number of other benefits, in the form of feedback to the project design process, which are noted further in the next section.

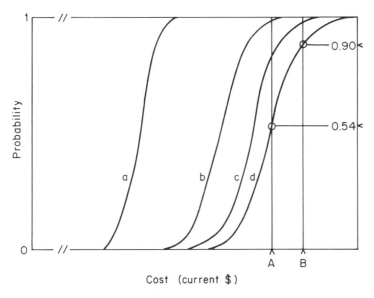

Figure 9.9 Risk analysis results—the total cost distribution for the hydroelectric development. (Curve a, direct cost; curve b, a plus indirect cost; curve c, b plus E, M and O cost; curve d, total cost; A, revised estimate; B, estimate plus contingency)

THE COST ESTIMATION PROCESS

The form of analysis described above could have been undertaken at the same time as the original cost estimate was obtained. This could have provided a direct measure of the risk contingency, as well as the cost estimate, with little change to the estimators' procedures. A great deal of additional information could have been obtained, without much additional estimating effort. This section discusses some of the main issues in this area.

Table 9.4 shows a typical calculation scheme that might be used in estimating the cost of concrete for a powerhouse substructure. The volume of concrete, V, has been estimated at 1800 m^3 from the design drawings (line 1). V is used in a series of calculations (lines 2–8); V is also used to determine placing time, T, in line 10, and this appears subsequently in lines 14, 19 and 20.

Now suppose that there is some risk associated with the estimate, in the form of uncertainty about the exact concrete volume V, perhaps due to possible design variations, estimation errors, or overbreak during excavation, and uncertainty about various unit costs. The same calculation

Table 9.4 Example cost estimation calculation process

Power house substructure concrete

Concrete volume		$V = 1800$ m^3	(1)
Material			
Cement	$1800 \times$ (unit cost)		(2)
Gravel and sand	$1800 \times$ (unit cost)		(3)
Additives	$1800 \times$ (unit cost)		(4)
Total material		(2) + (3) + (4)	(5)
Batch and mix			
Labour	$1800 \times$ (unit cost)		(6)
Equipment	$1800 \times$ (unit cost)		(7)
Total batch and mix		(6) + (7)	(8)
Placing			
Rate (including preparation, excluding cleanup) = 15 m^3 h^{-1}			(9)
Time $T = 1800/15$ = 120 h			(10)
Labour			
1 $\times$ Supervisor	(unit cost)		(11)
2 $\times$ Foremen	(unit cost)		(12)
12 $\times$ Labourers	(unit cost)		(13)
	(11) + (12) + (13) $\times$ 120		(14)
Equipment			
1 $\times$ 25T Crane	(unit cost)		(15)
1 $\times$ Bucket	(unit cost)		(16)
4 $\times$ Vibrators	(unit cost)		(17)
	(15) + (16) + (17) $\times$ 120		(18)
Total placing		(14) + (18)	(19)
Total concrete cost		(5) + (8) + (19)	(20)
Summary			
Labour		(6) + (14)	(21)
Material		(5)	(22)
Equipment		(7) + (18)	(23)
Total		(20)	(24)

structure as before can be used to estimate the total concrete cost. V, T and most intermediate line costs have become distributions rather than single numbers, and suitable computer software is needed instead of a hand calculator, but, in principle, the estimating process itself has changed very little.

The computer software necessary to implement an estimating procedure of this kind must contain a number of special features. The operations which combine line-items to form sub-totals and totals must recognize that the individual line costs are not independent. For example, V has been used to calculate all three components of total material cost; consequently the costs of concrete, gravel and sand, and additives will all tend to be low or high together, depending on whether the volume estimate is low or high. In other words, when the cost distributions in lines 2, 3 and 4 are added to form the distribution of material cost in line 5, the calculation process must remember that the *same V* has been used to derive each component, and the software must remember not only the component cost distributions but where they came from. Similar considerations apply throughout the scheme in Table 9.4.

The computational models used in the hydro risk analysis were simple examples of controlled interval and memory (CIM) models, and the structure of the analysis was such that it was not necessary to remember how particular distributions were derived. However, the wider family of CIM models can accommodate the kind of memory that would be needed in a combined approach to risk analysis and cost estimation. A more detailed description of this aspect of CIM models is the subject of the next chapter.

A risk-based cost estimating procedure does not require major changes in current estimating practice. Computer data-bases are frequently used to determine labour, equipment and material rates, and computer-based estimating systems are becoming more common for the management and control of the progress of large cost estimation projects. Risk analysis could be built into such packages, and with good software it could be almost transparent to the estimators.

A combined risk analysis and cost estimating process would have a number of major benefits. A direct measure of risk, in the form of a distribution of project cost, could be obtained at the same time as the basic cost estimate was formed. This would allow any particular contingency value to be interpreted quantitatively in relation to the possible spread of project costs and probability of a cost over-run, as illustrated by Figure 9.9.

As well as the traditional cost estimate form of Table 9.4, insight into project cost risk can be provided by enabling sources of risk to be identified and examined in the style of Figures 9.4, 9.6 and 9.7. This can also give a better feel for the important interdependencies between cost items, which can have large combined effects on the overall cost distribution, such as might be caused by common underlying factors like common technology, common labour forces, or common economic and market effects.

Feedback of risk analysis results can have important benefits for the project as a whole. The analysis provides additional information about sources of risk, and it highlights sensitive parts of the project plan and areas where design uncertainty is greatest. Design changes or reconsideration of the base plan may be indicated, allowing improvements in overall project risk performance.

Two examples from the hydro study illustrate the range of improvements that are possible. At the detailed engineering level, the risk analysis showed that a different concrete placement method from that specified in the original engineering design might be more suitable in terms of its implications for the quarrying and processing of aggregates, its equipment requirements, its reliability, and its consequences for the costs of all concrete structures. At the level of the broad design concept, the analysis demonstrated that there were major sources of risk associated with the planned method of access across the river in the early stages of the project, and that several critical activities might be affected. The cost and schedule implications were such that it was recommended that this aspect of the access plan be re-examined, and that an alternative site layout which reversed the relative positions of the powerhouse and spillway be considered.

As well as identifying major cost and economic uncertainties, analysis of cost risks frequently provides valuable indications of where risks might profitably be spread or shed. Depending on who is doing the analysis, this might influence how the owner calls for tenders, how the contractor responds to tender invitations, and how detailed contract negotiations are conducted. These aspects were considered explicitly in the hydro study under items 5 and 6 in Table 9.2: indirect costs; and engineering, management and owner's costs.

CONCLUSIONS

This chapter has described a general method for the risk analysis of a construction cost estimate. Although it has been discussed here in the context of a hydroelectric development project, the approach has wider applicability. It has been used in substantially the same form to examine offshore hydrocarbon production structures.

Risk analysis of a project cost estimate has a number of benefits. It provides an indication of the reliability of the cost estimate and the adequacy of the contingency allowance, in an independent audit process. Sensitivity analysis can be undertaken with respect to important economic parameters; in the hydro context, for example, the analysis was conducted assuming a very competitive heavy construction market, and again under more normal market conditions. Distributional results can be used directly in more general economic risk analyses and related to wider regional power generation planning. A range of benefits at the project level is possible, in terms of feedback to the design, tendering and contract setting processes. Other less specific organizational benefits appear in the form of study documentation, which provides a structured database of corporate knowledge that usually resides in the minds of various individuals and might otherwise not be revealed explicitly.

Risk analysis of this form could be combined with regular cost estimation procedures, to produce both a risk analysis and a cost estimate at the same time, with little change to the estimators' methods of working. The general technology exists in the form of CIM models, and specific software has been written. The benefits of a combined approach could be substantial.

It is arguable that the exclusion of extreme risks embodied on the approach of this chapter is inappropriate. If this is deemed to be the case, the approach can be modified to embrace such risks. However, in addition to complicating the analysis to some extent, this introduces a degree of realism not common in most preliminary feasibility studies. Such realism is appropriate if alternatives are viewed with similar realism, and desirable. However, such realism can prove traumatic, and must be introduced with care.

CIM models for structural dependence

Summary

This chapter provides an extended example of structural dependence in the context of an offshore construction schedule. It indicates the importance of retaining a memory of structural links, by comparing a full analysis with one based on expected values. This leads into a discussion of general specification structures for dependent risks, and methods for schedule risk analysis.

INTRODUCTION

The last case study looked briefly at an example in which the calculation process needed to remember how distributions were derived and where they came from. The computation scheme had a particular structure, which led to dependence between distributions. This was not a statistical dependence, of the kind discussed before, but a form of structural dependence.

In this chapter dependence is examined in more detail. The chapter starts with an example involving an activity network model, where structural dependence arises in a natural and obvious way in network merge events, and considers the CIM treatment of it. This leads into a consideration of the time rate of progress of activities, in the following chapter.

The example concerns part of the construction of an offshore oil platform. This specific application area is incidental: the example was designed to illustrate the CIM approach to structural dependence, to indicate the importance of structural dependence in risk calculations, and to provide a basis for discussion, basing the example on a real application familiar to the authors which illustrates the issues of interest in a compact manner. The numbers provide an outline framework for discussion; insights are the major objective.

Table 10.1 Activity list for an offshore platform, with finish-to-start precedence relationships

Number	Label	Predecessors
Modules sequence		
1	Design	
2	Materials	1
3	Fabrication	2
Jacket sequence		
4	Design	
5	Materials	4
6	Fabrication	1, 5

The example involves six activities: the design, materials acquisition, and fabrication of the topsides modules for an offshore platform; and the design, materials acquisition, and fabrication of the steel jacket itself. Finish-to-start precedence relationships are specified in Table 10.1, and shown in the precedence (activity-on-node) diagram of Figure 10.1.

Table 10.2 shows the durations of the activities in the modules sequence, with time expressed in half-year units. Under 'modules fabrication', the second and third lines show conditional probabilities, conditional on the modules design duration D_1; for example,

$$P(D_3 = 3 \mid D_1 = 4) = 0.3.$$

Modules sequence

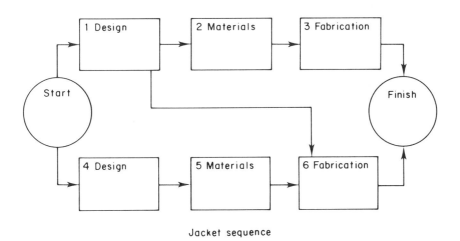

Figure 10.1 Activity-on-node precedence diagram, with finish-to-start links

Table 10.2   Modules sequence activity durations, in half-year units

1. Modules design	$D_1 =$	4	5	
	$P =$	0.6	0.4	$E = 4.4$
2. Modules materials	$D_2 =$	2	3	
	$P =$	0.3	0.7	$E = 2.7$
3. Modules fabrication	$D_3 =$	3	4	
P given modules design	$D_1 = 4$	0.3	0.7	$E = 3.7$
	5	0.8	0.2	3.2
	$P =$	0.5	0.5	$E = 3.5$

The fourth line shows unconditional probabilities; for example,

$$P(D_3 = 3) = P(D_3 = 3 \mid D_1 = 4)P(D_1 = 4)$$
$$+ P(D_3 = 3 \mid D_1 = 5)P(D_1 = 5)$$
$$= 0.3 \times 0.6 + 0.8 \times 0.4$$
$$= 0.5.$$

There is *negative* statistical dependence between modules fabrication and modules design: if design takes a long time, then fabrication can be speeded up, at additional cost. The table shows expected values: it is useful to keep track of expected values, and this can be done automatically with appropriate software.

Table 10.3 shows the durations of the activities in the jacket sequence. There is *positive* statistical dependence between jacket design and modules design, and between jacket fabrication and modules design. Problems with the design of the modules, particularly if they involve changes in the number or size of modules affecting their total weight, will lead to related

Table 10.3   Jacket sequence activity durations, in half-year units

4. Jacket design	$D_4 =$	2	3	
P given modules design	$D_1 = 4$	0.7	0.3	$E = 2.3$
	5	0.2	0.8	2.8
	$P =$	0.5	0.5	$E = 2.5$
5. Jacket materials	$D_5 =$	2	3	
	$P =$	0.3	0.7	$E = 2.7$
6. Jacket fabrication	$D_6 =$	4	5	
P given modules design	$D_1 = 4$	0.7	0.3	$E = 4.3$
	5	0.2	0.8	4.8
	$P =$	0.5	0.5	$E = 4.5$

Table 10.4   Activity precedence relationship overlaps

1–2	Modules design and modules materials			
	$L =$	0	1	
	$P =$	0.5	0.5	$E = 0.5$
2–3	Modules materials and modules fabrication			
	$L =$	0	1	
	$P =$	0.5	0.5	$E = 0.5$
5–6	Jacket materials and jacket fabrication			
	$L =$	0	1	
	$P =$	0.5	0.5	$E = 0.5$

problems with the design and fabrication of the jacket. Again, the dependence is specified in terms of conditional probabilities, and unconditional probabilities and expected values are also shown.

The simple six-activity structure of this example may be appropriate in practice. A coarse activity structure is often used in practice in order to facilitate a detailed treatment of the risks associated with each activity. Because the activities used here are composites of many lower level (more detailed) activities, there may be precedence relationship overlaps, as shown in Table 10.4. To examine all the activities at a level of detail which avoids the overlaps would often be too complicated and unnecessary for risk analysis purposes. The same distribution of overlap has been assumed in each case here, for simplicity. Expected values are shown, for ease of interpretation.

EXPECTED VALUE CALCULATIONS

Given the expected activity durations and the expected overlaps, standard network calculations can be performed to provide an initial assessment of the project schedule. A forward pass calculates activity earliest start times and project earliest finish time, and a backward pass calculates activity latest start times. Link float can be computed using

$$\begin{aligned} \text{FLOAT (link } i - j) = {} & \text{Latest Start (node } j) \\ & - \text{Earliest Finish (node } i) \\ & + \text{Overlap (link } i - j) \\ = {} & \text{LS}(j) - \text{ES}(i) - \text{D}(i) + \text{OL}(i, j). \end{aligned}$$

Expected activity durations and overlaps, earliest and latest activity start times, project finish time and floats are shown in Figure 10.2. The floats indicate that the modules sequence is critical, and that the jacket sequence is not critical. On the basis of this expected value assessment, the link 1–6 has the largest link float and looks irrelevant.

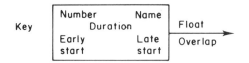

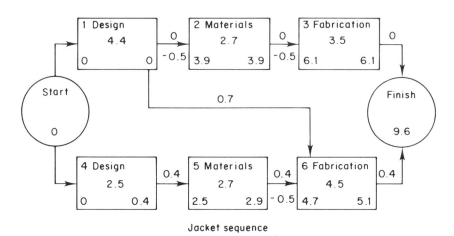

Figure 10.2   Expected activity durations and overlaps, activity early and late start times, project finish time, and link floats

DISTRIBUTION CALCULATIONS

The expected value calculations of Figure 10.2 are easy to perform. However, they do not take into account the probabilistic aspects of the dependence relationships that exist between the activities in the project network structure. It is necessary to examine the distributions of start and finish time for the activities and for the project network as a whole if the effects of these relationships are to be understood fully.

Modules sequence

Table 10.5 shows the time distributions for the modules sequence. Table 10.5A, modules materials start time, S_2, is the Modules Design distribution minus the overlap between Design and Materials, performed as a standard CIM subtraction calculation, of the kind seen before. This calculation format keeps a memory of the modules design aspect of S_2 uncertainty, needed later in the computation sequence. The probabilities computed in Table 10.5 in the $D_1 = 4$ and 5 columns are joint probabilities, rather than conditional probabilities like those in Tables 10.2, 10.3, and 10.4; for example,

$$P(S_2 = 4 \text{ and } D_1 = 4) = P(\text{no overlap}) P(D_1 = 4)$$
$$= 0.5 \times 0.6$$
$$= 0.3.$$

Because these are joint probabilities, the expected value calculations are a little different; for example,

$$E(S_2 \mid D_1 = 4) = (3 \times 0.3 + 4 \times 0.3)/(0.3 + 0.3)$$
$$= 3.5.$$

Tables 10.5B, 10.5C and 10.5D show the distributions of modules materials finish time (5A plus the modules materials duration distribution), modules fabrication start time (5B minus the overlap between materials and fabrication), and modules fabrication finish time (5C plus the modules fabrication duration distribution). The memory of the modules design duration is retained throughout, for later use.

Table 10.5A   Modules materials start time

	$P \mid$ Modules design		Unconditional P
	$D_1 = 4$	$D_1 = 5$	
$S_2 = 3$	$0.5 \times 0.6 = 0.3$		0.3
4	$0.5 \times 0.6 = 0.3$	$0.5 \times 0.4 = 0.2$	0.5
5		$0.5 \times 0.4 = 0.2$	0.2
$E =$	3.5	4.5	3.9

Table 10.5B   Modules materials finish time

	$P \mid$ Modules design		Unconditional P
	$D_1 = 4$	$D_1 = 5$	
$F_2 = 5$	$0.3 \times 0.3 \qquad\qquad = 0.09$		0.09
6	$0.3 \times 0.3 + 0.7 \times 0.3 = 0.30$	$0.3 \times 0.2 \qquad\qquad = 0.06$	0.36
7	$0.7 \times 0.3 = 0.21$	$0.3 \times 0.2 + 0.7 \times 0.2 = 0.20$	0.41
8		$0.7 \times 0.2 = 0.14$	0.14
$E =$	6.2	7.2	6.6

Table 10.5C   Modules fabrication start time

	P | Modules design		
	$D_1 = 4$	$D_1 = 5$	Unconditional P
$S_3 = 4$	$0.5 \times 0.09 = 0.045$	$0.5 \times 0.06 = 0.030$	0.045
5	$0.5 \times 0.09 + 0.5 \times 0.30 = 0.195$	$0.5 \times 0.06 + 0.5 \times 0.20 = 0.130$	0.225
6	$0.5 \times 0.30 + 0.5 \times 0.21 = 0.255$	$0.5 \times 0.20 + 0.5 \times 0.14 = 0.170$	0.385
7	$0.5 \times 0.21 = 0.105$	$0.5 \times 0.14 = 0.070$	0.275
8			0.070
$E =$	5.7	6.7	6.1

Table 10.5D   Modules fabrication finish time

	P | Modules design		
	$D_1 = 4$	$D_1 = 5$	Unconditional P
$F_3 = 7$	$0.3 \times 0.045 = 0.0135$	$0.8 \times 0.03 = 0.0240$	0.0135
8	$0.3 \times 0.195 + 0.7 \times 0.045 = 0.0900$	$0.8 \times 0.13 + 0.2 \times 0.03 = 0.1100$	0.1140
9	$0.3 \times 0.255 + 0.7 \times 0.195 = 0.2130$	$0.8 \times 0.17 + 0.2 \times 0.13 = 0.1620$	0.3230
10	$0.3 \times 0.105 + 0.7 \times 0.255 = 0.2100$	$0.8 \times 0.07 + 0.2 \times 0.17 = 0.0900$	0.3720
11	$0.7 \times 0.105 = 0.0735$	$0.2 \times 0.07 = 0.0140$	0.1635
12			0.0140
$E =$	9.4	9.9	9.6

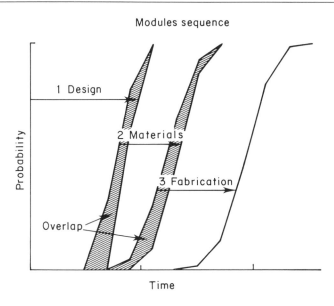

Modules sequence

Figure 10.3   Time distributions for the modules sequence

Figure 10.3 illustrates the start and finish time distributions for the modules sequence in Table 10.5. In Figure 10.3, the overlap allows a 'jump back' in the time sequence of activities. Remember that the 'curves' plotted here are based on histogram intervals, centred on whole numbers of half year units. They could be smoothed for output purposes, as discussed in Chapter 3, but this has not been done here.

The contributions of each of the component activity variations to the modules sequence finish time are shown in Figure 10.4. The lines shown are the design start time S_1, the design finish time F_1, the materials finish time F_2, and the fabrication finish time F_3 (which is the modules sequence finish time), all plotted from a common zero probability point. The areas between the lines indicate the variation contributions of each activity plus associated contributions from the overlap with prior activities.

In the modules sequence, the expected start times derived from the distributional results in Table 10.5 are the same as the start times calculated from the expected activity durations and expected overlaps of Figure 10.2.

Modules sequence

Finish time components

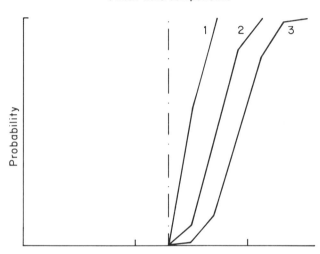

Figure 10.4   Contributions of each activity variation to the modules sequence finish time variation. (Note that the materials and fabrication components include a variation due to overlap.) Curve 1, design; curve 2, materials; curve 3, fabrication

Jacket sequence

Table 10.6 shows a sequence of calculations similar to Table 10.5, for the jacket sequence. Again, the calculations keep a memory of modules design. Table 10.6A, jacket design finish time, converts the Table 10.3 values from conditional probabilities to joint probabilities; for example

$$P(F_4 = 2 \text{ and } D_1 = 4) = P(D_1 = 4)P(F_4 = 2 \mid D_1 = 4)$$
$$= 0.6 \times 0.7$$
$$= 0.42.$$

Table 10.6A   Jacket design finish time

	$P\mid$ Modules design		Unconditional P
	$D_1 = 4$	$D_1 = 5$	
$F_2 = 2$	$0.6 \times 0.7 = 0.42$	$0.4 \times 0.2 = 0.08$	0.5
3	$0.6 \times 0.3 = 0.18$	$0.4 \times 0.8 = 0.32$	0.5
$E =$	2.3	2.8	2.5

Table 10.6B Jacket materials finish time

| | P \| Modules design | | Unconditional |
	$D_1 = 4$	$D_1 = 5$	P
$F_5 = 4$	$0.3 \times 0.42 = 0.126$	$0.3 \times 0.08 = 0.024$	0.15
5	$0.3 \times 0.18 + 0.7 \times 0.42 = 0.348$	$0.3 \times 0.32 + 0.7 \times 0.08 = 0.152$	0.50
6	$0.7 \times 0.18 = 0.126$	$0.7 \times 0.32 = 0.244$	0.35
$E =$	5.0	5.5	5.2

Table 10.6C Jacket fabrication start time, considering materials only

| | P \| Modules design | | Unconditional |
	$D_1 = 4$	$D_1 = 5$	P
$S_6' = 3$	$0.5 \times 0.126 = 0.063$	$0.5 \times 0.024 = 0.012$	0.075
4	$0.5 \times 0.126 + 0.5 \times 0.348 = 0.237$	$0.5 \times 0.024 + 0.5 \times 0.152 = 0.088$	0.325
5	$0.5 \times 0.348 + 0.5 \times 0.126 = 0.237$	$0.5 \times 0.152 + 0.5 \times 0.224 = 0.188$	0.425
6	$0.5 \times 0.126 = 0.063$	$0.5 \times 0.224 = 0.112$	0.175
E	4.5	5.0	4.7

Table 10.6D Jacket fabrication start time

	$P \mid$ Modules design		Unconditional P
	$D_1 = 4$	$D_1 = 5$	
$S_6 = 4$	$0.063 + 0.237 = 0.300$		0.300
5	0.237	$0.012 + 0.088 + 0.188 = 0.288$	0.525
6	0.063	0.112	0.175
E	4.605	5.280	4.875

Table 10.6E Jacket fabrication finish time

	$P \mid$ Modules design		Unconditional P
	$D_1 = 4$	$D_1 = 5$	
$F_6 = 8$	$0.7 \times 0.300 = 0.2100$		0.2100
9	$0.7 \times 0.237 + 0.3 \times 0.300 = 0.2559$	$0.2 \times 0.288 = 0.0576$	0.3135
10	$0.7 \times 0.063 + 0.3 \times 0.237 = 0.1152$	$0.2 \times 0.112 + 0.8 \times 0.288 = 0.2528$	0.3680
11	$0.3 \times 0.063 = 0.0189$	$0.8 \times 0.112 = 0.0896$	0.1085
$E =$	8.905	10.080	9.375

Table 10.6B, jacket materials finish time, is Table 10.6A plus the jacket materials duration distribution. Table 10.6C, the jacket fabrication start time considering materials only, is 6B minus the overlap. Table 10.6D, jacket fabrication start time, takes into account the modules design finish time. Because this is a merge event, a 'greatest' operation is used rather than addition, but the CIM principles are the same; for example,

$$P(S_6 = 4 \text{ and } D_1 = 4) = P(S_6' = 3 \text{ and } D_1 = 4)$$
$$+ P(S_6' = 4 \text{ and } D_1 = 4)$$
$$= 0.063 + 0.237$$
$$= 0.300.$$

The 'greatest' operation was encountered earlier, in the LNG system reliability case study in Chapter 4, where it corresponded to a particular parallel response repair regime. Table 10.6E, jacket fabrication finish time, is 6D plus the jacket fabrication duration distribution.

Figure 10.5 shows the start and finish times for the activities in the jacket sequence. Between materials and fabrication, there is a 'jump back' due to the overlap between these activities, and a 'jump forward' due to the precedence link from modules design. The modules design component, shown shaded in Figure 10.5, is a variation attributable to structural dependence of a more complex form than the additions and subtractions considered prior to this in the precedence network framework.

Jacket sequence

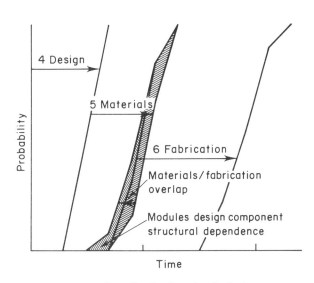

Figure 10.5   Time distributions for the jacket sequence

Modules sequence

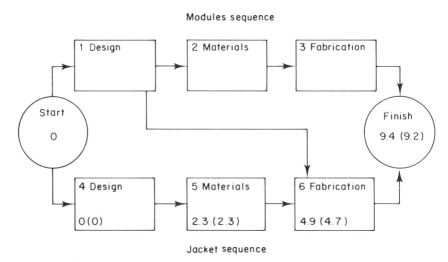

Jacket sequence

Figure 10.6 Expected activity start times and sequence finish time for the jacket sequence, calculated using CIM models, with the previous values shown in brackets

The expected activity start times for the jacket sequence calculated from the CIM distributional results in Table 10.6 are shown in Figure 10.6, with the values calculated from the expected activity durations shown in parentheses. The structural dependence embodied in the link 1–6 has increased the expected duration of the jacket sequence from 9.2 to 9.4 half-year time units. At the merge event at the start of jacket fabrication, there is an expected delay of 0.2 due to modules design delays. The link 1–6 will be critical at least some of the time, although link 1–6 seemed irrelevant when judged solely on the basis of expected values.

Table 10.7 Jacket fabrication start time criticality indices, joint probabilities

	Modules design								
	$D_1 = 4$			$D_1 = 5$			$D_1 = 4$ or 5		
Link	1–6	5–6	Both	1–6	5–6	Both	1–6	5–6	Both
$S_6 = 4$	$P = 0.300$	0.237	0.237				0.300	0.237	0.237
5		0.237		0.288	0.188	0.188	0.288	0.425	0.188
6		0.063			0.112			0.175	
Total	$P = 0.300$	0.537	0.237	0.288	0.300	0.188	0.588	0.837	0.425
Criticality index	$C = 0.500$	0.895	0.395	0.720	0.750	0.470	0.588	0.837	0.425

Criticality indices

To further examine the links leading into the merge events at the start of jacket fabrication, the criticality indices of the links can be calculated. The criticality index of a link indicates the conditional probability that the link will be critical. Calculations based on joint probabilities are shown in Table 10.7, and criticality is illustrated in Figure 10.7. For example, when the modules design duration $D_1 = 4$ and the jacket fabrication start time

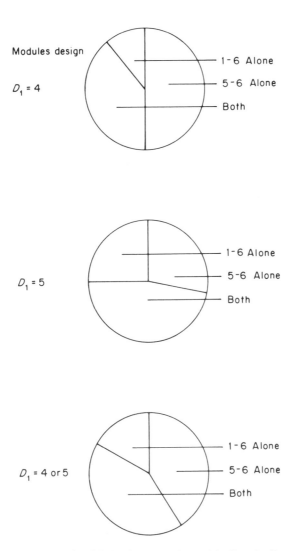

Figure 10.7   Jacket fabrication start time criticality pie diagrams

$S_6 = 4$, the probability that the jacket fabrication start time is constrained by link 1–6 (link 1–6 is critical) is

$$P(\text{constrained by } D_1 = 4) = P(S_6' = 3 \text{ and } D_1 = 4)$$
$$+ P(S_6' = 4 \text{ and } D_1 = 4)$$
$$= 0.063 + 0.237$$
$$= 0.300;$$

the probability that it is constrained by link 5–6 is $P(S_6' = 4 \text{ and } D_1 = 4) = 0.237$; and 0.237 is also the probability that it is constrained by both. In Table 10.7, the 'total' row indicates the joint probability that a link is critical and the particular modules design duration D_1 is obtained. The criticality index is the corresponding conditional probability, calculated by dividing the joint probability by the probability associated with the particular D_1 value; for example,

$$C(\text{link 1–6} \mid D_1 = 4) = P(\text{1–6 is critical and } D_1 = 4)/P(D_1 = 4)$$
$$= 0.3/0.6$$
$$= 0.5.$$

When the modules design duration $D_1 = 4$, the link 1–6 alone is critical for only a small proportion $(0.500 - 0.395 = 0.105)$ in comparison with link 5–6 alone $(0.895 - 0.395 = 0.500)$. Link 1–6 looks more important when the modules design duration is longer $(D_1 = 5)$, which is not surprising. Overall, link 1–6 has a criticality index of nearly 0.6, in marked contrast to the initial expected-value assessment.

THE PROJECT AS A WHOLE

It is now possible to look at the project as a whole, using Table 10.8. Tables 10.8A and 10.8B convert the joint distributions for modules fabrication finish time (from Table 10.5D) and jacket fabrication finish time

Table 10.8A Modules fabrication finish time rounded conditional distributions

		$P \mid$ Modules design	
		$D_1 = 1$	$D_1 = 5$
$F_3 =$	7	0.02	
	8	0.15	0.06
	9	0.36	0.28
	10	0.35	0.40
	11	0.12	0.23
	12		0.03
$E =$		9.4	9.9

Table 10.8B Jacket fabrication finish time rounded conditional distributions

		$P \mid$ Modules design	
		$D_1 = 4$	$D_1 = 5$
$F_6 =$	8	0.35	
	9	0.43	0.14
	10	0.19	0.64
	11	0.03	0.22
$E =$		8.9	10.1

Table 10.8C Project finish time conditional distributions

		$P \mid$ Modules design
		$D_1 = 4$
$FP =$	8	0.35×0.17 $= 0.0595$
	9	$0.35 \times 0.36 + 0.43 \times 0.53$ $= 0.3539$
	10	$0.35 \times 0.35 + 0.43 \times 0.35 + 0.19 \times 0.88$ $= 0.4402$
	11	$0.35 \times 0.12 + 0.43 \times 0.12 + 0.19 \times 0.12 + 0.03 \times 1.00 = 0.1464$
	12	
$E =$		9.7

		$D_1 = 5$
$FP =$	8	
	9	0.14×0.34 $= 0.0476$
	10	$0.14 \times 0.40 + 0.64 \times 0.74$ $= 0.5296$
	11	$0.14 \times 0.23 + 0.64 \times 0.23 + 0.22 \times 0.97 = 0.3928$
	12	$0.14 \times 0.03 + 0.64 \times 0.03 + 0.22 \times 0.03 = 0.0300$
$E =$		10.4

Table 10.8D Project finish time joint distributions

		$P \mid$ Modules design		Unconditional
		$D_1 = 4$	$D_1 = 5$	P
$FP =$	8	0.035 70		0.04
	9	0.212 34	0.019 04	0.23
	10	0.264 12	0.211 84	0.47
	11	0.087 84	0.157 12	0.25
	12		0.012 00	0.01
$E =$		9.7	10.4	10.0

(from Table 10.6E) to rounded conditional distributions; for example, in Table 10.8A,

$$P(F_3 = 11 \mid D_1 = 4) = P(F_3 = 11 \text{ and } D_1 = 4)/P(D_1 = 4)$$
$$= 0.0735/0.6$$
$$= 0.1225$$
$$= 0.12.$$

Table 10.8C gives the project finish time conditional distribution, calculated using a CIM 'greatest' operation at the merge event; for example,

$$P(F_3 \leqslant 9 \mid D_1 = 4) = P(F_3 = 7 \mid D_1 = 4) + P(F_3 = 8 \mid D_1 = 4)$$
$$+ P(F_3 = 9 \mid D_1 = 4)$$
$$= 0.02 + 0.15 + 0.36$$
$$= 0.53,$$

$$P(F_6 \leqslant 8 \mid D_1 = 4) = P(F_6 = 8 \mid D_1 = 4)$$
$$= 0.35,$$

$$P(FP = 9 \mid D_1 = 4) = P(F_6 = 8 \mid D_1 = 4)P(F_3 = 9 \mid D_1 = 4)$$
$$+ P(F_6 = 9 \mid D_1 = 4)P(F_3 \leqslant 9 \mid D_1 = 4)$$
$$= 0.35 \times 0.36 + 0.43 \times 0.53$$
$$= 0.3539.$$

Table 10.8D shows the corresponding joint distribution for project finish time; for example,

$$P(FP = 9 \text{ and } D_1 = 4) = P(FP = 9 \mid D_1 = 4)P(D_1 = 4)$$
$$= 0.3539 \times 0.6$$
$$= 0.21234.$$

The modules sequence, jacket sequence and project finish time distributions are illustrated in Figure 10.8.

Table 10.9 shows the criticality calculations for the project as a whole. The computation process is similar to that used for the criticality indices of the links leading into the jacket fabrication activity (Table 10.7), but joint probabilities are used here instead of conditional probabilities. The approach illustrated is slightly different, but the principles are the same. For example, in Table 10.9A with the modules design duration $D_1 = 4$ and a project duration $FP = 9$,

$$P(FP = 9 \text{ and jacket sequence critical} \mid D_1 = 4)$$
$$= P(F_6 = 9 \mid D_1 = 4)P(F_3 \leqslant 9 \mid D_1 = 4)$$
$$= 0.43 \times 0.53$$
$$= 0.2279,$$

$$P(FP = 9 \text{ and modules sequence critical} \mid D_1 = 4)$$
$$= P(F_6 = 8 \mid D_1 = 4)P(F_3 = 9 \mid D_1 = 4)$$
$$+ P(F_6 = 9 \mid D_1 = 4)P(F_3 = 9 \mid D_1 = 4)$$
$$= 0.35 \times 0.36 + 0.43 \times 0.36$$
$$= 0.2808,$$

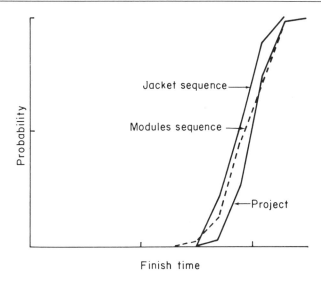

Figure 10.8   Sequence finish time distributions and project finish time distribution

$P(FP = 9$ and both sequences critical $\mid D_1 = 4)$
$= P(F_6 = 9 \mid D_1 = 4)P(F_3 = 9 \mid D_1 = 4)$
$= 0.43 \times 0.36$
$= 0.1548.$

The criticality indices are illustrated in Figure 10.9. When the modules design duration is short ($D_1 = 4$), the modules sequence is more important than the jacket sequence, but when the modules duration is longer ($D_1 = 5$), then the jacket sequence is more important! This counter-intuitive result arises for a number of reasons: the negative statistical dependence between modules design and modules fabrication offsets the effect of increased modules design duration on the modules sequence; the positive statistical dependence between modules design and both jacket design and jacket fabrication means modules design delays have a large positive impact on jacket sequence delays; the structural precedence link between modules design and jacket fabrication introduces further positive dependence. Thus modules design delays impact the jacket sequence more than the modules sequence, due to both statistical and structural dependence.

Figure 10.10 shows the expected activity start and project finish times calculated using the CIM approach as just outlined, with the previous estimates in brackets. The expected values are higher than the original estimates for both merge events. The structural dependence relationships have had a big impact on expected values, with an increase of 0.2 at each merge. Criticality indices are also shown. These criticality indices indicate that the jacket sequence is almost as important as the modules sequence

Table 10.9A   Project finish time criticality indices, Part 1 of 3

	$P \mid$ Modules design $D_1 = 4$		
	Jacket sequence	Modules sequence	Both
$FP =$ 8	$0.35 \times 0.17 = 0.0595$	$0.35 \times 0.15 \qquad\qquad\qquad\qquad = 0.0525$	$0.35 \times 0.15 = 0.0525$
9	$0.43 \times 0.53 = 0.2279$	$0.35 \times 0.36 + 0.43 \times 0.36 \qquad\qquad = 0.2808$	$0.43 \times 0.36 = 0.1548$
10	$0.19 \times 0.88 = 0.1672$	$0.35 \times 0.35 + 0.43 \times 0.35 + 0.19 \times 0.35 \qquad = 0.3395$	$0.19 \times 0.35 = 0.0665$
11	$0.03 \times 1.00 = 0.0300$	$0.35 \times 0.12 + 0.43 \times 0.12 + 0.19 \times 0.12 + 0.03 \times 0.12 = 0.1200$	$0.03 \times 0.12 = 0.0036$
$C =$	0.4846	0.7928	0.2774

Table 10.9B   Project finish time criticality indices, Part 2 of 3

	$P \mid$ Modules design $D_1 = 5$		
	Jacket sequence	Modules sequence	Both
$FP =$ 8		$0.14 \times 0.28 \qquad\qquad\qquad\qquad = 0.0392$	$0.14 \times 0.28 = 0.0392$
9	$0.14 \times 0.34 = 0.0476$	$0.14 \times 0.40 + 0.64 \times 0.40 \qquad\qquad = 0.3120$	$0.64 \times 0.40 = 0.2560$
10	$0.64 \times 0.74 = 0.4736$	$0.14 \times 0.23 + 0.64 \times 0.23 + 0.22 \times 0.23 = 0.2300$	$0.22 \times 0.23 = 0.0506$
11	$0.22 \times 0.97 = 0.2134$	$0.14 \times 0.03 + 0.64 \times 0.03 + 0.22 \times 0.03 = 0.0300$	
12			
$C =$	0.7346	0.6112	0.3458

Table 10.9C   Project finish time criticality indices, Part 3 of 3

	P | Modules design D_1 = 4 or 5		
	Jacket sequence	Modules sequence	Both
FP = 8	0.035 70	0.031 50	0.031 50
9	0.155 78	0.184 16	0.108 56
10	0.289 76	0.328 50	0.142 30
11	0.103 36	0.164 00	0.022 40
12		0.012 00	
C =	0.584 60	0.720 16	0.304 76

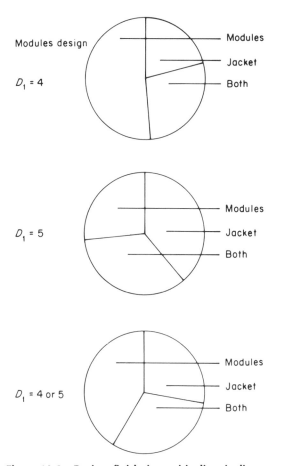

Figure 10.9   Project finish time criticality pie diagrams

Modules sequence

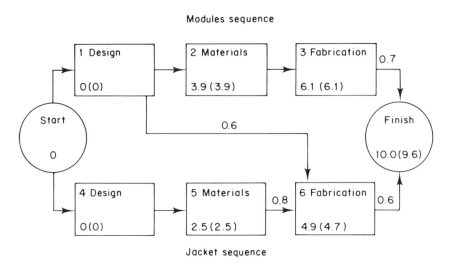

Figure 10.10 Expected activity start and project finish times, calculated using CIM models, with the previous values shown in brackets. Link criticality indices are also shown

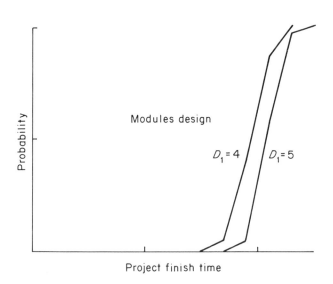

Figure 10.11 Project finish time conditional distributions

Modules sequence

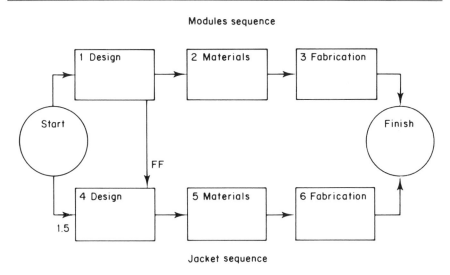

Figure 10.12   Revised project plan, with a delayed start to the jacket sequence and a finish-to-finish precedence link

for project completion, a very different picture from the misleading representation of Figure 10.2.

Figure 10.11 shows project finish time distributions conditional on modules design duration. The gap between these curves and the associated difference in expected values, from $E = 9.7$ when $D_1 = 4$ to $E = 10.4$ when $D_1 = 5$, indicates that the modules design activity is very important. This might lead to a change in plans, to avoid problems at the outset. For example, a revised precedence arrangement between sequences and a delayed start to the jacket sequence might be considered, as illustrated by Figure 10.12. This would change the structural dependence relationships, and ought to affect the statistical dependence of the jacket sequence on modules design as well.

EXTENSIONS TO COSTS

The memory capabilities which are used to handle structural dependence allow more complex dependence structures for cost estimating, with more levels of memory. The practical computational and data handling problems become more complicated, principally in keeping track of the data, but no new theoretical issues are involved.

For example, a cost composition example is given in Table 10.10, and illustrated in Figure 10.13. Several levels of memory are required, but the specification flexibility is greatly increased.

Table 10.10   Cost composition example requiring several levels of memory

Number	Item	Dependence	Definition
10	Jacket weight		
11	Manpower level	10	
12	Timescale	10, 11	
C13	Manmonths		11 × 12
14	Labour unit cost	10	
C15	Contractor cost		C13 × 14
16	Contractor revenue	11, C15	
C17	Contractor margin		16 − C15

CONCLUSION

This chapter has provided an illustration of the importance of structural dependence relationships using an activity precedence context. It has demonstrated how such relationships can interact with statistical dependence relationships to produce important effects which cannot be detected and understood using simple expected value calculations. These effects are complex, but they can be identified, modelled and understood in a CIM framework. They could be modelled in a Monte Carlo simulation

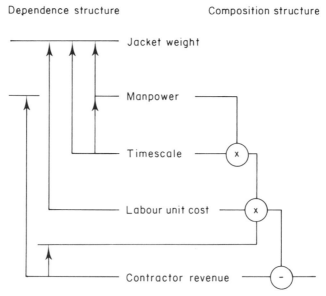

Figure 10.13   A cost composition example, showing composition and dependence structures

framework, but such a framework is unlikely to provide the same depth of insight.

Only one limitation of the CIM approach relative to a Monte Carlo simulation approach need be noted, but it is an important limitation. The retention of a single memory dimension for the activity precedence example of this chapter involved preserving and working with a matrix of probabilities at each stage. This involved a slight increase in computational effort. The cost composition example of Table 10.10 and Figure 10.13 involves two levels of memory at several stages, requiring a three-dimensional matrix of probabilities. In general, n levels of memory involve $(n + 1)$-dimensional probability matrices. Large values of of n make this approach computationally demanding. Computer software which will handle largish values of n is in use, but the size of value of n at which Monte Carlo simulation would be a preferable computational approach remains a research issue. Further, some forms of structural dependence may not lend themselves to modelling via this memory concept, in which case Monte Carlo simulation is the only viable alternative.

A risk engineering approach embraces the use of a Monte Carlo simulation procedure as and when necessary or appropriate. Since the development of the memory aspect of the CIM approach the authors have not had occasion to need to resort to Monte Carlo simulation, and such procedures are not considered in this book. However, an example application area where the authors would recommend and use a Monte Carlo approach on its own or in conjunction with CIM methods is the assessment of expected durations for very large and complex activity networks.

Chapter 11

CIM models for processes through time

Summary

This chapter introduces an alternative method for specifying uncertain activity durations, based on the progress in a fixed interval of time rather than on the time required to complete a fixed amount of work. The approach is particularly appropriate for 'continuous' activities, and those for which it is desired to embed preventive and contingency response decisions in the analysis.

INTRODUCTION

In the previous chapter, probability distributions for activity durations were specified directly. This may not be the easiest or the most effective way of dealing with uncertain activity durations.

Rather than attempting to specify the uncertainty associated with the time required to complete a fixed amount of work, it is often easier to specify the uncertainty associated with the amount of work that can be achieved in a fixed interval of time. This is a more natural way of thinking about many activities, particularly when deterministic duration estimates are based on a calculation of the total work to be done divided by a rate of progress.

An approach based on fixed time intervals rather than fixed work units can be more effective in a number of ways. It permits a more explicit consideration of individual sources of risk, which may arise at different stages of completion of the activity or at different times, in a stage- or time-dependent manner. It also allows preventive and contingency response decisions to be embedded in the analysis, for both responses related to a general lack of progress and responses specific to particular sources of risk. This leads to a better understanding of the inherent risk structure of the activity, and provides a more suitable framework for risk quantification. Further, such an approach allows a much clearer treatment of activity precedence relationships involving possible overlaps.

This approach is particularly appropriate for those activities which are in some sense continuous or repetitive processes, such as pipelaying, drilling, tunnelling, or the construction of multi-level tower buildings, but it is not restricted to these. It has been used successfully for activities like the construction of an offshore oil production platform.

A pipe coating activity in an offshore oil project context will be used to illustrate the approach. The example was introduced in Chapter 3. It is based on an example used in Chapman and Cooper (1983 and 1985), which was in turn based upon actual studies.

EXAMPLE PROBLEM

A 200 km offshore pipeline is to be laid. Before it can be laid, it must be coated with concrete and other anti-corrosive materials. There are three main sources of uncertainty: when a yard will be available, the productivity of the yard when it is operating on a normal shift basis, and whether overtime working or a second shift will be required. Once delivery of uncoated pipe begins, an inventory of uncoated pipe is assured by a delivery rate much faster than the coating rate, so coating can overlap delivery without concern for uncoated pipe stockout. However, overlap between coating and laying pipe does require attention.

EXAMPLE ANALYSIS

To model the time dependent nature of coated pipe inventory assuming single shift working with no overtime, the rate of coating, R km per month, might be specified as in Table 11.1. If the rate of coating is independent of time, then $P(S_t)$, the probability of having a stock of coated pipe S_t at the end of time period t, can be calculated by a series of independent additions: the distribution of stock at the end of an interval is the distribution at the start of the interval plus the production as specified in Table 11.1. Assuming a zero inventory at time 0, the stock of coated pipe at

Table 11.1 Coating rate distribution, R km per month

R	$P(R)$
30	0.2
35	0.2
40	0.3

Table 11.2   Stock of coated pipe at the end of months 1, 2 and 3

t	S_t	Computation			$P(S_t)$
0	0				1
1	30	0.2 × 1			0.2
	35		0.5 × 1		0.5
	40			0.3 × 1	0.3
2	60	0.2 × 0.2			0.04
	65	0.2 × 0.5 + 0.5 × 0.2			0.20
	70	0.2 × 0.3 + 0.5 × 0.5 + 0.3 × 0.2			0.37
	75	0.5 × 0.3 + 0.3 × 0.5			0.30
	80	0.3 × 0.3			0.09
3	90	0.2 × 0.04			0.008
	95	0.2 × 0.20 + 0.5 × 0.04			0.060
	100	0.2 × 0.37 + 0.5 × 0.20 + 0.3 × 0.04			0.186
	105	0.2 × 0.30 + 0.5 × 0.37 + 0.3 × 0.20			0.305
	110	0.2 × 0.09 + 0.5 × 0.30 + 0.3 × 0.37			0.279
	115	0.5 × 0.09 + 0.3 × 0.30			0.135
	120	0.3 × 0.09			0.027

the end of months 1, 2, 3, . . ., is given in Table 11.2. Formally, this is a Markov process.

Assuming a 10 per cent over-ordering of pipe for losses due to pipe buckles while laying, coating will cease when 220 km of pipe have been coated. The coating rate distribution of Table 11.1 can be generalized to that of Table 11.3 to incorporate this cut-off decision. The result is a semi-Markov process, with a state-dependent transition distribution. It will provide results identical to Table 11.1 until $t = 5$; for $t = 6, 7, 8, S = 220$ becomes an absorbing state, as shown in Tables 11.4 and 11.5. The second $P(S_t)$ column provides rounded results for the calculations for the next period for illustrative simplicity, using a rounded procedure based on cumulative probabilities discussed earlier, so that $P(S_t)$ values sum to one.

Table 11.3   Conditional coating rate distribution

S	R	P(R)
<220	30	0.2
	35	0.5
	40	0.3
220	0	1

Table 11.4   Stock of coated pipe at the end of months 4 and 5

t	S_t	Computation		$P(S_t)$	
4	120	0.2 × 0.008	0.0016	0.002	
	125	0.2 × 0.060 + 0.5 × 0.008	0.0160	0.016	
	130	0.2 × 0.186 + 0.5 × 0.060 + 0.3 × 0.008	0.0696	0.069	
	135	0.2 × 0.305 + 0.5 × 0.186 + 0.3 × 0.060	0.1720	0.172	
	140	0.2 × 0.279 + 0.5 × 0.305 + 0.3 × 0.186	0.2641	0.264	
	145	0.2 × 0.135 + 0.5 × 0.279 + 0.3 × 0.305	0.2580	0.258	
	150	0.2 × 0.027 + 0.5 × 0.135 + 0.3 × 0.279	0.1566	0.157	
	155	0.5 × 0.027 + 0.3 × 0.135	0.0540	0.054	
	160	0.3 × 0.027	0.0081	0.008	
5	150	0.2 × 0.002	0.0004	0.000	
	155	0.2 × 0.016 + 0.5 × 0.002	0.0042	0.005	
	160	0.2 × 0.069 + 0.5 × 0.016 + 0.3 × 0.002	0.0224	0.022	
	165	0.2 × 0.172 + 0.5 × 0.069 + 0.3 × 0.016	0.0737	0.074	
	170	0.2 × 0.264 + 0.5 × 0.172 + 0.3 × 0.069	0.1595	0.159	
	175	0.2 × 0.258 + 0.5 × 0.264 + 0.3 × 0.172	0.2352	0.235	0.740
	180	0.2 × 0.157 + 0.5 × 0.258 + 0.3 × 0.264	0.2396	0.240	0.505
	185	0.2 × 0.054 + 0.5 × 0.157 + 0.3 × 0.258	0.1667	0.167	0.265
	190	0.2 × 0.008 + 0.5 × 0.054 + 0.3 × 0.157	0.0757	0.075	0.098
	195	0.5 × 0.008 + 0.3 × 0.054	0.0202	0.021	0.023
	200	0.3 × 0.008	0.0024	0.002	0.002

Table 11.5   Stock of coated pipe at the end of months 6, 7 and 8

t	S_t	Computation		$P(S_t)$	
6	180	0.2 × 0.000	0.0000	0.000	1.000
	185	0.2 × 0.005 + 0.5 × 0.000	0.0010	0.001	1.000
	190	0.2 × 0.022 + 0.5 × 0.005 + 0.3 × 0.000	0.0069	0.007	0.999
	195	0.2 × 0.074 + 0.5 × 0.022 + 0.3 × 0.005	0.0273	0.027	0.992
	200	0.2 × 0.159 + 0.5 × 0.074 + 0.3 × 0.022	0.0754	0.076	0.965
	205	0.2 × 0.235 + 0.5 × 0.159 + 0.3 × 0.074	0.1487	0.148	0.889
	210	0.2 × 0.240 + 0.5 × 0.235 + 0.3 × 0.159	0.2132	0.214	0.741
	220	0.2 × 0.265 + 0.5 × 0.505 + 0.3 × 0.740	0.5275	0.527	0.527
7	210	0.2 × 0.000	0.0000	0.000	1.000
	215	0.2 × 0.001 + 0.5 × 0.000	0.0002	0.000	1.000
	220	0.2 × 0.999 + 0.5 × 1.000 + 0.3 × 1.000	0.9998	1.000	1.000
8	220	0.2 × 1.000 + 0.5 × 1.000 + 0.3 × 1.000	1.0000	1.000	1.000

The third $P(S_t)$ column provides reverse cumulative values to the extent required for the calculations for the next period, a slight modification of the procedure of Table 11.2 required to deal with the absorbing state. In practice a slightly different computation procedure would be followed.

Coated pipe inventory is defined by $P(S_t)$ for each t. The value of $P(S_t)$ for $S_t = 220$ defines the probability that coating is finished by the end of month t. This allows the duration distribution for the coating activity of Table 11.6 to be extracted from Table 11.5, via CP values, using four places of decimals for the values in Table 11.6 to clarify their source.

Table 11.6   Probability of pipe coating duration D

D	P(D)	CP(D)
6	0.5275	0.5275
7	0.4723	0.9998
8	0.0002	1.0000

The distribution of Table 11.6 is the basic activity duration uncertainty distribution obtained directly in Chapter 10. However, it is clearly easier to specify the distribution of Table 11.3 and use appropriate computer software to derive Table 11.6.

The distribution of Table 11.6, perhaps in the format of Figure 11.1, is an interesting output from this computation process, but it is not the only output of interest. Probability distributions indicating the stock of coated pipe available in each period t, assuming none is taken away for pipelaying purposes, is also provided by Tables 11.2–11.5, as illustrated in Figure 11.2.

Relating this analysis to the start of pipe delivery and the availability of the coating yard involves a further condition associated with the transition

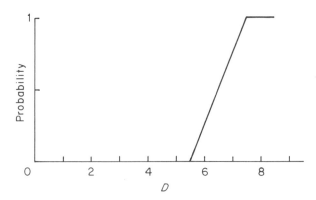

Figure 11.1   Probability of pipe coating distribution D

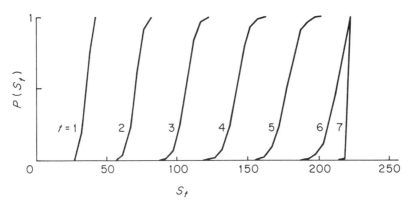

Figure 11.2   Distribution of coated pipe stock S_t

distribution, this time probabilistic in nature. For example, if the joint effects of pipe delivery delays and coating yard availability delays were the pipe coating start distribution defined by Table 11.7, Table 11.8 would be the equivalent of Table 11.2.

In addition to being easier to use and richer in information, this approach makes it easier to consider responses to realized risks. For example, suppose that the $P(S_t)$ distributions suggest that pipe laying might be held up by a lack of coated pipe. A decision to use overtime or second-shift working might be considered. This could involve testing an immediate decision for the whole of the coating activity, by changing the probability values in Table 11.3 and recomputing Tables 11.4–11.6. More subtle decision rules could also be used, and embedded in Table 11.3. Supose that a second shift with performance comparable to the first will be mobilized if less than 140 km of pipe have been coated by the end of April. Table 11.3 is revised to Table 11.9. Computing the equivalent of Table 11.8 involves successive addition, but independent addition is no longer appropriate. Now the coating rate R is conditional on the inventory level S_t and the month M, and the calculation must allow for this. No additional memory dimensions, not already preserved in Table 11.8, are required.

Table 11.7   Start of coating distribution, month M

M	$P(M)$
January	0.5
February	0.3
March	0.2

Table 11.8   Stock of coated pipe at the end of month *M*

M	S_t	Computation			$P(S_t)$
Jan	0		0.3 × 1	0.2 × 1	0.50
	30	0.5 × 0.2			0.10
	35	0.5 × 0.5			0.25
	40	0.5 × 0.3			0.15
Feb	0			0.2 × 1	0.200
	30		0.3 × 0.2		0.060
	35		0.3 × 0.5		0.150
	40		0.3 × 0.3		0.090
	60	0.5 × 0.04			0.020
	65	0.5 × 0.20			0.100
	70	0.5 × 0.37			0.185
	75	0.5 × 0.30			0.150
	80	0.5 × 0.09			0.045
Mar	30			0.2 × 0.2	0.0400
	35			0.2 × 0.5	0.1000
	40			0.2 × 0.3	0.0600
	60		0.3 × 0.04		0.0120
	65		0.3 × 0.20		0.0600
	70		0.3 × 0.37		0.1110
	75		0.3 × 0.30		0.0900
	80		0.3 × 0.09		0.0270
	90	0.5 × 0.008			0.0040
	95	0.5 × 0.060			0.0300
	100	0.5 × 0.186			0.0930
	105	0.5 × 0.305			0.1525
	110	0.5 × 0.279			0.1395
	115	0.5 × 0.135			0.0675
	120	0.5 × 0.027			0.0135

Table 11.9   Coating rate with second shift option

M		S_t	*R*	$P(R)$
April or earlier			30	0.2
			35	0.5
May or later	and	⩾100	40	0.3
May or later	and	<100	60	0.1
			65	0.2
			70	0.3
			75	0.2
			80	0.2
May or later	and	220	0	1.0

If uncertainty about the coating rate would be partially resolved in the first few periods, then R might be conditional on previous R values, or decision rules relating to previous R values might be used. In either case, some memory retention of R values will be needed, but not necessarily for the whole process.

Specifying all possible decision rules in advance is not practical. However, observing the results without embedded decision rules will allow reasonable and rational decision rules to be developed. Further refinements can be added subsequently if desired.

This framework makes the assessment of dependence easier, since obvious sources appear explicitly in a causal structure. The interdependence of coating rate and associated decisions also appears explicitly as the basis for duration assessment.

FURTHER EXTENSIONS

The case study on which the example was based made use of all the features described above. Other case studies made use of further features, some of which are outlined briefly below.

Weather windows

The ability to specify progress distributions for an activity which depend on the particular time period allow complex weather effects to be modelled. For example, in the context of offshore pipelaying, the effect of weather variations might be specified in terms of different distributions of kilometres of pipe laid according to the month in which laying was attempted, thus incorporating the ability of the lay barge to operate in different wave conditions, as indicated in Table 11.10.

Table 11.10 Distributions of lay days available each month $P(L)$

L	March	April	May	June	July	etc
0	0.3	0.2	0.1			
5	0.4	0.3	0.2	0.1		
10	0.2	0.3	0.3	0.1		
15	0.1	0.2	0.2	0.2	0.1	
20			0.1	0.3	0.2	
25			0.1	0.2	0.4	
30				0.1	0.3	

Sources of uncertainty

Direct specification of semi-Markov processes to describe the progress through time of an activity may not be any easier than direct specification of the duration of the activity, because of time, state, and joint time and state dependencies. It may be necessary to probe the risk structure more deeply, if it is to be probed at all.

The basis for activity duration uncertainty is a set of sources of uncertainty, specific reasons for deviations from the target plan. Decisions concerning responses to these deviations may be general in nature, in that a particular response might be used to overcome the combined effect of a number of problems. Other decisions may involve responses specific to the source of the uncertainty. For example, second-shift working is a general response to a range of problems including labour availability, labour productivity, equipment reliability, and so on. Providing additional supervision might be a specific response to quality control problems.

The effect of both specific and general responses can be examined in relation to specific sources of uncertainty and their joint effect net of specific responses, within the same basic framework. Responses specific to the risk sources can be considered and decision rules developed as necessary when each new risk source is added. General responses can be considered last, in relation to all the risk sources modelled net of the specific responses modelled. A generalized PERT–GERT framework incorporates responses without distinguishing between specific and general responses. This can obscure more than it reveals.

Modelling these decisions involves secondary risks with secondary responses, tertiary risks with tertiary responses, and so on. Even in an offshore pipeline context, there is a limit to the extent to which the pursuit of such decision trees is useful. However, they are there in real life even for comparatively simple tasks. They can be ignored but they cannot be wished out of existence, and their implications can be central to sound decision making.

Some risk sources and responses which require quantitative treatment may be best treated probabilistically, but others may be more conveniently treated via sensitivity analysis. For example, if the ability to begin construction in one year or the next depends upon obtaining government approval, probabilities might be estimated, but most project managers would prefer separate analyses based on the two different start dates. Comprehensive identification of sources of risk is of obvious operational importance here too, even if measurement is not undertaken. It is important to distinguish between decisions which can be embedded in the analysis directly and those which need indirect treatment as separate options.

This kind of approach may seem complex, but it is the simplest way to understand how risks affect activity durations, particularly when weather

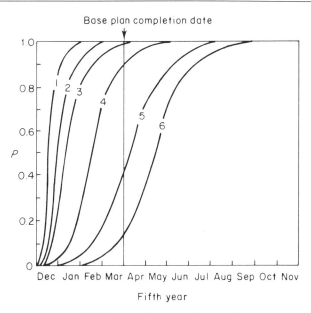

Figure 11.3 Cumulative probability distribution with six risk source components. The components are: 1, yard not available/mobilization problems; 2, construction problems/adverse weather; 3, late delivery of subcontracted items; 4, material delivery delays; 5, industrial disputes; 6, delayed award of contract

windows are involved, and to consider the relationship with other activities.

It is much easier to answer a structured series of detailed questions on specific components of the risk than to answer general questions about gross combined effects. It is more accurate, and it yields more insight. Moreover, the partial answers, as the analysis proceeds, may give important clues about what further questions need to be asked. Areas for detailed decision analysis are identified as part of the process of risk measurement. Risk measurement itself is possibly the least important product of the process as a whole, but measurement which incorporates sensitivity analysis of the kind illustrated by Figure 11.3 is extremely useful in practice.

Curve 6 in Figure 11.3 indicates the overall probability of completion in relation to the base plan completion date at the end of March. Curves 1–6 indicate the relative importance of the sources of risk associated with this overall picture. The large gap between curves 4 and 5 highlights 'industrial disputes' or a key source of uncertainty. The small gap between curves 2 and 3 indicates construction problems and adverse weather are comparatively minor sources of uncertainty.

CONCLUSION

It may seem counter-intuitive, but representations of uncertainty which are more complex in a modelling and computation sense can be much easier to use than apparently simple direct representations. They can provide much richer results, and much better understanding of what is involved. They can also lead to much better decisions because they facilitate the explicit modelling of complex decision rules and the identification of areas which need to be addressed in terms of such decision rules. This chapter has attempted to clarify these quite general notions.

Chapter 12

Economic risk evaluation for large projects

Summary

This chapter discusses decision making for project evaluation. It uses the economic and political uncertainties associated with offshore hydrocarbon development projects as an illustrative context. Economic and political conditions are treated in terms of broad scenarios, and an evaluation approach is outlined. The choice of an economic decision criterion for project acceptance is discussed in detail, concentrating on the project's net present value (NPV) and its rate of return (ROR). The reasons for preferring an NPV to an ROR criterion under conditions of uncertainty are indicated.

INTRODUCTION

Offshore hydrocarbon development projects invariably involve a lack of information which leads to uncertainty about the size and characteristics of the oil or gas field, the development costs and schedule, the reliability of the technology to be employed, and the economic, political and fiscal environments in which development and production will take place. Uncertainty is an important problem for offshore developments because they involve large capital outlays, and once a decision has been made to proceed, a large portion of the total outlay is required before production is possible and any returns are realized. In addition, the cost of acquiring more information to reduce risk and uncertainty before development begins is extremely high. These factors emphasize the need for assessing the nature and extent of the uncertainties and risks affecting the development before committing large sums of money.

The starting point for most risk analysis is a deterministic description of the development scenario to be examined, including the cost estimate, the project schedule, and the production profile. From this information a

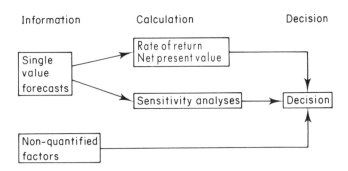

Figure 12.1   Traditional decision process

deterministic economic evaluation can be performed. This serves as a base case for comparison for the risk analyses. Sensitivity analysis of important parameters like capital cost, production volume and oil and gas prices may be carried out at this stage.

A deterministic evaluation of the project yields point estimates of costs, schedule duration and production rates, and can indicate sensitivities of the project economics to variations in these parameters. However, no probabilities of outcomes are specified, so the decision maker must rely on his own intuition to put these sensitivities into perspective, and to assess what might happen to cause such variations and with what likelihood. With many inter-related sources of uncertainty, this can be a very difficult task. Figure 12.1 shows this 'traditional' decision process.

Risk analysis provides a tool by which uncertainties and risks which can impact on project estimates of costs, schedule, and production can be quantified. Economic and financial parameters can also be quantified, and the joint impact of these uncertainties on project economics can in turn be examined. In more detailed analyses, the sources of uncertainty are identified and possible responses are assessed. Ideally, the only intangible information will be that which is beyond the company's resources of time, money or skill to quantify, or which has no bearing on the project outcome. This leads to quite a different decision framework from the preceding one (Figure 12.2).

The relative importance of each source of uncertainty can be highlighted as part of the risk analysis procedure, providing a more definite perception of what overall risks really exist. In the process of identifying and modelling the risks, greater awareness of the assumptions made in the development scenario is engendered, weaknesses in the project are uncovered, and improvements can be incorporated in the form of project revisions and contingency plans. Through an interactive and iterative process of examining the risks involved in various aspects of the project, calling for input

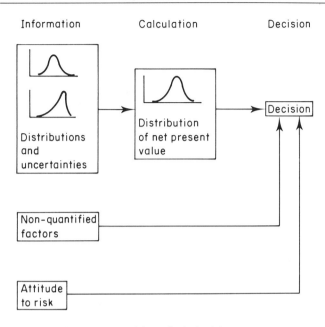

Figure 12.2   Risk analysis decision process

from the most knowledgeable people in each area and recycling the results back to them, decision making can proceed with more information about profitability and risks, a reduction in project risk is possible, and a degree of project optimization can be achieved. Most experienced users of risk analysis see these benefits as even more important than the direct benefits of quantification of uncertainty. It is not just a question of producing a richer and more useful description of the project plan; it is a question of improving the plan in the process of describing its implications.

A selection of areas to which risk analysis can make useful contributions in offshore developments is given in Table 12.1. Descriptions of the methods and models used to tackle some of them are provided in the references.

This chapter describes the economic risk evaluation process for an offshore project. The next section indicates how economic and political variables can be assessed and incorporated in a project risk analysis. The following section provides a brief discussion of decision criteria for project evaluation. More general discussion is given in a concluding section. The principles discussed in this chapter apply to any project, although the nature of the analysis must be adjusted to reflect differences in circumstances.

Table 12.1   Areas in which risk analysis can be applied to offshore
developments

Area	Example topics
Construction cost	Activity cost deviations
	Procurement cost deviations
Construction schedule	Activity duration deviations
	Resourcing implications
Pipelines	Pipelaying cost and schedule
Reservoir	Field size
	Recovery characteristics
Development schedule	Reservoir response
	Facility design
Operating costs	Abnormal events
	Extreme conditions
Technological reliability	Specific equipment risks
	System structure
Regulatory aspects	Licensing delay
	Certification delay
Environment and safety	Hazard risks
	Evacuation procedures
Political	Country risks
Economic and fiscal	Inflation and interest rates
	Oil and gas prices
	Taxes, incentives and royalties

ECONOMIC AND POLITICAL CONDITIONS

In order to evaluate the overall economic viability of a development project, uncertainty with respect to such global variables as economic and political conditions, oil and gas prices, and tax and royalty structures must be considered. These global variables differ from many project-specific factors in two main respects:

Specific risks are less important than long-term trends for the economic variables;
Whereas the impact of risks related to project-specific activities can be controlled to some degree through contingency planning and mitigating action, the global variables are largely beyond control.

Economic uncertainty

Economic uncertainty is best considered initially in terms of broad scenarios, in which are embedded forecasts of the key economic variables, such as inflation, oil and gas prices and the cost of capital. While short-term risks such as rapid increases or decreases in the world price of crude oil will

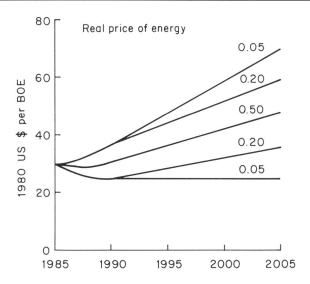

Figure 12.3   Energy price scenarios, 1985–2005. (BOE = barrel of oil equivalent)

affect the economics of the project to some extent, and actual economic conditions will show greater annual fluctuations than is represented by the long-term forecasts, it is the general trend that is of most interest. Detailed modelling of year-by-year departures from trends is usually unwarranted at the level of overall project evaluation considered here.

Figure 12.3 illustrates how economic uncertainty can be specified. Five 20-year scenarios are developed for each variable, and in some cases probabilities are assigned to each of them. Assigning probabilities to scenarios is a difficult and contentious exercise; frequently the results are evaluated conditional on each scenario, leaving the decision maker to use his own judgement about the weights to give them. Figure 12.3 was first produced in late 1984. When examined in early 1986, with oil at about 30 per cent of its 1984 levels, the need to interpret with care probabilities associated with long term trends rather than short term fluctuations was particularly clear.

The economic forecasts can be developed from a number of sources. In most cases the use of internal forecasts which are generally accepted for project evaluation is recommended. This facilitates comparison with other projects being considered, under similar sets of assumptions.

Political conditions

Political conditions present some of the greatest uncertainties facing offshore development projects. Many decision makers consider them to be some of the most important ones. However, they are often given inadequate attention because they are difficult to handle. To a large extent they are inter-related with the state of the domestic economy of the country with jurisdiction over the project and its extraction products. For example, subsidies and incentives may be available and the tax and royalty burden may be reduced when economic conditions are poor, while returns to the project may be restricted through increased taxes and royalties under good economic conditions.

Other key political uncertainties are the allowable production and future export policies. These depend on domestic supply and demand, as well as on economic conditions and government policy. Jurisdictional disputes between federal and state or provincial governments may also present risks to a project and there may be delays due to changing regulatory, licensing and certification requirements and procedures.

The impacts of political considerations on a project are difficult to assess, and they are often treated as conditions, to avoid quantification. However, it is possible to undertake further evaluation using sensitivity analyses, and more detailed quantification effort may be justified if political risks could have particularly serious consequences (for example, see Bunn and Mustafaoglu, 1978).

Evaluation approach

An evaluation process for economic and political risks is outlined in Figure 12.4. Detailed risk analyses can provide probability distributions for variations in direct construction costs, construction schedule duration, operating costs, reservoir size and the reservoir development schedule, as described in earlier chapters. More general assessments are made of potential variations in the long-term trends in global parameters such as oil prices, inflation and the cost of capital. Each of these distributions is then summarized using from three to six scenarios.

Each scenario may be interpreted as a conditional expectation within a given band of values, with an associated probability defined by the band of values. Combining scenarios from each distribution determines overall project scenarios, with associated probabilities.

In the combination process, appropriate assumptions must be made about the dependence between variables. For convenience some bias may be allowed with respect to individual assumptions, but an attempt should be made to avoid overall bias. For example, direct cost variations are not completely correlated with schedule duration variations, but the dependence is very high: complete dependence can be assumed, bearing in mind that this is a slightly conservative (pessimistic) assumption. To balance this bias, at least in part, direct costs may be taken as independent

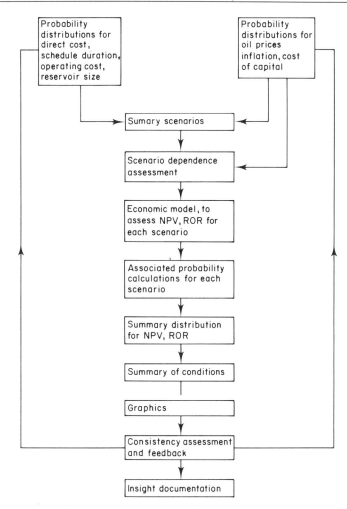

Figure 12.4   Economic risk assessment process

of operating costs, bearing in mind that this may be a slightly optimistic assumption if direct cost problems imply consequent operating problems. A case could be made for negative dependence between direct costs and operating costs if high capital spending, forced by regulatory conditions, implies low operating costs as a byproduct. If so, the pessimism associated with assuming independence should be borne in mind, and an attempt made to compensate in the overall assessment.

In some cases conditional probability distributions are used. For example, the various scenarios for oil prices are frequently specified conditional upon the rate of inflation and defined in terms of similar

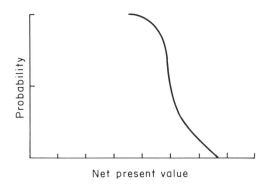

Figure 12.5   Probability distribution of project net present value

economic scenario levels. Ensuring consistency with prior unconditional probability assessments requires a careful examination of underlying assumptions and relationships.

Production profiles from the reservoir development schedules are combined with parameter values from the overall project scenarios in an economic model, to derive cash flow streams. These in turn are used to calculate various economic indicators, such as net present value (NPV), discounted rate of return (ROR), payback period, average return on capital, and discounted profit to investment ratio.

The project scenario probabilities and the associated indicator values are summarized as probability distributions and represented graphically, as indicated in Figure 12.5. All key assumptions and conditions should be noted. The assumptions should be reviewed in light of the results obtained, and any revisions incorporated in the analysis.

Once the results are accepted, further sensitivity analysis can be carried out to assess which variables have the greatest impact on overall project economics. This is done by looking at the change in the distribution of NPV or ROR when the distribution for each variable is changed. This is a further level of sophistication, examining uncertainty about uncertainty, which yields useful additional insight into project outcomes, but it may not be worthwhile pursuing uncertainty at this level of detail.

CHOICE OF DECISION CRITERION

This section considers the choice of a decision criterion for project evaluation. It concentrates on NPV and ROR, and indicates why NPV is preferable to ROR under conditions of uncertainty.

Suppose a development project has a projected annual cash flow stream $X_1, X_2, X_3, \ldots, X_n$. For most projects, the initial cash flows will be negative

Table 12.2   Net cash flows for typical offshore projects

	Year	Activity	Net cash flow
'Simple' project	1–3	Platform construction, installation, commissioning	Negative
	4–20	Production	Positive
	21	Platform salvage value or (more likely)	Positive
		Decommissioning cost	Negative
Phased project	1–3	Platform construction, installation commissioning	Negative
	4–6	Production, Phase 1	Positive
	7–8	Phase 1 production, and development of satellite facility	Negative
	9–25	Production, Phase 2	Positive
	26	Decommissioning cost	Negative

as money is invested, followed by positive cash flows as production begins and returns are realized. The final cash flows may be positive, or they may be negative, for example if there are large costs associated with decommissioning an offshore structure. As indicated in Table 12.2, intermediate cash flows may also be negative for a phased project. The net present value of the project's cash flows is

$$NPV = \sum X_t/(1 + R^t),$$

where R is the required corporate return. The project's rate of return is that value of R for which NPV = 0.

The rate of return used in NPV calculations represents an appropriate trade-off between returns in different time periods for the organization making the decision. For streams of cash flows which are single best-estimate values, R includes an appropriate risk-free rate of return, an appropriate corporate risk premium, and an appropriate debt capital rate, appropriately weighted. This is a corporate rate of return, given the assumptions about the company's balance between equity and debt financing. If the cash flows are uncertain, associated with probability distributions, as they will be if they are derived from a risk analysis, then no risk premium should be included in the corporate R, otherwise an improper double adjustment for uncertainty would be imposed on the project.

An alternative to NPV for project appraisal is the rate of return of the project's cash flows. The ROR attempts to measure the actual rate of return on the capital that is invested. It is the rate of discounting which equates the present value of the project's cash inflows with the present value of the investment. The ROR is the discount rate for which the project's NPV is zero. It is calculated by solving for R in the equation above. Solving this equation to determine the ROR generally requires an iterative trial-and-error approach.

The ROR is often interpreted as the maximum rate of interest that the firm should pay if the project was to be financed entirely by borrowing, and the project's cash flows were to be used to repay the initial loan and its interest charges. The firm would just break even on the project, which would have NPV = 0. If the ROR exceeds the cost of borrowing, it is assumed that project should be accepted. Alternatively, if the firm is providing its own finance, it is assumed that the project should be accepted provided the ROR exceeds the return the firm could get by lending on the market.

Even under assumptions of certainty these interpretations of ROR can be misleading. The basis of the problem is that the same discount rate is applied to positive cash flows as well as negative cash flows, implicitly assuming that the organization earns the ROR on its investments as well as paying the ROR for its borrowings. Put another way, ROR has a mathematical meaning for all values of R obtained by putting NPV = 0 and solving the resulting equation, but it has an economic meaning only in the region related to the appropriate cost of capital. ROR is often criticized because it can be shown that multiple roots associated with solving NPV = 0 exist when more than one sign change is associated with the cash flow, the number being equal to the number of sign changes. This is a symptom of the more fundamental difficulty noted above.

The ROR of a project can usefully be interpreted as a parametric assessment of NPV, as the return for which NPV = 0, as indicated in Figure 12.6. If the corporate rate of return is not clearly defined, but R_1

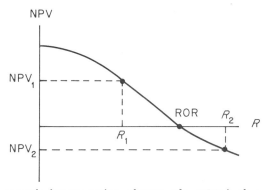

Figure 12.6 **Parametric interpretation of NPV. The ROR is that return for which NPV = 0, i.e. where the NPV curve crosses the horizontal axis**

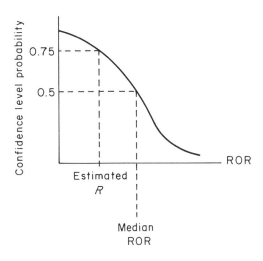

Figure 12.7   ROR distribution

seems more likely than R_2, then a positive NPV seems more likely than a negative one.

Under uncertainty, a probability distribution for rate of return can be obtained as indicated in Figure 12.7. Given the estimated corporate rate R, analysis indicates a 75 per cent chance of obtaining a positive NPV. If the median rate of return exceeds the corporate R, then a positive NPV is more likely than a negative one. However, while all rates of return on the probability distribution have a *mathematical* meaning, R has an *economic* meaning only in the region related to the appropriate corporate cost of capital. In any practical project evaluation, the rate of return must have an economic meaning. For this reason it is generally more helpful to consider probability distributions associated with NPV than ROR. Three cases illustrate the difference between the mathematical and economic interpretations of ROR.

Multiple rates of return

For 'simple' projects, with cash flow streams which involve an initial investment followed by positive returns, the NPV equation has only one solution, as in Figure 12.6. However, many offshore projects involve the phased development of a field, where an initial production platform is supplemented later by satellite platforms or wells, enhanced re-injection facilities, and additional flowlines and pipelines. In this case, where the project requires net cash outflows periodically through its life, there are sign changes in the cash flow stream as indicated in Table 12.2. As indicated

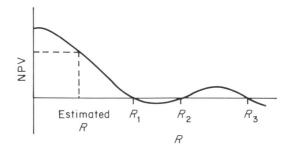

Figure 12.8 Multiple rates of return R_1, R_2, R_3

earlier, this means there will be more than one solution to the NPV equation as illustrated in Figure 12.8. Which is the appropriate project ROR, and what do the others mean? None of them means anything in practical economic terms unless it falls in the region of the estimated corporate rate of return. What is important in terms of project evaluation is that the NPV be positive for the estimated corporate R.

Negative rates of return

Of more importance in the context of uncertainty are negative rates of return, which result whenever $R = 0$ yields a negative NPV as illustrated in Figure 12.9. This implies that the company pays to invest, and pays to have its returns taken away, which clearly does not make practical sense. Thus a concept like expected rate of return, which might seem a useful summary statistic for a rate of return distribution, is misleading and confusing, because it incorporates negative rates of return which have no practical economic meaning.

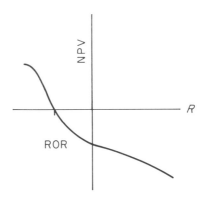

Figure 12.9 Negative ROR

Comparison of projects

Using rates of return which are not in the region of the corporate R can lead to decision errors. In Figure 12.10, Project A apparently has a higher rate of return than Project B. However, both ROR values are outside the region of the corporate R, where Project B has a higher NPV than A. Using an artificial risk premium when calculating the NPV of a project can have similar effects if it forces the rate of return outside the region of the corporate R.

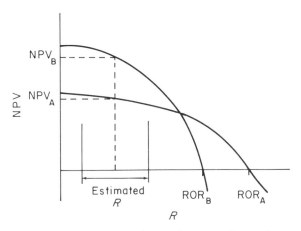

Figure 12.10   NPV and ROR for comparing projects

This brief discussion of some of the problems associated with the use of rate of return as a criterion for project evaluation indicates that net present value will be preferable in most circumstances. Many companies require rate of return information as well, but it must be interpreted with care.

REFERENCES

Bunn, D. W. and M. M. Mustafaoglu (1978) Forecasting political risk. *Management Science*, **24**(15), 1557–67.

Gebelein, C. A., C. E. Pearson and M. Silbergh (1978) Assessing political risk of oil investment ventures. *J. Petroleum Technology*, May, 725–30.

Jones, R. J. (1984) Empirical models of political risks in U.S. oil production operations in Venezuela. *J. International Business Studies*, **Spring/Summer**, 81–95.

Chapter 13

Some more general reflections on risk analysis applications

Summary

This chapter provides a summary of key prejudices or beliefs about risk analysis held by the authors, related to their evolution through experience. It describes the development of risk analysis models for a variety of clients and problems over a period of eight years, in ten case studies. The emphasis is on the relationships between the perceived problems and the structure of the models used, using contentions or statements of prejudice prior to and after each study.

INTRODUCTION

'Risk analysis' has many different meanings. Some differences are contextual. Some differences are the results of different prejudices about which models and methods are most appropriate for any given situation. These prejudices might be called beliefs, precepts, or hypotheses, and many other labels are possible. 'Prejudice' was chosen to clearly indicate they are neither sacred nor scientific in origin.

This chapter begins by attempting to summarize prejudices held by the second author at the outset of his first risk analysis in 1974, in terms of nine contentions. Ten sections then consider ten selected risk analysis studies. Discussion concentrates on how earlier prejudices were implemented, tested, revised and extended, leading to a new set, jointly held in 1982 when this chapter was drafted as a paper, and still jointly held. A concluding section provides final contentions and summary remarks.

INITIAL PREJUDICES: NINE CONTENTIONS

(1) The most useful basic definition of 'risk' is 'an undesirable implication of uncertainty'. Sometimes 'risk' is a convenient short form for 'source

220

of risk', and sometimes 'risk' is a convenient short form for 'the probability of realizing a source of risk'. However, 'risk' in its basic sense need not be measured. In general, measures of risk should be seen as surrogates unless special restrictive assumptions or conditions hold.

(2) Portfolio selection involves allocating a total amount of resource to each of a number of possibilities, as when investing in stocks or shares. One concern is risk efficiency: a minimum level of risk for a given expected return or cost. Another concern is an appropriate risk/return or risk/cost balance. A mean/variance approach provides the most effective basic conceptual model. In practice an indirect and much simplified approach to covariance estimation is essential. In an operational context, measurement of risk is not necessary, but a prescriptive model structure based on preference theory is useful.

(3) Option selection involves choosing a single strategy from a set of policies or selecting a sequential decision choice policy, as considered by decision theory. The prescriptive nature of approaches based on utility theory is attractive conceptually. In practice a descriptive modelling approach considering probability distributions for key variables is preferable, seeking risk efficiency and balance through informally applied dominance concepts. Portfolio and option selection are different in nature, and in practice they require very different approaches, despite some links at a theoretical level.

(4) Unconstrained aggregation involves adding the uncertainty associated with a number of items, some of which may be defined in terms of difference relationships, and price times quantity or other multiplication and division relationships, as encountered when assessing the cost or profit associated with capital investments. A mean/variance or higher moment approach provides the most effective basic conceptual model. In practice there is no effective way of dealing with correlation or covariance.

(5) Constrained aggregation is akin to unconstrained aggregation, but it usually involves 'items' which are 'activities' in the process through time sense, with constraints like the precedence and resource limitations encountered in a PERT framework. A Monte Carlo simulation approach provides the most effective conceptual and operational model. In practice there is no effective way to deal with correlation or covariance. Constrained and unconstrained aggregation are similar in principle, but in practice effective treatment requires very different approaches.

(6) Probabilistic modelling in general involves a wide range of different models for different circumstances. As these models take advantage of

the special characteristics of their circumstances, there is no virtue in attempting to use a common set of conceptual or operational models.

(7) Computer software systems which are tailored to efficient use of one kind of model are the key contribution to problem solving provided by computer scientists. PERT packages, simulation packages and linear programming packages are obvious examples.

(8) A basic statement of the 'scientific method' involves well known steps; observe the phenomenon of interest, form a hypothesis, test the hypothesis, reject the hypothesis or accept it as a theory, and start the cycle again. A basic statement of the 'OR method' also involves well known steps: describe the problem requiring a solution, develop a model, derive a solution, test the solution, implement and maintain the solution. Both are useful basic statements, but all they share is a systematic step structure which bears very little relationship to what happens in practice, for very good reasons.

(9) Scientists of any discipline like to hide their prejudices, unless someone else reveals contrary prejudices, when they are inclined to use them like a big stick. Non-scientists are more tolerant, because they recognize prejudices for what they are more readily. However, everyone finds prejudices difficult to deal with directly in discussion.

CASE 1.   SEISMIC RISK TO NUCLEAR POWER STATIONS

At the time of this study, relevant design procedures for nuclear power station components in relation to seismic risk were based upon a design base earthquake (DBE) or safe shut down earthquake (SSE) specified by a peak horizontal ground acceleration at the power station site. Safety factors related stress generated by these accelerations to deterministic models describing component failure. The study addressed the question 'Is the level of safety provided by such approaches appropriate?'.

An event tree model was used. It employed scenarios and conditional expectations, and a numerical computation procedure akin to the discrete probability distribution approach described by Kaplan (1981) and outlined in Chapter 2, a form of constrained aggregation model. The model traced seismic event occurrence, location, size, other characteristics like acceleration frequency, propagation to site, damage to the plant, and consequential radiation leakage. This model was embedded in an option selection model, using a sensitivity analysis approach for assessing the economic implications of damage and leaks. For a more detailed discussion see Charlewood, Anderson, and Chapman (1975).

The study was internally funded by an engineering consultancy firm as a public relations and marketing exercise. Appropriate computer software was not readily available, so a simple scenario structure was used to facilitate event tree computation. Despite the crude summary scenario structure, the model was plausible. Substantial insight was provided by the modelling process, allowing the assessment of strengths and weaknesses of conventional design methods, as well as the level of safety they provided. For example, it became evident that designs were highly sensitive to distribution function assumptions buried deeply within the mechanics of computing DBE or SSE.

The firm responsible for the study gained its first major nuclear power contract shortly after the study. This success cannot be attributed to the study, but the study certainly did not do any harm.

Two prejudice revisions took place. First, when a constrained aggregation model of the event tree variety is embedded in an option selection model, Monte Carlo approaches are not attractive. Representing uncertainty in terms of a very limited set of conditional expectation scenarios using conditional probabilities to capture dependence, with analytic computation procedures, is preferable conceptually and operationally.

Second, if used with sensitivity and limited scenario approaches, pocket calculators can cope with very complex problems, allowing the modelling restrictions imposed by the most general of computer software packages to be avoided. The first time a new kind of problem is modelled, using a calculator rather than a computer provides a great deal of insight, more than enough to reward the effort involved, provided time is available.

CASE 2.   LABOUR AVAILABILITY RISK FOR A COMPRESSED SCHEDULE

A major Arctic pipeline had a proposed 3 year construction schedule base plan. Meeting base plan labour requirements in a politically acceptable manner was a key issue. However, 2 and 2.5 year base plans needed consideration, in terms of labour availability risk and consequential cost and time (duration, programme or schedule) risk.

A discrete scenario form of generalized PERT model was used, embedding simple decision trees in a probabilistic activity network structure. Activities were defined in terms of work by a spread (a work team in one location) in a season. Within an available labour supply, planners specified resource level increases to meet problems associated with bad weather and other difficulties in a general manner. Several different levels of labour availability were considered, embedding a constrained aggregation structure in an option selection structure, as in Case 1. Cost and duration probability distributions were provided in independent and joint distribution form for each labour level considered. The chance of failing to meet duration targets for each labour level was a key summary statistic, associated with the expected delay given that delay occurred.

The risk analysis was initiated as a three week 'quick-and-dirty' study, to overlay a very substantial and intensive three-month study of associated schedules and costs. The risk analysis study clearly demonstrated the relationship between labour availability, cost and schedule risk. Perhaps more important, the risk analysis process became a central part of the larger schedule and cost study process. Demonstrating the importance of incorporating risk analysis in the ongoing planning process was generally accepted as a key benefit of the risk analysis study.

A further prejudice revision took place. When a constrained aggregation model of the generalized PERT variety is embedded in an option choice model, Monte Carlo approaches need not be the preferred choice. The approach of Case 1 is preferable, using conditional expectation scenarios, conditional probabilities, and analytic computation procedures, provided the activity network does not involve a lot of merge events and more than one path with a high criticality index.

The prejudice for pocket calculators early in a study involving a new problem was endorsed, although simple computer software was written and used after a few weeks.

A new prejudice was also firmly established. Risk analysis need not be about measuring risk any more than planning need be about producing plans. Both ought to be about developing an understanding of what might and should happen which is jointly understood by more than one person. This prejudice was initially based upon a sample of two studies, but it has sustained itself.

CASE 3.   CONTRACTUAL RISK FOR A MIDDLE EAST PROJECT

A consortium of engineering consulting firms were favoured bidders for a turn-key thermal electric power project in the Middle East. A fixed price tender was required. The consortium did not have the capitalization to undertake any significant financial risks, but the prospective client and the home government were making supportive offers. These included substantial advance payments to be invested in trust for the consortium to provide a hedge against inflation, and home government insurance on inflation of domestic content above specified ceiling rates. The study addressed the question 'Should the consortium bid, and if so, at what level?' For a more detailed description, see Chapman and Cooper (1985).

An event tree model was used, to attempt identification of all possible sources of risk. Decision tree models were embedded in this structure, to attempt identification of all possible responses to realized risk sources. Representative scenarios were employed, but not probabilities. The concern was avoiding or neutralizing all significant sources of risk via contractual arrangements with the client, the home government, sub-contractors and insurance companies. The model took a verbal form, in terms of structured lists of risk and responses, with backup discussion and documentation. Much of the initial input came from legal, insurance and economic advisors, but the formal lists and assessments were the product of extensive discussion at meetings involving the senior officers of the consortium companies.

The expected rewards were high, but the consortium decided not to bid. History suggests some wisdom in this decision, and the risk analysis was given credit for contributing to the process of acquiring it.

Three new prejudices were firmly established.

(1) Risk analysis need not use probabilities. Probabilities may be largely irrelevant.
(2) Structured verbal models can be extremely useful, especially when the nature of risks and associated responses may cause confusion or misunderstanding if an agreed definition is not provided.
(3) Risk analysis ought to be fun for all those involved, in the sense that all those involved ought to feel they are both gaining from and contributing to the process, in terms of insights gained and offered.

A sample of three studies gave rise to the last of these new prejudices, samples of two and one for the middle and first prejudices, but all three have sustained themselves.

CASE 4.   TIME RISK FOR A PASSIVE PROJECT

A major North Sea operator wanted to develop a set of risk analysis methods and models for projects exposed to significant risks.

Time risk analysis was performed on a 'passive' project, an offshore pipeline just completed. Planning and technical information was provided by two planning engineers just released from the project, who also acted as risk analysis users. The aim was development of time risk analysis methods and models based upon a synthesis of experience gained from earlier studies, to serve as a basis for further methods and models for other kinds of risk.

A decision tree model was used, embedded in a semi-Markov process model, embedded in a simple activity network structure. The method addressed the generation of comprehensive lists of risk sources, responses, and higher order risks associated with responses. It also addressed selective modelling, in relation to identified conditions or risks explicitly excluded from quantification. It distinguished between responses which were specific to particular sources of risk, and those which were relevant to a number of possibilities. It also distinguished between decisions which could be embedded in the model directly, and those which needed indirect treatment as separate options. Extensive verbal backup documentation was structured in list form, and special summary diagrams were developed to summarize the modelled problem structure. This study led to two other studies reported here (Cases 5 and 7), and initiated a consulting and joint development relationship which still flourishes.

A number of new prejudices were established which still persist.

(1) To understand an activity like 'laying 150 km of pipe' in relation to weather variations within uncertain weather windows, semi-Markov process representation of progress on a month by month basis is essential. Failure to consider any activity in a semi-Markov process framework is a simplification of the inherent problem structure which can cost a great deal in terms of lost insight, and make quantification of risk much more difficult.

(2) To understand monthly progress distributions for an activity like offshore pipelaying, individual sources of risk must be identified, because although some responses are general in the sense that they can be related to a general lack of progress, others are specific to particular sources of risk. Failure to consider any activity in terms of individual sources of risk heavily restricts our ability to model or understand uncertainty in a descriptive sense, and greatly limits our ability to consider preventive and contingency response decisions.

(3) Although option choice and constrained and unconstrained aggregation models must be used for project planning purposes, conceptually the project planning problem should be seen as a portfolio problem. The planner must allocate time and other resources to activities in a risk efficient manner which achieves a suitable cost risk balance. Project planning is much more difficult than conventional portfolio problems, because the risk associated with one allocation is not independent of other allocations, quite apart from statistical and causal dependence relationships given particular allocations. Prescriptive approaches to such complex problems are not possible. Descriptive modelling which maximizes insight maximizes the chance of an effective and robust set of base and contingency plans.

(4) Very complex problems can be tackled in an effective and efficient manner only if a method is developed which is specific to the situation and to the model. This method will bear some resemblance to the basic OR method, but it will take advantage of a prior judgement on the nature or class of problem and the relevant class of models. Within constraints implied by this prior judgement, the specific method will be primarily concerned with identification of the issues needing attention, if any, and the selection of an appropriate approach to them, from a

wide but integrated set of models and associated procedures. There need not be a 'problem' in the classic OR sense: the purpose of the exercise may be to see if such a problem exists. For this reason the term 'situation specific' is preferable to 'problem specific'.

(5) An approach specific to a situation and a model necessarily runs the risk of being inhibited by prior judgements about the model and the problem class. This makes a very flexible set of models essential.

(6) The modelling approach in the context of a specific method is necessarily interactive. Planners must develop, in stages, an understanding of the nature of the uncertainty associated with the tasks to be performed, each new stage building on the last. Putting all the numbers into the computer and turning the handle will guarantee nonsensical results, as near as anything is certain in this world.

(7) Developing models and methods in a 'passive' problem is a useful approach. It allows portions of an analysis to be redone in search of more efficient or effective methods to an extent not possible with a live problem. It also allows a range of models to be tried, before making commitments that must be maintained for the duration of the study in progress, if not longer.

The prejudice for using pocket calculators early in a study involving a new problem was sustained here, despite the complexity of the models. It was extended to the view that the more complex the models, the greater the need to use a calculator until no more insights are forthcoming. It was also extended to the view that in the long term, the situation and model specific method approach would benefit substantially from carefully designed and highly sophisticated computer software. Such software might integrate word processing and verbal data file facilities with automatic graphics of considerable complexity generated from the verbal input structure, in addition to providing flexible interactive computing capabilities. In the short term basic interactive computation abilities would be the first priority.

A further prejudice extension took place. Monte Carlo simulation has an operational role when a constraint structure becomes intractable for analytic approaches. Otherwise the approach of Cases 1 and 2 is preferable in most option selection or constrained or unconstrained aggregation contexts, using conditional expectation scenarios, conditional probabilities, and analytic computation procedures. This includes queuing, inventory and reliability structures, and situations normally involving many other kinds of probabilistic models. Whether Monte Carlo techniques or analytic procedures are employed, there should be no change in the conceptual model: the computational procedures should be invisible to the user, and a common conceptual framework should be preserved.

CASE 5. TIME AND COST RISK FOR AN OFFSHORE PROJECT

The North Sea operator involved in Case 4 wanted to apply the resulting model and method sets to a live project, involving a production platform as well as several pipelines, and cost risk as well as time risk.

Time risk analysis was performed by a planning engineer working full time for six months, assisted by the second author on a part-time basis. A simple cost risk analysis was superimposed on the time risk analysis in the last few weeks. Three or four days of input and feedback discussions took place with each of six groups of senior planners responsible for the project, in addition to several joint meetings. Other sources of information included data banks, weather models, and specialist engineering expertise. Most of the planners saw the feedback as useful, and at least one significant change to the base plan was attributed to the risk analysis. Analysis results went to the main board for assessment prior to the release of funds.

Immediately after the first study, computer software development began. Within two years, interactive computer software was in its fourth version, and the need for a new generation of software was being explored. Within the same period, a risk analysis group was established. Roughly comparable studies were being performed by a single experienced analyst in about eight weeks. More than twenty projects have now been assessed in this way, and the initial project study has been updated twice. More details of the approaches used are given in the next chapter.

Two extensions of earlier prejudices were established.

(1) Extensive verbal models not only provide a sound basis for immediate decision making: they provide a very useful store of corporate knowledge.

(2) Integrating non-probabilistic treatment of risk sources with a probabilistic treatment of risk is essential, because doing so makes explicit the conditions which always exist when subjective or objective probability estimates are made. At the extreme, any finite cost or duration estimate excludes a nuclear war leading to destruction of the world. In this study probabilistic treatment of more than 25 per cent of the identified sources of risk rarely proved appropriate. Deciding what should and should not be included was not always straightforward, emphasizing the importance of the task. Even within the context of a specific risk source, significant differences in subjective probability assessments could usually be related to different implicit conditions. Such differences were resolved by extending the precision of associated verbal definitions and discussions. 'Bias' associated with subjective probabilities is almost entirely due to different premises, and the only way to avoid bias is to be explicit about the premises or conditions involved.

CASE 6.   COST RISK FOR UNDERGROUND POWER STORAGE

An electric power authority was considering two alternative forms of underground storage of electric power, one based on compressed air, the other on pumped hydro. Two largely separate studies were being conducted in different parts of the country. Capital cost differences were of particular interest. The main sources of cost variations were technological uncertainties asssociated with unknown geotechnical conditions and the need to extrapolate current practice to larger machines. Separate risk analyses were conducted to compare potential cost variations.

An event tree model was used, embedded in an unconstrained aggregation model for item costs. The event trees identified the reasons for cost variations within items. Elements of the offshore project method (Case 5) were employed.

The two risk analyses went to very different levels of detail, and neither involved a clearly defined method design phase prior to the start of the main study. Relating the two studies proved difficult. In one case the analysis provided useful insights, but neither of the engineers charged with the risk analysis tasks had great confidence in the results.

The treatment of dependence posed particular difficulties. Most of the dependence involved in earlier cost risk studies was modelled in a direct causal manner within the semi-Markov process and activity network structure; residual dependence was not important and reasonably easy to treat. The model structure of this study implied a mixture of statistical and causal dependence, both important, but neither accommodated effectively.

Two further prejudices resulted.

(1) Cost risk which is not closely related to time risk is best considered using a statistical dependence structure, rather than a causal dependence structure like that applied to time risk. In a descriptive sense, it is easier to picture dependence in a portfolio selection framework than in an option selection framework.
(2) If risk analysis is to perform a comparative audit function, a method carefully specified prior to starting the studies themselves is essential to ensure comparability.

The latter prejudice persists, but the former has been modified in an important manner.

CASE 7.   COST RISK FOR A GAS COMPRESSION PLANT

As part of the development of computer software following the first offshore study (Case 5), an interpolation approach to statistical dependence was developed, akin to that discussed by Hull (1980). Independence was equated to 0 per cent dependence, complete positive dependence was equated to 100 per cent dependence and interpreted in terms of common percentile values, and any intermediate percentage dependence specification was allowed (Chapter 7).

The first onshore project to which this software was applied involved a gas compression plant. It was seen as a method development study, but it was a live problem. The cost risk study was superimposed upon a time risk study, but time risk did not dominate. The software showed some initial weakness in this new role, but a rapid revision met the obvious difficulties.

The offshore method was substantially revised in the course of the study, drawing upon the experience with the underground power storage study. Event tree identification of risk sources was dropped. Identification of correlation or covariance structures within an appropriate level of cost item and element decomposition was the main thrust of the new method. Both the method and the model set embedded in the software proved successful, to the extent that they have since been extended to incorporate exchange and inflation issues, applied, and deemed well worthwhile. However, the meaning and implications of 75 per cent dependence or 95 per cent dependence worried the risk analysts. It was agreed from the outset that a conditional probability structure should be explored as a means of avoiding percentage dependence when necessary, and understanding what it meant when its use was appropriate. Nevertheless, the limitations of such structures in terms of the number and variety of dependence links which can be modelled was a source of concern.

The prejudice for a statistical dependence approach to cost risk maintained itself, with some reservations.

CASE 8. RELIABILITY ANALYSIS OF AN LNG FACILITY

Reliability analysis of a proposed Arctic gas gathering, processing, liquefication and storage facility was required to confirm the sizing of LNG storage. The purpose of the storage was a buffer between production and LNG icebreaking tanker arrivals, absorbing normal production and shipping variations. This case was described in detail in Chapter 4.

The offshore method and model set was modified to suit the problem, taking about two man weeks. Software used for Cases 5 and 7 was mounted on a new computer local to the study. Word processing facilities to handle the verbal data files were integrated with the interactive computation software. Event trees for risk sources were related to system components, incorporating outage probabilities, probability distributions for the proportion of production capability lost given an outage, and repair time distributions. Components and event trees were defined so as to avoid dependence issues. Sources of outage which storage was and was not designed to cope with were distinguished. Sensitivity analysis revealed that sparing in one subsystem should reduce unscheduled downtime by a factor of three. The study could not confirm the storage sizing decision on its own, as the results had to be related to separate tanker studies. A further study was commissioned by the client.

An earlier prejudice was strengthened. The offshore model easily adapted to reliability problems.

An earlier suspicion became a prejudice. The offshore method also adapted with remarkably few changes of significance, although an entirely new set of terminology had to be generated, and detailed procedure notes had to be prepared for the study team to follow. Situation and model specific methods can be created for new problem situations as a pre-main-study phase. A relatively small early investment of effort in this way provides a considerable increase in efficiency and effectiveness during the main study. The key is the need to ensure the model set is general enough to cope.

CASE 9.   RIVER CROSSING RISK FOR A PIPELINE

A large diameter Arctic pipeline had to cross a major river. The favoured approach was putting it on an existing bridge, already carrying a large diameter pipeline. This approach and several alternatives required comparison. Apart from cost and reliability, the political and opportunity cost implications of lost production, potential pollution, and other non-monetary factors required consideration. This case was described in detail in Chapter 5.

The reliability analysis method and model sets were modified to suit the problem, taking about four man weeks. New software was written to cope with multiple criterion treatment of consequences. A component structure was used for reference purposes, but complete physical systems were treated directly for the purpose of assessing risk source/impact/consequence sequences. Each event tree for a source of risk incorporated uncertain occurrence of the event, uncertain physical impacts including common mode effects, and uncertain repair times. All sources of risk identified were considered in probabilistic terms. Dollar transformations of 'natural' variables like oil spillage and interrupted production flow were used, in addition to natural variable distributions, to provide guidance on the relative importance of different criteria. Sensitivity analysis was provided for dollar transformations and for those probabilities which were largely subjective. The study provided a sound basis for logically argued engineering judgements, which the client accepted.

In some ways this study was closer to the Case 1 study than any of the intervening ones. The prime distinction between the model used and earlier event tree structures was the natural and dollar transformation treatment of multiple criteria. The use of the dollar transformations was not intended as a formal basis for criterion aggregation; it was provided as a sensitivity assessment, to yield insight on the orders of magnitude of importance for each natural criterion. Had criterion aggregation been required, appropriate trade-off uncertainty might have dominated other sources of uncertainty. Causal dependence in such functions, even in deterministic forms, would have been a major problem, because the implications of each criterion measure are not independent of the source of risk. For example, when comparing loss of supply and pollution consequences, damage caused by sabotage in a time of war and major energy shortages has very different implications to comparable seismic damage in a time of peace and plenty.

Advances in multiple criterion decision theory are tempting because of their prescriptive nature. However, apart from the difficulties raised by conflicting points of view, and the obscuring effect criterion aggregation can have, it is important to realize that prescriptive models of this kind are not reality, and the existence of higher order models involving uncertainty necessarily makes lower-order models myopic as prescriptive devices. Raiffa (1970) makes the point about higher-order models clearly, although he obviously draws somewhat different conclusions.

Despite the similarity between the seismic study and the river crossing study in terms of approach, two recent prejudices were strengthened.

(1) The set of models used for earlier studies easily generalized to a multiple criterion treatment, reinforcing the view that the models explicitly and implicitly associated with the set cover a very wide range.
(2) The method used was not as easy to adapt as the models, but it was possible to do so fairly quickly, and doing so was very worthwhile.

CASE 10.   COST AND TIME RISK FOR A HYDRO PROJECT

A large hydroelectric project required several tiers of risk analysis. The most general dealt with very long term energy supply and demand issues in parametric terms. The most specific one, considered here, dealt with comparatively short term (15 year) time and cost risk issues, providing a probabilistic treatment of uninflated cost for comparison with other energy sources. This case was described in detail in Chapter 8.

The river crossing method was modified to suit the situation, taking about eight man weeks. The river crossing software was extended to incorporate percentage dependence assessments, as for the gas compression cost risk study (Case 7). A simple activity structure was used. Risk sources were associated with activities in conjunction with previously constructed facilities, decomposing longer activities to portray the completed facilities reasonably precisely. Within this framework, models akin to those used for the river crossing study were used, bearing some relation to the underground approach (Case 6). Direct cost was treated as one criterion. Time delays with indirect cost implications were treated as a second criterion. Delayed or lost energy production was treated as a third criterion. Transformations to indicate total actual and opportunity cost were used. All risks were identified probabilistically. This included a 'residual risk', which attempted to capture the gap between the sum of identified specific risks and an overall risk distribution embodying all but the most extreme conditions, like major wars: statistical data on project estimate/cost relationships over time were assessed, and the current estimate was related to the process of cost growth with information and time.

The model did not accommodate changes easily this time. Both time and cost risk were involved, but the time and cost risk approach used for the offshore and gas compression studies (Cases 5 and 7) was not feasible, in part because of a tight study timetable, in part because the construction schedule was not very tightly defined. The only expedient alternative was adapting the river crossing approach, but the need to mix state and process concepts in a simple activity framework took some time to resolve. For example, a flood realized during the early phase of main dam construction had to be related to other effects which were quite different if the same flood was considered two years later. A semi-Markov process model would have been easier to deal with conceptually.

Method development posed no difficulties, apart from those generated by model development and interpretation.

Suspicions and concerns dating back to the underground storage study, and concurrent work on desirable features for a new generation of software, led to one new prejudice with wide ranging implications. All the features of all the above models need to be properly integrated into a single 'controlled memory' computation structure, using a 'controlled interval' computation procedure. Some of the notions involved in these concepts have been illustrated in earlier chapters. Others will be developed in a book currently in draft and papers in preparation. The controlled memory framework allows a semi-Markov process approach to cost risk with a mixture of conditional probability and percentage dependence specifications, in addition to sources of risk modelled in a causal manner as and when required. A sequence of distribution integrations (convolutions) preserves all 'memories' required for subsequent conditions. In the context of processes through time, dependence induced by separating and merging activity paths can be handled in this way. Although Monte Carlo simulation techniques may preserve an advantage for other complex networks requiring limited distribution precision, and for other constrained aggregation models, substantial penetration into this area should be possible for controlled interval and memory (CIM) models.

CONCLUSION

The previous sections have indicated how our prejudices have developed in specific case studies. A number of trends can be identified, which reflect our broad approach to risk analysis, and have the status of a summary contention. We have moved away from formal numerical models within a general method, towards the use of situation-specific methods which employ far more general models and structured verbal information. Thus we no longer see a numerical 'solution' to a 'problem' as the most important part of an analysis. Instead, a major purpose is to provide a framework within which to approach a specific situation, a structure which will allow a variety of people with diverse disciplinary backgrounds to communicate and gain insight. With this perspective the models used may be traditional numerical ones, but they are frequently informal, non-numerical, graphical or verbal. Models should not be viewed as ends, but rather as general means to a wide range of ends, and of these ends, 'insight' is often more important than 'numbers'.

REFERENCES

Bell, D., R. L. Keeney and H. Raiffa (1977) *Conflicting Objectives in Decisions*, Wiley, New York.

Chapman, C. B. and D. F. Cooper (1985) Contract risk analysis for a turnkey project bid: a case study. *Geneva Papers on Risk and Insurance*, **10**(37), 293–305.

Charlewood, R. G., D. L. Anderson and C. B. Chapman (1975) On seismic risk analysis of nuclear plant safety systems. *Canadian Journal of Civil Engineering*, December.

Freedman, R. J. (1959) A generalised PERT. *Operations Research*, **9**, 281–90.

Gadsdon, J. and C. B. Chapman (1982) Risk analysis as a control feature in project management. *Transactions of the 7th International Cost Engineering Conference, London*. C3.1–C3.11.

Hull, J. C. (1980) *The Evaluation of Risk in Business Investment*. Pergamon, New York.

Kaplan, S. (1981) On the method of discrete probability distributions in risk and reliability calculations—application to seismic risk assessment. *Risk Analysis*, **1**(3).

Keeney, R. L. and H. Raiffa (1976) *Decisions with Multiple Objectives*, Wiley, New York.

Markowitz, H. M. (1959) *Portfolio Selection*, Wiley, New York.

Moder, J. J. and C. R. Philips (1970) *Project Management with CPM and PERT*, Van Nostrand, New York.

Raiffa, H. (1970) *Decision Analysis: Introductory Lectures on Choices under Uncertainty*, Addison-Wesley, New York.

Van Slyke, R. M. (1963) Monte Carlo methods and the PERT problem. *Operations Research*, **11**, 839–60.

US Nuclear Regulatory Commission Reactor Safety Study (1975) *An assessment of accident risk in US commercial nuclear power plants.* WASH-1400, NUREG-75/ 014.

An overview: selecting an approach to project time and cost planning

Summary

The final chapter summarizes the risk analysis processes discussed in the book in the context of project time and cost planning. Other contexts could be summarized in a similar manner, but a single context is essential for expository convenience. It illustrates the main steps in a risk analysis study, using examples from a time-based schedule analysis for an offshore construction project. Short-cut methods of risk analysis are outlined, and the benefits which accrue from a risk analysis study are reviewed.

A portfolio of methods for project planning is outlined and related to two approaches to project management. The focus of the discussion is the need to treat uncertainty and risk at different levels of modelling complexity. The need for methods that are tailored to the circumstances is emphasized, no single approach being best in all circumstances.

INTRODUCTION

A recent paper by Lichtenberg (1983) argues that alternative concepts of good project management should be sought that are not necessarily based on traditional Western ideas. He suggests a Scandinavian alternative, based upon the 'successive principle' of project management, starting with a perspective kept as simple as possible, expanding the detail in the light of successive analyses. Gilbert (1983) addresses the importance of the environment of a project with respect to management systems. He argues for an approach based upon cybernetics, concerned with control theory and communications in the context of self-regulating and self-adjusting systems with 'distributed intelligence'. Both urge a departure from a conventional deterministic critical path method (CPM) planning framework. Instead they want uncertainty to be addressed directly, but their perspectives and suggestions are somewhat different, despite important areas of agreement.

This chapter argues that key differences between the approaches suggested by Gilbert and Lichtenberg should be seen as deliberate choices which are a function of the uncertainty associated with the project together with other project characteristics. Further, it argues that these two possibilities are part of a much wider set of choices. This wider set spans extremely detailed approaches deliberately avoided by Lichtenberg and expressly dismissed as impossible by Gilbert, as well as simpler conventional CPM methods. This view is based upon the development and application of planning procedures that treat uncertainty in a very detailed manner. These have been used by the BP International Projects Department for offshore projects for the past seven years. It also draws upon preceding and subsequent experience with a range of simpler approaches and examines the role of simpler approaches as used by BP, which include that of Lichtenberg, Ashley's influence diagramming, conventional CPM and conventional programme evaluation and review techniques (PERT).

The next section outlines the synergistic contingency evaluation and response technique (SCERT) development for time (schedule or programme) risk analysis of offshore oil projects and associated cost risk analysis, the most detailed of those considered here. This is followed by a discussion of the advantages and disadvantages of such an approach. Successive simplifications are then addressed, in relation to appropriate conditions for simplification, focusing on the degree of uncertainty associated with a project. Method modification to complement model simplification is considered next. A penultimate section concludes the discussion of alternatives suggested by Lichtenberg and Gilbert begun earlier. A final section emphasizes the need to use a portfolio of approaches in a selective manner. In contexts other than project time and cost planning similar issues arise, but a specific context is essential for discussion without an excessive degree of abstraction.

DETAILED METHODOLOGY

A technique like CPM can be associated with a model (activity network) and a method (steps used to make use of the model for project management). When designing new techniques or approaches, it is useful to distinguish carefully between the model and the method and focus attention on their relationship, as discussed in Chapters 4 and 5. In the present context, similar considerations apply.

The time risk analysis method of interest here involves two main phases. Each phase is divided into a number of steps, each step involving clearly specified tasks which are described in more detail in preceding chapters.

The first phase is qualitative. The project is divided into a very limited number of key activities (see Figure 14.1); each activity is then described in

Activities associated with platform structure and topside facilities:

* conceptual design
* steel procurement and delivery
* procurement and delivery of long lead time items
* other material procurement and delivery
* detailed design
* fabrication, erection, onshore testing
* load out, tow to site, installation
* hook-up and commissioning

Activities associated with subsea pipelines:

* design and award contracts
* surveys for route selection
* steel procurement and delivery
* other material procurement and delivery
* pipe coating and delivery to onshore base
* pipe laying
* pipe trenching or burying
* pipeline tie-ins to platforms and/or shore
* pipeline tests

Figure 14.1   Activities for an offshore project

detail (see Figure 14.2); all significant sources of risk associated with each activity are listed and described (see Figure 14.3); all feasible responses to each source of risk are then listed and described (see Figure 14.4). Where appropriate, secondary sources of risk associated with responses are similarly considered. The overall problem structure is then studied, distinguishing responses that are specific to single sources of risk from those general responses that apply to sets of risks. The responses are then ordered, and associated decision rules are studied.

This structure is summarized in diagrammatic form in Figure 14.5. Circles portray sources of risk associated with the activity; 'yard not available' and 'mobilization' problems, for example, illustrate mutually exclusive risks, all others being additive or multiplicative in effect. Specific mitigating responses are shown in the boxes below the associated risks, in preference order, with associated circles indicating secondary risks. General mitigating responses are collected together under a 'net delay' circle at the extreme right of the last of the pages for an activity, not shown in

Number	Title/Details
8.0	*Fabrication, erection and tests*
	This activity covers fabrication of the platform structure including offsite fabrication of nodes, erection of the structure, installation of all associated equipment, cathodic protection, flooding, grouting, internal leg inspection, strain gauges, environmental monitoring and 'J' tubes/risers, painting of the structure, inspection of welds and any resulting repairs and testing all equipment prior to float and tow-out.
	The award of the fabrication contract is planned for the beginning of November, 1986. The subcontract(s) for rolling jacket tubulars, rolling and fabricating nodes/piles and assembly of the structure should be in accordance with the procedures summarized in Activity No. 5 Details List.
	Fabrication of the jacket assembly has a planned duration of 29 months available and should be complete by the end of March 1989. The principal keydate associated with this activity is 1 April 1989 planned float-out in preparation for the tow to site.
Prepared by	**Date**

Figure 14.2 Activity details list

Number	Title/Description and notes
8.0	*Fabrication, erection and tests*
8.1	Yard availability: Contracted yard may not be available at the required fabrication start date (e.g. because of modifications necessary to accommodate the platform or work on a previous contract).
8.2	Mobilization: Yard may have been idle for some time leading to equipment and manpower mobilization problems.
8.3	Productivity: Contractor's ability to proceed at expected rate to the required specifications (speed and effectiveness of work and minor interruptions).
8.4	Industrial disputes: Significant interruptions not covered under productivity (8.3).
8.5	Equipment breakdowns: Significant breakdowns under productivity (8.3).
Prepared by	**Date**

Figure 14.3 Risk list

Number	Title/Description and notes	Secondary risks
8.0	*Fabrication, erection and tests*	
8.1	*Yard availability:*	
8.1.1	Mobilize: Mobilize as much equipment/ personnel as possible (preferred if delay is likely to be short).	No
8.1.2	Alternative yard: Search for an alternative yard if delay is likely to be very long—this will depend on activities in offshore structure fabrication yards N.B. The costs involved in implementing the above and/or compensation for delays could be (partially) recovered from contractor, if appropriate contractual clauses are incorporated.	Yes
8.1.3	Accept delay: In awaiting availability of contracted yard.	No
Prepared by		Date

Figure 14.4   Risk/response list

Figure 14.5. Preventive responses and other notes appear along the top, while further notes and assumptions appear along the bottom. Links in from other activities and links out to other activities may also appear on these diagrams. A distinction is made between minor sources of risk; major sources of risk, the non-realization of which will be a condition of the quantitative analysis; and major sources of risk to be modelled quantitatively. All project staff with relevant information are involved at appropriate stages, and the problem perception captured by this documentation is agreed with management before the qualitative phase ends.

The second phase is quantitative. The first step is to assess the probabilities of the risks occurring and the probabilities of various consequences, given assumed decision rules for responses. Both causal and statistical dependencies are considered. The cumulative effect of successive sources of risk is then computed, to provide a portrait of the relative role of each source of risk within an activity (see Figure 11.3) and the relative contribution of each activity to total time risk (see Figure 14.6). At intermediate stages in this accumulation process, feedback begins. Feedback continues until everyone is satisfied with the assumed probabilities and decision rules in relation to the conditions identified earlier.

The models used for the quantitative phase belong to the CIM (controlled interval and memory) family of models. These range from simple procedures for the addition of independent distributions to processes that

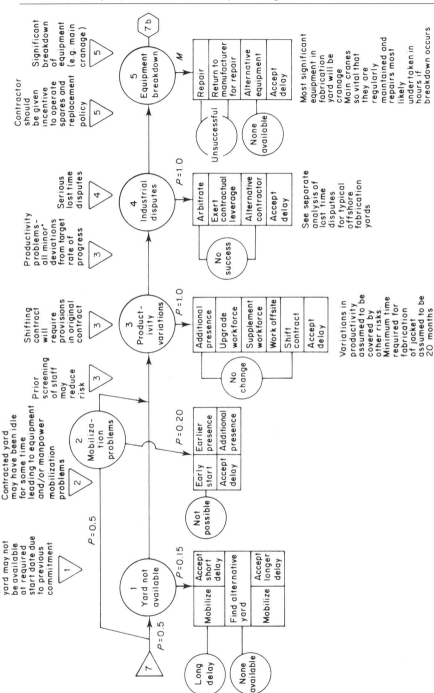

Figure 14.5 Risk/response diagram for an offshore project

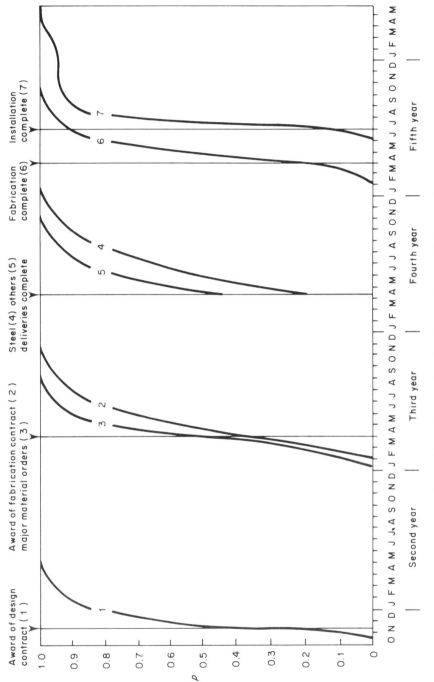

Figure 14.6   Intermediate level output for an offshore project

incorporate a variety of more complex techniques as necessary. The latter include fault trees, event trees, decision trees, semi-Markov processes and activity networks in their most general forms. Monte Carlo simulation could be used, but it would be more expensive and less accurate. BP, Acres and K&H Project Systems have developed special computer software packages to perform these calculations in an interactive manner.

When the project team is satisfied with the time risk analysis, associated cost risk is considered. For example, activity duration distributions are combined with unit of resource distributions and unit cost per unit of resource per unit time distributions, and probabilistic treatment of exchange rates and inflation rates is used if appropriate. The relative impact of each source of cost risk is portrayed as in Figure 11.3 and 14.6. Project managers generally want to be satisfied that they have an understandable and justifiable case for all major decisions inherent in this overall result.

ADVANTAGES OF THE METHODOLOGY

Some advantages of this detailed methodology accrue directly, some are spin-offs. Both are summarized below.

Outside influences, technical, environmental, and political, are specifically considered in direct relation to internal technical and political issues, and appropriate strategies to deal with these complex interactions are developed. This provides a balanced view of the total project.

The integration of planning and costing in estimating and control terms is improved. This builds cooperation. Members of the project team develop an understanding of likely problems and responses in their own area and those in other areas that will affect them. Teamwork is developed.

Attention is focused on specific problem areas, and further analysis is pursued until the project team is confident that it can cope with all foreseeable events it ought to be able to handle, clearly identifying all events beyond the scope of their plan. This builds morale and responsibility.

Project management is provided with a means of signalling trends without redefining objectives. This helps to avoid crises.

Knowledge and judgements are formalized and documented, making similar projects at a later date much easier to deal with, even if the personnel involved are not available. Corporate knowledge is captured.

A probability distribution is provided for completion date and cost estimates but this may be a less important aspect of the exercise. The approach described here is an enhanced and enriched planning process, intended to provide a basis for developing a risk-efficient and cost-effective approach which is robust and credible. It is based upon a need for insight, creativity, balanced judgement and technical skills in a thoughtfully managed manner.

DISADVANTAGES OF THE METHODOLOGY

Engineers with appropriate experience and suitable risk analysis training are required, together with computer software and specialist consulting advice as necessary. A single fairly simple study may take six weeks elapsed time, involving 12 weeks of analyst time and several weeks of other staff time for input and review. Until the staff are familiar with the approach, the time requirements may be two or three times greater. In addition, a large complex project of long duration may require several update studies at different points through its life.

This detailed approach is expensive, in terms of both staff time and information requirements. Nevertheless, it has many advantages which frequently outweigh the costs. BP have used this approach on more than 20 major studies to date, and they continue to believe it is worthwhile for all large, complex or sensitive projects involving significant uncertainty.

A SEQUENCE OF MODEL SIMPLIFICATIONS

Clearly, not all projects justify such a detailed approach. As uncertainty and risk decline, the approach required becomes simpler. A reduction in project size, complexity or sensitivity accelerates the need for simplifications, as do limits on planning time, personnel or computing resources.

The point at which further simplifications become appropriate is a complex judgement which must reflect a wide range of factors. However, the ordering of appropriate simplifications is reasonably unambiguous, because, to a considerable extent, it depends upon the logic of the model structure. The following subsections describe the sequence of model simplifications.

Assumed responses

Dropping response analysis and assuming a single suitable response, with any secondary risk effects built into the consequences associated with the response, is a reasonable first level of simplification, provided there is no reason to believe that significant erroneous response assumptions will be made, and provided that it is not worth developing contingency plans. Even for very large, complex and sensitive projects, these conditions may apply in the early planning stages, when the broad implications of alternative plans are being studied. At this stage, uncertainty does not imply risk except insofar as the wrong plan is selected, assuming that subsequent detailed planning will take place prior to implementing the selected plan.

Such an approach has been used for several Canadian and US clients in the gas and electric power industries. A detailed example was seen in Chapter 5, where secondary risks and responses were embedded in the assessment of each risk event/damage scenario/response combination for the alternative river crossing configurations.

Limited search for sources of risk and aggregation of residual risk

Making risk lists as exhaustive as possible requires considerable initial effort, and if it results in 40 or 50 sources of risk, considerable subsequent analysis is required as well. A reasonable second level of simplification involves concentrating on five to ten key sources of risk at the outset and aggregating all the others into a single 'residual risk' category. A potential danger of this is that a significant risk might be overlooked, and so this approach is not recommended unless the study team has extensive familiarity with risk analyses of projects of a similar kind. More experience is required than for the first simplification, but in the early planning stages this approach may be justified, even in the context of large, complex, and sensitive projects, because the risk of choosing the wrong plan is not the same as the risk associated with implementing the plan, and loosely defined preliminary plans may not warrant more rigorous treatment. A Canadian client has used this approach in conjunction with assumed responses since establishing their risk analysis team at the end of 1982 for offshore oil and gas projects in the Arctic and off the east coast of North America.

Reordering the simplifications of this and the previous subsection is possible; analysing responses in detail after a limited search for sources of risk and aggregation of residual risk. However, such an approach is effective only in special circumstances, because many responses are specific to the nature of the source of risk. We have no experience of such an approach, a practical reflection of the rationale for the ordering of this and the last subsections.

No disaggregation of risk sources

No disaggregation of sources of risk, addressing activity duration variability and other cost component variability directly, is a reasonable next stage of the simplification process. The authors have used this approach when time risk is not a significant component of cost risk, when the estimators have considerable experience of cost component variations, and all that is required is a probabilistic cost estimate for preliminary project assessment purposes. However, experience is needed if this approach is to provide reasonable results, unless it is based upon a detailed analysis of the kind discussed earlier. In particular, it is never clear which risk sources have been quantified and which have not, unless a detailed analysis has been undertaken beforehand. This is an issue of some importance, as illustrated by studies in which only half a dozen risk sources were quantified of some four dozen identified, half of which were major, and considerable discussion preceded the selection of risk sources requiring quantification.

We have used assumed responses in the context of no risk source disaggregation where only one response was feasible, but this would not seem advisable in general, an inherent limitation of early generalized PERT or graphical evaluation and review (GERT) models. It is for this reason that the ordering of this and the previous two subsections was selected.

No statistical dependence

Statistical independence, in conjunction with all the previous subsection simplifications, is a very strong and generally very misleading assumption, unless considerable experience or prior detailed analysis allows activities or cost components to be defined so as to avoid dependence. However, statistical independence in conjunction with all the previous subsection simplifications is a very powerful assumption in the sense that it makes assessment very much easier. Time risk analysis models simplify to conventional PERT models. Cost risk analysis simplifies to the extent that simple mean-variance or higher moment models become viable, like the successive estimating approach recommended by Lichtenberg.

In the time risk context, conventional PERT models are acceptable, provided a rich experience base is available or prior, more detailed, analysis has been undertaken, the activities are simple in nature and a probability distribution for project end date is all that is required. For this purpose, probabilistic Monte Carlo methods have been used to establish variations in the project end date and levels of confidence in given programmes. The successive estimating approach described by Lichtenberg has been used to establish cost estimate variations caused by project uncertainty. The method provides a quick means of identifying uncertainty, and in many industries it is often a fast, ballpark result that is required rather than an unnecessary degree of accuracy. It also provides a means of concentrating effort on areas that will produce the greatest benefit.

We have used other mean-variance based approaches without much success. In our view, the reported reduction in uncertainty associated with successively redefining areas of uncertainty in greater detail may be largely a spurious result associated with an erroneous independence assumption. Most users of mean-variance cost models limit the level of decomposition, explicitly or implicitly acknowledging the bias associated with assuming independence, which grows as the number of components increases. However, Lichtenberg claims to overcome this by isolating general conditions, and dependence could be introduced in this framework.

Statistical independence without previous subsection simplifications is generally much more acceptable, because the implications of the independence assumption are easier to see in terms of causal relationships. In some cases the structuring of primary sources of risk and secondary sources of risk can be used to ensure independence, as in the LNG case described in Chapter 4 and the river crossing case described in Chapter 5. The simplification of this subsection becomes easier and more appropriate as earlier subsection simplifications are abandoned.

No probabilities

The ultimate simplification involves abandoning probabilities altogether, using a deterministic CPM approach to scheduling and a traditional deterministic approach to costing. This approach has been used successfully in cases where probabilistic treatment is not warranted.

Even if probabilities are not required or desired, the identification of risk sources and responses may be useful.

In a method known as risk assessment, BP use Ashley's influence diagramming approach illustrated by Figures 14.7 and 14.8 for identifying

---

Section A1 — Client factors
1. Who is the client?
2. How important is the product to the client?
3. How 'cooperative/flexible' is he likely to be?
4. How well does the client know what he wants?
5. How well does he appreciate what it will take to achieve his objectives?
6. Has the client full authority to proceed as he wishes independently of any other authority?
7. What are/will be his approval procedures?
8. Has he rigorous ideas as to how the project will function, i.e. will he dictate standards/purchasing procedures, etc?
9. What is the quality of his in-house technical expertise? Will he be using consultants to support them?
10. Does the client appreciate what constitutes a change of scope?

Figure 14.7   Primary risk assessment — typical questionnaire

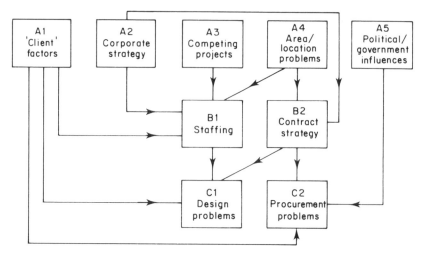

Figure 14.8   Influence diagram showing the project risk structure: A, B and C indicate
primary, secondary and tertiary sources of risk

risk factors and their relationships, when quantifying risks is not an immediate concern or when time is not available, but a general under-standing of the importance of risk sources is required. This method is useful in establishing, in a qualitative manner, the type and seriousness of the various risks involved. The method can be used to evaluate possible options for establishing a clear identification of the project strategy at an early stage, where preferred options can be selected on the criterion of minimizing risks. We have used a less formalized version of the SCERT approach without probabilities when any risk was deemed unacceptable and responses involving contractual and insurance arrangements and government guarantees needed careful examination (Chapman and Cooper, 1985). Hence, this section's simplification need not follow any of the previous ones.

The choice between various methods depends on the level of definition of the project, its value and other factors. There is no hard and fast rule about which method to use in which circumstances. Effort must be tailored to suit the project, to ensure that the most appropriate methods are employed. However, for simplicity, four main approaches can be con-sidered, as portrayed by Figure 14.9. Non-probabilistic risk assessment can be useful for major projects at low levels of definition, a 'successive' method for minor projects with a low level of project definition, a prob-abilistic schedule appraisal for minor projects which are well defined, and a full detailed risk analysis for reasonably well defined major projects.

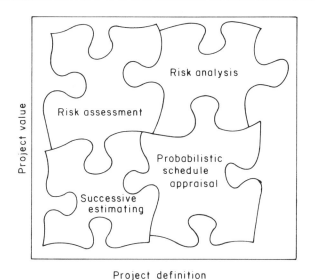

Figure 14.9   Simplified choices form a portfolio of methods

METHOD MODIFICATIONS TO COMPLEMENT MODEL SIMPLIFICATIONS

There is a natural tendency to simplify methods when simplifying models. For example, the conventional steps associated with basic CPM analysis are much simpler than those associated with SCERT analysis. However, if the model is too simple for the task at hand, the method ought to be made more complex, to compensate for the model's shortcomings. Sometimes simple models that do not capture important aspects of a problem are desirable. For example, there are cases where it may be desirable to avoid CPM models that allow the use of activity crash costs and times, as well as normal costs and times, in order to optimize activity costs plus project indirect costs: if there is scope to redefine activity diagrams and the activities themselves, and to adjust activity durations; and if it is not appropriate to use all these possibilities via formal modelling in a decision CPM framework. However, if uncertainty and risk are important, the uncertainty should be modelled in as much detail as possible, because it is simpler to provide the necessary probabilities with confidence. For example, asking an engineer to define directly a probability distribution for the duration of a 300 km offshore pipelaying activity is posing a very difficult question. However, it is much easier if the task is split up and considered at a level like: 'How much progress is expected in the month of June, given 20 good weather days and no breakdowns, buckles or other interruptions?', 'What is the probability of a buckle in these cir-cumstances?', and so on. Having decided upon the maximum feasible level of treatment for uncertainty, an appropriate method can then be designed.

Neither Gilbert nor Lichtenberg address this issue, because they are not directly concerned with selecting an approach from a portfolio of possi-bilities, and other authors providing a comprehensive catalogue of models and techniques normally do so indirectly. However, in our experience it is an issue deserving explicit and careful consideration.

GILBERT AND LICHTENBERG ALTERNATIVES

The Lichtenberg alternative was discussed earlier and its place within a portfolio of approaches identified. However, it is worth emphasizing the quite different perspectives of the portfolio approach discussed here and the successive estimation principle. We recommend selecting a model that provides as much detail about uncertainty as possible within the time and resources available, bearing in mind the cost of the analysis and the risk implications of uncertainty. If an approach that distinguishes sources of risk is selected, the analysis can be abandoned when the analyst is convinced that no related problems warrant further attention, but the search for potential problems is pursued at a detailed level. The successive estimation process is in a sense a mirror image, starting with a very simple picture lacking detail, successively developing detail only as a need to do so is perceived.

The Gilbert alternative was not placed within the portfolio of approaches discussed earlier. This is largely because of our lack of familiarity with it. However, it is worth noting that the self-regulating self-adapting view of a project that Gilbert adopts would seem to be the antithesis of the SCERT approach. Gilbert suggests that one should avoid preplanning, on the grounds that it will inevitably be shortsighted, and concentrate on reactive control without assessing what went wrong when departures from plans occur. We would argue that this approach is not necessarily correct, given the above armoury of tools to cope with the problem. However, there may be more differences in the words and concepts than in what occurs in practice.

CONCLUSION

In our view, Lichtenberg and Gilbert are quite right to argue for alternative approaches, and we support them in general terms, although disagreeing on some important points of principle. A key difference is the need to make a considered and conscious choice from a set of alternatives, bearing in mind the project's risk and uncertainty in relation to other project characteristics. There is no single best way to manage all projects.

REFERENCES

Ashley, D. B. (1982) *Risk distribution and influence diagramming.* Presented at Construction Risk Identification and Prevention Techniques Seminar, Hamburg, FRG.

Chapman, C. B. and D. F. Cooper (1985) Contract risk analysis for a turnkey project bid: a case study. *The Geneva Papers on Risk and Insurance,* **10**(37), 293–305.

Gilbert, G. P. (1983) The project environment. *International Journal of Project Management,* **1**(2), 83–7.

Lichtenberg, S. (1983) Alternatives to conventional project management. *International Journal of Project Management,* **1**(2), 101–2.

Lichtenberg, S. *et al.* (1981) *Risk Management—Terminology, Methods and Examples.* Danish Project Management Society, Danish Technical Press, Denmark.

Moder, J. J. and C. R. Philips (1970) *Project Management with CPM and PERT.* Van Nostrand, New York.

ACTIVITY: a component of a project; a process through time; the term 'activity' includes non-engineering tasks like obtaining approvals, obtaining equipment, waiting for material deliveries and so on.

ACTIVITY DETAILS: all the information about an activity required for analysis and record purposes.

ACTIVITY LABEL: brief title and number for identification.

ANALYSIS FOR PLAN APPROVAL: the second stage in a project's development, after project approval but prior to detailed planning; emphasis is on the overall shape of plan.

ANALYSIS FOR PROJECT APPROVAL: the first stage in a project's development, prior to approval; the emphasis is on the go-no go decision.

BAR CHART: a line chart showing timing relationships by means of a time scale; schedule graph; Gantt chart.

BASE PLAN: the plan to be followed if no risks are realized.

BUDGET CONTINGENCY SUM $C_1 + C_2 + C_3 + C_4 = BC - TC$; an amount added to the sum of a project's target costs to reflect the uncertainties associated with target figures in terms of an appropriate budget level; $C_1 + C_2 + C_3$ adjusts the sum of target costs to EC, an expected cost estimate, C_4 provides an adjustment to reflect the cost of overshooting versus the cost of undershooting.

BC: project budgeted cost; $BC = TC + C_1 + C_2 + C_3 + C_4$

C_1 CONTINGENCY ALLOWANCE: the difference between activity target costs and activity expected costs summed over all activities; reflects skewness of the measured activity probability distributions.

C_2 CONTINGENCY ALLOWANCE: the difference between $TC + C_1$ and the project expected cost as computed via joint consideration of all activities during the first steps of the manipulation and interpretation phase; reflects and measures probability distribution implications of activity interactions.

C_3 CONTINGENCY ALLOWANCE: the difference between $TC + C_1 + C_2$ and EC, the true project expected cost; reflects all risks not considered in probabilistic terms, in terms of the skewness of the true cost probability distribution less $C_1 + C_2$; reflects non-measured effects analogous to C_1 and C_2.

C_4 CONTINGENCY ALLOWANCE: a budgeted amount over and above the expected cost which balances the expected cost of committing more money than necessary with the expected cost of not committing enough.

EC: project expected cost; $BC = EC$ plus an allowance to reflect the cost of

252

overshooting a budget versus the cost of undershooting a budget and the associated probabilities.

TC: project target cost; the sum of activity target costs.

C RISKS AND RESPONSES: probabilistic treatment not contemplated, all such analysis being conditional upon not realizing the risk or response in question.

COMMON INTERVAL (CI): an early version of the Controlled Interval and Memory (CIM) approach to combining probability distributions, used to illustrate the CIM approach in this book.

COMPLEX DECISION RULE: a decision rule which cannot be explicitly defined prior to analysis.

COMPUTATION AND INTERPRETATION PHASE: this phase is concerned with combining probabilities and probability distributions, and interpreting the implications of risks, responses and controls.

CONDITIONAL EXPECTATION: expected value (of cost or time for example) given some condition, like bad weather, good weather, etc.

CONDITIONAL TREATMENT: an approach to risks and responses or controls which are only loosely specified, involve high consequences with low probability, or have implications which are beyond the responsibility of those interested in the analysis. The results of the study are conditional on the risks not arising, or conditional on the responses or controls working as intended.

CONSEQUENCE RANGE: range of cost and time values associated with the conditional expectation defining a scenario.

CONSEQUENCES (of a risk): cost and time deviations from the base plan, considered first in physical scenario terms when possible.

CONTINGENCY ALLOWANCES: See budget contingency sum above.

CONTROL: a system or organization or procedure designed to prevent risks arising, or to detect their occurrence, or to mitigate their effects; a form of response.

CONTROLLED INTERVAL AND MEMORY (CIM): generalized version of the approach to combining probability distributions used in this book.

COST: direct or indirect cost.

CP RISKS AND RESPONSES: indirect probabilistic treatment contemplated after considerable analysis conditional upon not realizing the risk or response in question.

CRITERION: a measure of the consequences of a risk.

DECISION RULE: definition of the circumstances when a response will be implemented.

DEPENDENCE: the relationship between sub-systems, risks, controls or responses by which the probability or distribution of one is conditional on another. Sources of dependence include:

Cause/effect relationships;
Common antecedents;
Common modes of operation;
Compounding consequences.

DETAILED PLANNING AND IMPLEMENTATION: last stage in a project's development; planning with an emphasis on implementation and control.

DIAGRAMMING: producing a risk/response diagram.

DIRECT COST: material, labour, equipment and other costs generated directly by an activity.

EFFICIENCY: risk efficiency; minimum level of risk for a given level of expected cost or profit; maximum level of expected profit or minimum level of expected cost for a given level of risk.

EFFICIENCY BIAS: cost overestimation because the plan is not efficient.

ESTIMATION BIAS: systematic estimation error; persistent tendency to overestimate or underestimate; the expected value of the parameter of interest is not equal to the estimate.

EVENT TREE: chains of consequences following from an initiating event.

EXPECTED VALUE: mathematical expectation; the balancing point (first moment about the origin) of the associated probability distribution; a best estimate of what should happen on average.

FAULT TREE: chains of conditions leading to a specific failure or fault.

GENERAL CONTROL/RESPONSE: control or response which is applicable to a set of risk sources.

INDIRECT COST: overhead; cost of capital and other costs generated indirectly by an activity or directly by a project as a whole; may include lost revenue in opportunity cost form.

INHERENT RISK: risk of material errors inherent in the existing system.

INTERNAL CONTROL RISK: risk that internal control will fail to detect material errors.

LINK RESEARCH: identification of dependence relationships by examining all pairs of sub-systems, risks, controls and responses.

MAJOR RISK: any risk identified during the scope phase which is not classified as a minor risk. A major risk will either be quantified, or treated as a study condition.

MANIPULATION AND INTERPRETATION PHASE: combines the relevant cost and time probability distributions, drawing decision rule inferences in the process.

MINOR RISK: a risk identified during the scope phase but deemed not worth further separate treatment during the structure phase. A risk with negligible effect, or negligible probability of arising. Minor risks are not quantified, unless there is a large number of them.

P RISKS: to be given probabilistic treatment, directly and immediately.

PARAMETER PHASE: phase concerned with associating probabilities and distributions of consequences with those risk/control combinations to be assessed quantitatively.

PC RISKS: direct probabilistic treatment contemplated after initial analysis conditional upon not realizing the risk or response in question.

PERVASIVE RISK: risk associated with more than one activity; general risk.

PHASE (of risk analysis): scope, structure, parameter, manipulation and interpretation; defined in terms of a change in analysis orientation.

PRECEDENCE DIAGRAM: flow chart showing precedence relationships in activity-on-node form.

PRIMARY RESPONSE: a response to a primary risk.

PRIMARY RISK: a self-initiating source of risk related to the initial list of activities or sub-systems.

RESPONSE: procedure or plan for meeting a specific risk or the combined effect of a set of risks. A response may involve action prior to risk occurrence, or after it, or both.

RISK: potential source of material error, or cost, or deviation from expectation; an undesirable implication of uncertainty.

RISK ANALYSIS: the modelling and quantification of risk.

RISK BALANCE: the trade-off between risk and expected cost or profit to derive risk efficient plans.

RISK BALANCE BIAS: cost overestimation or underestimation because the plan involves an inappropriate tradeoff level between expected cost and risk.

RISK EFFICIENT: a plan is risk efficient if it involves the minimum level of risk for any given level of expected cost or profit, or the minimum level of expected cost or the maximum level of expected profit for any given level of risk.

RISK EFFICIENCY BIAS: overestimation of cost or underestimation of profit because the plan is not risk efficient.

RISK ENGINEERING: the identification, structuring, classification and modelling of risks, and associated controls, responses, and consequences, with a view to better risk management.

RISK EXPOSURE: exposure to uncertainty with undesirable implications.

RISK/RESPONSE DIAGRAM: a diagram showing the relationship between risks and responses; may include relevant parameters.

SCENARIO: a representation of a range of possible outcomes in terms of a specific set of circumstances.

SCOPE PHASE: defines the scope of the analysis, provides an outline definition of the study task, and identifies the activities, risks, responses and control systems of interest.

SECONDARY RISK: a risk which arises as a consequence of a primary risk, or as a consequence of implementing a control or response.

SECONDARY RESPONSE: a response to a risk associated with a response plan for a primary risk or another secondary risk.

SELF-INSURANCE: a means of decreasing expected cost by increasing risk, where contractual arrangements to provide insurance may not be possible.

SIMPLE DECISION RULE: a decision rule which can be explicitly defined.

SPECIFIC CONTROL/RESPONSE: control or response to a single specified risk.

STRUCTURE DIAGRAM: diagram showing the relationships between activities or sub-systems, risks, controls, responses and consequences.

STRUCTURE PHASE: defines the relationships between activities or sub-systems and relevant risks, controls, responses and consequences.

SUB-SYSTEM: part of the installation or organization to be treated as a unit for analysis purposes.

TARGET VALUE: base plan estimate; used as target figure for control purposes; based upon most likely value assuming a minimal level of problems.

Chapman, C. B. (1974) Modular portfolio selection: an introduction. In J. P. Dickenson (Ed.), *Portfolio Analysis*, Saxon House, Farnborough, Hampshire.

Chapman, C. B. (1975) *Modular Decision Analysis: An Introduction in the Context of a Theoretical Basis for Consumer Demand Analysis*. Saxon House, Farnborough, Hampshire.

Chapman, C. B. (1979) Large engineering project risk analysis. *IEEE Transactions Engineering Management* **EM-26**(3), 78–86.

Chapman, C. B. (1980) *Risk analysis of offshore ventures*. Channel Offshore '80 Conference, Southampton, February.

Chapman, C. B. and D. F. Cooper (1983) Risk engineering: basic controlled interval and memory models. *J. Operational Research Society* **34**(1), 51–60.

Chapman, C. B. and D. F. Cooper (1983) Parametric discounting. *Omega* **11**(3), 303–10.

Chapman, C. B. and D. F. Cooper (1983) Risk analysis: testing some prejudices. *European J. Operational Research*, **14**, 238–47.

Chapman, C. B. and D. F. Cooper (1985) A programmed equity-redemption approach to the finance of public projects. *Managerial and Decision Economics* **6**(2), 112–18.

Chapman, C. B. and D. F. Cooper (1985) *Identification and estimation of risk: issues and illustrations from North Sea and Arctic engineering projects*. Proceedings of the 7th International IFAC/IFORS Symposium on Identification and System Parameter Estimation, York, UK, 3–7 July.

Chapman, C. B. and D. F. Cooper (1985) Contract risk analysis for a turnkey project bid: a case study. *The Geneva Papers on Risk and Insurance*, **10**(37), 293–305.

Chapman, C. B., D. F. Cooper and A. B. Cammaert (1984) Model and situation specific OR methods: risk engineering reliability analysis of an LNG facility. *J. Operational Research Society*, **35**(1), 27–35.

Chapman, C. B., D. F. Cooper, C. A. Debelius and A. G. Pecora (1985) Problem-solving methodology design on the run. *J. Operational Research Society*, **36**(9), 769–78.

Chapman, C. B. and J. Del Hoyo (1972) Progressive basic decision CPM. *Operational Research Quarterly*, **23**, 345–59.

Chapman, C. B., E. D. Phillips, D. F. Cooper and L. Lightfoot (1985) Selecting an approach to project time and cost planning. *International J. Project Management*, **3**(1), 19–26.

Charlewood, R. G., D. L. Anderson and C. B. Chapman (1975) On seismic risk analysis of nuclear plant safety systems. *Canadian J. Civil Engineering,* December.

Cooper, D. F. and C. B. Chapman (1985) An overview of risk analysis for underground projects. *Underground Space* **9**(1), 35–40.

Cooper, D. F., C. B. Chapman and A. B. Cammaert (1983) *Reliability analysis of an LNG facility.* Proceedings of the 6th National Conference, Australian Society for Operations Research, Brisbane, 43–53.

Cooper, D. F., D. H. Macdonald and C. B. Chapman (1985) Risk analysis of a construction cost estimate. *International J. Project Management* **3**(3), 141–9.

Gadsdon, J. and C. B. Chapman (1982) *Risk analysis as a control feature in project management.* Transactions of the 7th International Cost Engineering Conference, London, C3.1–C3.11.